RICHARD'S BICYCLE BOOK

Cover bicycle: frame by F. W. Evans, London; gears by Shimano

Richard Ballantine

Richard's bicycle book

Pan Books London and Sydney

First British edition published 1975 by Pan Books Ltd,
Cavaye Place, London SW10 9PG
Revised edition 1976, 1977
© Richard Ballantine 1972, 1975, 1976, 1977
ISBN 0 330 24203 2
Printed in Great Britain by
Richard Clay (The Chaucer Press) Ltd, Bungay, Suffolk

Mechanical illustrations by John Batchelor;
old bicycles and cycling scenes from the author's library,
with contributions from Heywood Hill and Sherry Rubin

HLQ

B

S0788

This book is dedicated to
Samuel Joseph Melville,
hero

Contents

Prices of the bicycles mentioned in this book were as correct as possible at the time of going to press.

Foreword

Fair notice: I am an American, and despite Scottish and English grandparents and an English mother, some of my notions differ from those of the British, just as Italians can be distinguished from Swedes.

Book One

1. Get a Bike!

There is a bicycle boom throughout the world. In America it is like the 1849 California Gold Rush: sales in 1971 were 8·9 million, double the number sold in 1960, 13·9 million in 1972, and 1973 sales hit 15·8 million. The total number of bikes in use in the United States is nearing 100 million! In the Netherlands 75 per cent of the population own bicycles. In Japan the government is energetically promoting bicycles, with 30 million in use. No figures are available, but news films from China show clearly that it is literally a country on bicycle wheels.

And now there is a boom in Great Britain. The pattern is unique and distinctive. In America, for example, the typical pre-World War II bike was sturdy but cumbersome. Equipped with a single pedal-operated coaster brake and one low, slow gear, these 'balloon tyre bombers' hit the scales at about 5 stone plus. Used primarily by youngsters not old enough to drive, they were wonderful workhorse machines tough enough to withstand jolting rides over kerbs and

through fields, frequent nights out in the rain, and a generally high level of abuse. Fond nostalgia permeates memories of these bikes, but for the most part only people who had no other alternative used them. Pre-World War II sales could not have exceeded 500,000 per annum. In contrast, in much smaller Great Britain, 1935 was the heyday of the bicycle, with a record sale of 1·6 million. The bicycle was then a transportation staple in widespread use. The basic design established by 1910 had been subject to a long evolutionary series of minor improvements. Most machines were middleweights with lightened frames, roller lever rim brakes, and $1\frac{1}{2}$ in tyres, and fancier models had calliper cable-actuated rim brakes, gears, and $1\frac{1}{4}$ in or $1\frac{3}{8}$ in tyres. Tipping the scales at 45 to 50 pounds, they were dubbed 'English Racers' by Americans because of their startlingly better performance over the domestic product. Here, they were just the ordinary ride-around bike for local use, to and from work, shopping, mail delivery, police work, light touring, and the like.

The bottom dropped out of the market after the war. Although in America the 'English Racer' provided the foundation for the growth of cycling as an adult sport and means of transport, after World War II sales in Great Britain dropped below 500,000 per annum. Cycles were out, and cars were in. Perhaps it would not have happened if, as in consumer America, cars had been easily available. (I shall never forget my shock when an English uncle of forty-two told me he was buying his first car – a used Humber. I was then fifteen, and in an entirely casual and not at all unique fashion had already owned and used up three or four motorcars.) But it did. Britain went car-crazy, and the bicycle went the way of the Dodo bird. Roads, car parks, petrol stations, motorways, and cars, cars, cars proliferated, so that now Britain is a world leader in number of cars per mile of road, and many of her towns and villages have been transformed into mazes of one-way motordromes. Some of the traffic and parking schemes are marvellously efficient, but serve only to perpetuate the motorcar and further refine a continuous, gigantic traffic jam.

Re-enter our Dodo bird the bicycle. In 1972 sales were 700,000. In 1973 they were 1 million.* And while a fair number of bikes in

* Statistics are nasty things. A critic might point out that while the number of cycles in use is increasing, so is the population, and hence the *per capita* use is declining (at about 5 per cent per annum). But population growth is slowing down and bike sales, steadily increasing, will catch up sooner or later. In towns such as Stevenage, where there is special provision for cyclists, the decline in *per capita* use has fallen to $2\frac{1}{2}$ per cent.

use today are old middleweight workhorses, the new bikes come in a sparkling variety of shapes and sizes. There are sporty 10- and 15-speed racing and touring bikes which weigh about 20–25 pounds and are almost incomparably faster and easier to ride than other bikes. The standard 3-speed is now a lightweight at about 35 pounds. The 'chopper' or 'dragster', with small wheels, long banana seat, and high-rise handlebars is the delight of youngsters. Shoppers and commuters are whirling around on natty mini-bikes. Folding bikes are another hit. And to get mounted on a new machine you can spend anywhere from £40 to £300.

Why? How come the bicycle is coming back like Mrs Grundy's spinach? For the moment, let's concentrate on the personal advantages of cycling and discuss broader social benefits later. A full list of the vastly extended applications and uses for lightweight bikes would be dull. The main ones are:

Economics

With even moderate use a bike will pay for itself. Suppose you use a bike instead of public transportation or a car to get to work and back. Figure public transport costs at 75p a day. Say it rains once a week* and you lay up the bike from December through February. That's 4 days × 4 weeks × 9 months × 75p or £108 which buys a very nice bike. On a 10-mile round trip (the national commuting average) at 8p a mile, a car costs 80p a day. Using a bike four days a week saves £115. And eliminating the car altogether saves £144 per annum. These are conservative figures, for a 8p per mile cost is calculated over all types of driving, including motorways. The man who drives five miles to the station and pays parking fees as well is shelling out a lot more. A hundred and forty-four pounds will buy two to four bikes, each guaranteed for anywhere from one to five years. Put another way, the British Cycling Bureau reckons that the average annual cost of commuting by cycle is £8.

Travelling to and from work is just one application. Bikes are just dandy for visiting friends, light shopping, nipping down to the

---

* A generous allowance. There is no measurable rainfall twenty days a month. Cycling is out of the question only fifteen days a year. And in the time between 8–9 AM and 5–6 PM it rains only twelve days a year. In towns such as Stevenage where cycles are a popular form of transport, the variation in use is at most 5 per cent, and is not related to the weather.

cinema, and so on. You save money every time and it can add up to an impressive amount. Besides easing many of your chores and tasks, bikes are worthwhile in themselves, so that a bike easily 'pays for itself' in rides taken just for fun and pleasure.

Convenience

Speed. In heavy traffic you can expect to average 10 mph, and in lighter traffic 15 mph. I used to ride from my London flat near Westbourne Park Grove to Oxford Circus in 20 minutes, usually less. The bus or Tube usually took about 35 or 40 minutes. (And in these days of deteriorating public services you can set out for the bus or Tube and not have the bloody thing come at all. A bike is not only faster, but also more reliable.) When I lived in New York City, a regular 2½-mile ride from the Lower East Side to midtown Manhattan took less than 15 minutes as against 30 to 40 for the bus and 25 to 35 for the Subway. It used to be my delight to race Subway-travelling friends from 120th street to Greenwich Village – about 6 or 7 miles – and beat them. The story is the same everywhere. There have been many bike versus bus, Tube and/or sportscar contests in many cities, and in each case I know about the bike has always won.

One reason a bike is so fast is that it can wiggle through the traffic jams that now typify cities and towns. Another is the fact that a bike is door-to-door. Use of public transportation involves walking to the local stop, waiting around for the bus or train, possibly incurring a change with another wait, and then a walk from the final stop to your destination. Cars have to be parked. On a bike you simply step out the door and take off. No waiting, no parking problems.

The bike's capabilities make it a real freedom machine. Your lunch hour: tired of the same company cafeteria slop or local sandwich bar? Cycling to a new and interesting café a mile or so away is a matter of minutes. Or how about a picnic in the park? Lots of errands to do? A bike can nip from one place to another much faster than you can hoof it, and has a car beat hollow in traffic and for parking. What might ordinarily take an hour or more is only 15 minutes on the bike. And if there is a lot to lug around, it is the bike and not you that does the work. Last-minute decision to catch a film or visit friends? Boom! Ten minutes and you're there before the Tube even gets going. If, like me, you are at all nocturnal, a bike is a tremendous advantage. Trains and buses tend to become elusive as the wee hours approach. There is also a powerful contrast between a journey on a noisy and often dirty train or bus, and a graceful rhythmic ride in which you glide through calm and silent streets or through the stillness of a country night under the moon and stars.

Medical

All right, you say. So it takes less time than the Tube. But I've got to work for a living and the Tube is easier, takes less out of me. You expect me to get up in the morning and crack off 5 miles? Finish a day of hard work and do another 5? I'd never make it.

Get this. Even a moderate amount of exercise makes life *easier*. It gives your body tone and bounce which makes daily work and chores a breeze. Simply put, this is because exercise increases your range of possible effort, putting daily activities towards the centre rather than the peak of your capabilities. So as you go through the day you are just cruising. It's something like the difference between a 25- and 100-horsepower automobile engine. At 60 mph the 25 horse is working hard but the 100 is just loafing. It is important to realize that you can get this increased bounce, verve, and good feeling with relatively little time and effort. Bicycling will make your work and day easier, not harder.

Are you familiar with 'cleaning out' a motor vehicle? Cars today often operate in stop-and-go traffic for long periods of time. The engine becomes clogged with carbon and other residue. The car stumbles and staggers, it works harder than it needs to, and petrol consumption goes up. The best thing for any such car is to be taken out on a motorway and run fast, for at higher speeds the engine cleans itself out. Your body is a machine with exactly similar characteristics, and you will literally become more fagged out and tired just sitting still than if you run around the block a few times.

According to Eugene Sloane in his *Complete Book of Bicycling*, if you get in some sort of regular exercise you can expect:

to live for up to five years longer;
think better (more blood to the brain – and if you think this is crazy, go out and run around for a while and then think it through again);
sleep better, and in general be more relaxed;
be stronger and more resistant to injury;

reduce the incidence of degenerative vascular diseases responsible for or associated with heart attacks, strokes, and high blood pressure.

As cardiovascular problems account for over 50 per cent of all deaths each year, this last point is worth some elaboration. The basic deal with the cardiovascular system is movement, the flow of blood through your heart, veins, arteries, and so forth. The heart normally pumps about 5 quarts per minute and, during exercise, up to 30 quarts per minute. If this flow is sluggish and slow, the system clogs up. In arteriosclerosis, for example, the walls of the system become hardened and calcified. This decreases the bore of the arteries and veins, resulting in a diminished capacity to carry blood. The heart must therefore pump harder and higher blood pressure results. High blood pressure is a cause of stroke or rupture of brain blood vessels. Arteriosclerosis happens to everybody, but extent is governed by the rate of flow of the blood. Exercise stimulates the blood flow, and does not permit calcification to occur as rapidly.

Atherosclerosis is a related malady. This is when fatty substances are deposited on the lining of the blood vessels. Clots in the blood may be formed as a result, and these can jam up the system at critical points, such as the brain or heart, causing a stroke or heart attack. Again, exercise by stimulating the blood flow helps prevent fatty deposits.

So, the main benefits of regular exercise are first, that it will help keep your blood circulatory system cleaned out; secondly, the heart muscle, like any other, responds to exercise by becoming larger and more efficient, so that each heartbeat delivers more oxygen to the body; and thirdly, lung-filling capacity is restored or enlarged. In short, you can do more, and recover more quickly from doing it.

Bicycling, in particular, is a complete exercise. Not only are the legs, the body's largest accessory blood-pumping mechanism, used extensively, but also arm, shoulder, back, abdominal and diaphragmatic muscles. At the same time there is enough flexibility so that muscle groups can be worked individually, and of course pace can be set to suit the rider.

A word about weight control. Bicycling or other exercise will help your body's tone and figure. But for weight loss, eat less food. A brisk ride does not entitle you to apple pie and ice cream. Regular cycling burns about 300 calories per hour and hill climbing or racing about 600 per hour. Your body uses up about 150 calories per hour anyway, and so in the case of regular cycling this means a burn-up of an extra 150 calories per hour. At 3,600 calories per pound, it would take 24 hours of riding to lose this amount. It's much simpler just to eat less. Curiously enough, cycling may help you to do this. Regular exercise can change the metabolic balance of the body and restore normal automatic appetite control so that you eat no more than you actually need.

A serious health hazard for the urban cyclist is hyperventilation of highly polluted air. See Traffic Jamming (p 94) for more information on this subject.

Ecology

Great Britain is literally drowning in pollutants and many of them come from transportation machinery. In cities the internal combustion engine is a prime offender, contributing up to 85 per cent of all air pollution,* and of an especially noxious quality. The effluents from petroleum engines hang in the air and chemically interact with other substances and sunlight to form even deadlier poisons. Living in a major city is the same thing as smoking two packs of cigarettes a day.†

All city transportation contributes to pollution. Trains run on electricity generated in plants fired by fossil fuels or deadly atomic reactors. But as anyone who has been lucky enough to live through a taxicab strike or vehicle ban knows, cars and buses are the real problem. I shall never forget a winter a number of years ago when a friend and I came driving into New York City late at night after a holiday in Canada. To my amazement, the lights of the city shone like jewels and each building was clear and distinct. From the west bank of the Hudson river I could for the first (and perhaps only) time in my life see Manhattan and the Bronx in perfect detail from beginning to end, and even beyond to Brooklyn and her bridges. As we crossed the George Washington Bridge the air was clean and fresh, and the city, usually an object of horror and revulsion, was astoundingly beautiful and iridescent. The explanation was simple: enough snow had fallen to effectively eliminate vehicle traffic for a couple of days. No vehicles, no junk in the air. A better world.

* Reinow, L. & L., *Moment in the Sun* (Ballantine, New York).
† Commoner, Barry, *The Closing Circle* (Jonathan Cape, London).

Arguments against motorized transport are usually dismissed as idealistic and impractical and on the grounds that the time-saving characteristics of such vehicles are essential. The fact is that even pedestrians are easily able to drone past most traffic, and of course bicycles can do even better. A saving in physical effort is realized, but few of us are healthy enough to need this, or dismiss inhaling the poisons (equivalent to two packs of cigarettes a day) which necessarily accompany the internal combustion engine.

Walking, roller-skating, or riding a bicycle is an efficient use of energy and reduces wastage. Professor Rice in *Technology Review* has calculated that a cyclist can do 1,000 miles on the food energy equivalent of a gallon of petrol, which will move a car only some 20 or 30 miles. His figures are based on a 40-pound bicycle, and could probably be doubled for a 20-pound lightweight. Facts and figures be as they may, utilizing a 100-horsepower, 3,000-pound behemoth to move one single 150-pound person a few miles is like using an atomic bomb to kill a canary. Great Britain runs neck and neck with the United States in its ability to consume and waste, and in relation to the size of her population utilizes a disproportionately large proportion of the world's resources. For example, we import fish meal from African countries where people are starving, to feed beef herds, and then wonder why people down there don't like us. Great Britain's dependence on imports needs no documentation. The point is, many of the commodities we take for granted are gained at considerable expense to a world hurting badly for food and other necessities. Using a bicycle is a starting antidote to the horrors of consumerism.

Which brings us to the most positive series of reasons for trying to use bicycles at every opportunity. Basically, this is that it will enhance your life, bringing to it an increase in quality of experience which will find its reflection in everything you do.

Well! You have to expect that I would believe bicycling is a good idea, but how do I get off expressing the notion that bicycling is philosophically and morally sound? Because it is something that *you do*, not something that is done to you. Need I chronicle the oft-cited concept of increasing alienation in our lives? The mechanization of work and daily activities, the hardships our industrial society places in the way of loving and fulfilling relationships and family life, the tremendous difficulties individuals experience trying to influence political and economic decisions which affect them and others?

Of course there will always be people who say that they like things the way they are. They find the Tube really interesting, or insist on driving a chrome bomb and rattling everybody's windows. But the fact is that trains are crowded, dirty, impersonal and *noisy*, and nearly all cars are ego-structured worthless tin junk (with bikes the more you pay the less you get).

The most important effect of mechanical contraptions is that they defeat consciousness. Consciousness, self-awareness, and development are the prerequisites for a life worth living. Now look at what happens to you on a bicycle. It's immediate and direct. *You* pedal. *You* make decisions. *You* experience the tang of the air and the surge of power as you bite into the road. You're vitalized. As you hum along you fully and gloriously experience the day, the sunshine, the clouds, the breezes. You're alive! You are going some place, and it is *you* who is doing it. Awareness increases, and each day becomes a little more important to you. With increased awareness you see and notice more, and this further reinforces awareness.

Each time you insert *you* into a situation, each time *you* experience, you fight against alienation and impersonality, you build consciousness and identity. You try to understand things in the ways that are important to you. And these qualities carry over into everything you do.

An increased value on one's own life is the first step in social conscience and politics. Because to you life is dear and important and fun, you are much more easily able to understand why this is also true for a Vietnamese, a black, or a Tobago islander. Believe it. The salvation of the world is the development of personality and identity for everybody in it. Much work, many lifetimes. But a good start for you is *Get a bicycle*!

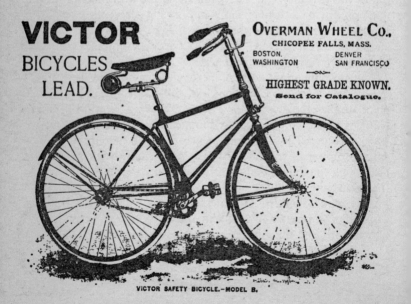

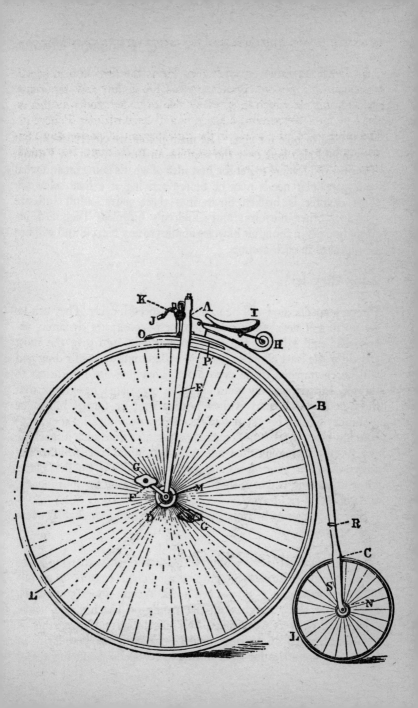

What kind of bike for you? The main points are covered here, but you should also look over the sections on Buying, Riding, Fitting, Touring and Racing to get the best idea of what's going on and what your particular needs may be before arriving at a final selection. This chapter is broken down into three parts: adult full-size bicycles; other bicycles; and children's bicycles. Technical information given for adult bicycles applies to any bicycle and will not be repeated in each section.

Adult Bicycles

I hope your decision will be to get a 10-speed bicycle. They can be set up to suit nearly any rider, job, or purpose; are dynamic, responsive, and vibrant, the most comfortable, and give the most speed for the least effort so that you will get more out of riding and will be encouraged to do even more. They are also the easiest to service. Initial cost may seem high, but experience has shown that most people who start with a heavyweight or tourist model or gimmicky folding bike soon find themselves desiring (and acquiring) a racing bike. It takes no longer than the first time such a machine sweeps by them going up a hill. Although initial cost is higher my advice is to *save your money* and get a racing bike in the first place. More important, you have the most fun and turn-on for your money, and you get it right away.

Bicycle categories by function break down into four slightly overlapping groups:

(1) The heavy roadster, built entirely of steel, with wide 1½-in tyres, roller lever brakes, a totally-encased chain running in an oil-filled gear case, and 1- or 3-speed gears. Weight about 50 pounds. Suitable for really tough work like riding on beaches and fields, newspaper delivery, collisions, and absolutely no care, this is sometimes called an 'Africa' model because of its popularity in developing countries for transporting heavy loads, bouncing across

deserts and through jungles and the like. A frame and forks designed for taking the sting out of bumps make them particularly steady and graceful; and for this reason they are also very popular with Netherlands housewives. The Netherlands are mostly flat however, and pedalling them elsewhere is HARD WORK!

(2) The sports roadster, also called tourist model or English racer, with a lighter frame and mudguards, cable calliper brakes, flat handlebars, 26-in × 1⅜-in tyres, and 1-, 3-, or 5-speed hub gearing. This is the one for utility use such as local errands, shopping, lots of stop-and-go riding, short trips, good durability, and minimal maintenance. Weight about 35 pounds.

(3) Club sports or semi-racer, light frame, 27-in × 1¼-in high pressure tyres, cable brakes, dropped handlebars, 5- to 15-speed derailleur gears, some alloy components, mudguards or not depending on model, and weight between 25 and 35 pounds. Touring and general use, but overall not of the first water.

(4) Racing bikes, flat out. In road versions these have ultra-light frames, all alloy components, cable brakes, 10- or 15-speed close ratio derailleur gears, dropped handlebars, and tubular tyres. Many of these machines, modified with wide ratio gears, mudguards and pannier racks, make lovely touring and utility bikes. Weight from 20 to 30 pounds, depending on equipment. Track racing bikes are utterly stark, with a single fixed gear, no brakes, and a weight of approximately 17 pounds.

These categories overlap somewhat. A manufacturer may bring out a 5-speed derailleur bike with flat handlebars and call it a 'tourist' model. The same machine with dropped bars becomes a 'racer'. For the sake of simplicity I am going to speak of 3-speed bicycles, by which I mean those with 3- to 5-speed internal hub gears; and 10-speed bicycles, those with a 5- to 15-speed derailleur gear system. If this is Greek to you, hold on for just a moment.

The 10-speed models are for longer trips over 25 miles, touring, racing, hilly terrain; durability is dependent on model, and maintenance is moderate. Actually, a 10-speed can be set up for almost any job or purpose except beach riding. The same machine, with minor modifications, can compete in a race, go on a camping tour, and haul groceries or newspapers. It can even pull a trailer. The only crucial difference between the 3- and 10-speed is the method of operation for the gears: the 3-speed can be shifted to the correct

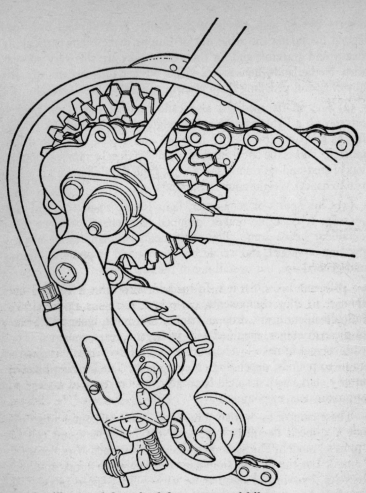

Rear derailleur and freewheel for a 10-speed bike

gear at any time; the 10-speed must be shifted while the bicycle is in motion. It's easy once you get the knack, and the 10-speed's efficiency outweighs the disadvantage of initial unfamiliarity. If you get stopped in a 'wrong' (inefficient) gear, it is easy to shift once you are under way again.

The question of durability is largely a function of bicycle model and weight and rider sense. 10-speeds range from ultra-light (20 pounds) alloy models to heavy (35 pounds) steel models. My

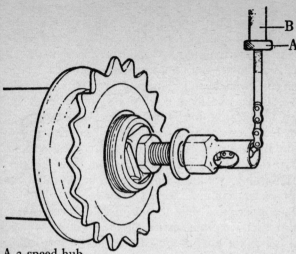

A 3-speed hub

first 10-speed was a sturdy machine with steel wheels which I not only rode hard and fast over bumpy streets, but also used for games of bicycle tag in the woods and fields, as well as just plain cross-country and back-trail riding. It held up just fine.

The classic down-swept handlebars of the 10-speed are not a requirement; you can equip or buy such a bike with conventional tourist handlebars, although it wouldn't be to your advantage to do so (more on handlebars later). With the exception of the cheaper models, 10-speed bikes have the much better centre-pull calliper brakes, rather than the coaster or side-pull calliper brakes usually supplied with 3-speed bikes. Comfort is sometimes cited in favour of the 3-speed. The fact is that the 10-speed has a wider variety of riding positions, allows you to utilize more muscles to greater advantage, and is therefore much less tiring to ride than a 3-speed.

A choice between the 3- and 10-speed bike is therefore largely governed by the type of person you are and how heavy you want to get into bicycling, the contents of your wallet, and real-life physical factors such as the quality of your neighbourhood and the number of stairs you climb every day. It is the first of these which is the most relevant, and what you must assess is how much consciousness you want to bring to bicycling. Not everybody is interested in the boiling scald of blood through their veins as they sprint up the road, or the eerie desolation of a chill night. Get a 3-speed if: you are not terribly interested in bicycling and just want something you can stick in the shed or basement to use for local jaunts once or twice a month (if you're really in this category and can do so, rent machines); you or the prospective rider are not at all mechanically inclined and don't care to be; you need a knock-around bike for use by several different people; or just want a worry-free machine. There is nothing degenerate about this last state of affairs. There are times when I prefer the totally casual spirit of the 3-speed, where one can just drop it on the spot, bash it around, and in general not think about what is going on. But this is the exception, not the rule. Over the long haul, the 10-speed is just so much better, so much more rewarding, that it will surely overcome any diffidence you feel about bicycling and make you an enthusiast.

Expense is a consideration only if your absolute maximum is £20·00, which restricts you to a serviceable used 3-speed. If you have £25·00 to £30·00 you can buy a used bike that at least has 10 speeds, if nothing else. More on this later.

Most of the more pragmatic considerations in type of bicycle are physical:

For hilly terrain get a 10-speed, no matter what.

If you live at the end of a long, rocky dirt road you may want a sturdier model 10-speed. This is also a question of rider weight. For example, I gave a Peugeot UO-8 to a thirteen-year-old, 100-pound

RUSHING A RISE.

cousin five years ago. At 27 pounds this is closer to an ultra-light 20-pound racer than a 35-pound heavyweight. My cousin's family lives at the top of a steep, winding, rocky dirt road about one-eighth of a mile long, and my cousin's idea of fun is to blaze down the hill as fast as he can. The Peugeot is holding up fine, but I am sure that if I tried the same stunt with my 150 pounds, wear and tear on the machine would be noticeably greater. Bear in mind that 'sturdier' bikes are built that way because they have to be in order to overcome inherently inferior materials and manufacturing techniques. The amount of extra strength gained is debatable, and only at considerable costs to the power-to-weight ratio. I myself would stick with a lighter machine – and take it easy over the bumps.

Carrying the bicycle is a problem largely confined to stair-climbing flat dwellers. There's only one answer, and that's a light 10-speed. Folding bikes and 3-speeds run to 35–45 pounds. I'm not Charles Atlas, but I'm certainly of average strength or better, and I assure you that the difference between 20 and 45 pounds up two to four flights of stairs is very noticeable. Unless you are particularly athletic, get a 10-speed.

Using a car or public transportation to reach a departure point for a trip is also part of carrying. Any 10-speed is easier to take apart than a 3-speed, and if your bike is even of minimal quality, it will have quick-release wheels which come off at the flick of a lever. Or it can be equipped with lever-nuts for 50p. A folding bike takes up a little less room, true, but has innate limitations (look 'em up in Other Bicycles, pp 54–57), so you lose more than you gain.

Storage is also an issue only for flat dwellers. Again, although the folding bike takes up less room, on balance the 10-speed wins out. With the wheels off it can be hung in the closet. If you are really cramped, hang it from the ceiling or wall via brackets or pulleys. Stick it in the shower cabinet or bathtub. Look afield. Your building (or one nearby) should have a basement or broom closet or some other niche. You can work something out and under any circumstance will find the 10-speed easier to deal with than the 3-speed.

For frequency of repair the 3-speed has it all over the 10-speed. All the 3-speed hub will need for years is a monthly shot of oil. Once it does break down, however, it is much too complicated to fix, and most bicycle shops will simply replace it. It is also considerably less efficient than the 10-speed design, and transmits less pedal effort to the rear wheel. The 10-speed, while more efficient, requires more frequent adjustment and servicing. However, because the parts are all quite simple and out in the open where they are easy to get at, this is easy to do. In fact, it is part of the fun of riding. The vitality and responsiveness of the 10-speed is such that you come to enjoy fine-tuning your bike.

Perhaps now you have started to form a notion of what kind of bike you would like to have. But there are still more types: mini-bikes, folding bikes, tandems, tricycles, and prices for this bewildering array vary from £40 to £300. I will discuss these under Other Bicycles (pp 54–60), but first here is some technical information to guide you through the maze and help you to get your money's worth.

The significant components of a bicycle are the frame, brakes, rims, tyres and hubs; gears and gear-changing hardware, chainwheel, cranks, and pedals; and stem, handlebars, and saddle. According to the grade of component selected by the manufacturer, the price for a 3-speed will range from £50 to £65, from £70 to £140 for production line 10-speeds, and £140 and up for custom-made bikes. Manufacturers tend to assemble rather than manufacture bicycles, getting the components from a number of independent companies. Hence, two bikes in the same price category from two different brand name 'manufacturers' sometimes have exactly the same parts.

The Frame

The frame is the heart and soul of a bicycle. It is the determining factor of bicycle weight, and the more you pay the lighter the weight for the same strength. Frames are not meant to be rigid or unyielding, but rather to absorb irregularities from the road surface. Called resiliency or twang or flex, this is a function of quality of materials and manufacturing methods, and gives better bikes more springiness and vitality. There is no way to improve a cheap frame. Other components can be modified or changed but the frame endures, and it should be the first focus of your attention when considering a prospective bike.

Inexpensive coaster brake, 3-speed, and cheap 10-speed bikes use seamed tubing, made by wrapping a long, flat strip of steel into a tube and then welding it together (electrically) at high

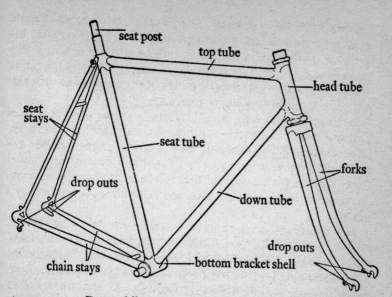

temperature. Better bikes use a seamless tubing which is even in bore throughout. The best bikes use special, cold-drawn alloy steel seamless double-butted tubing. Double-butted means that while the outside diameter of the tube remains constant, it is thicker on the inside at the ends, where greater strength is needed.

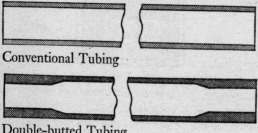

Conventional Tubing

Double-butted Tubing

The method by which the frame parts are attached to each other is important. Bikes with seamed tubing are usually just stuck together and welded, leaving a smooth joint. This is the commonest and weakest type of assembly. The welding, done at high temperatures, robs the metal of strength. High-carbon bike tube steel becomes brittle and subject to fatigue when heated. With better bikes the frame is lugged and brazed, rather than welded. Lugging is the

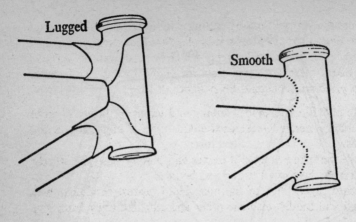

Lugged

Smooth

addition of reinforcing metal at stress points, and brazing is done at lower temperatures than welding. Make sure that the job has been done cleanly and neatly on any prospective bike you examine.

The very, very best frames are Reynolds 531, Columbus, or Falk, double-butted, with Reynolds generally considered the finest. Reynolds 531 comes in several grades. Read the label to see what you are getting:

Only the top tube, seat tube, and down tube are Reynolds 531 plain gauge tubing.

Only the top tube, seat tube, and down tube are Reynolds 531 double butted tubing.

All the tubing is Reynolds 531 plain gauge.

All the tubing is Reynolds 531 double butted.

Chances are you will not be getting double-butted tubing unless you have elected to spend upwards of £140. However, you should at least get seamless lugged tubing, which is used even on low-cost quality bikes. Here are three tests for frame quality. Differences between price ranges should be evident.

(1) Weight. Electric welded tubing and joints are heavy in order to overcome inherent weaknesses of this type of construction and materials.

(2) Lift the bike a couple of inches and bounce it on the wheels. Better frames have more twang and bounce.

(3) Stand to one side of the bike. Hold nearest handlebar with one hand and saddle with the other and tilt bike away from you.

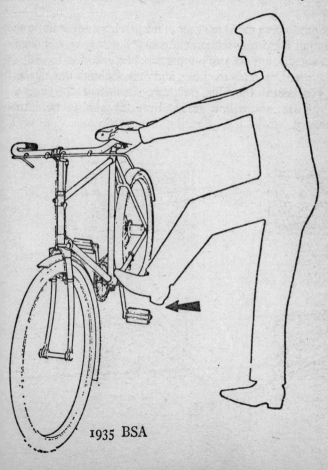

1935 BSA

Place one foot on end of bottom bracket axle and give a *gentle* push. A good frame will flex and then spring right back. Try several different bikes to get the feel of it and *be careful*; the idea is to find frames that will give with a gentle push, not bend anything you may encounter. If enough force is applied, cheap frames will bend – permanently.

Bicycle frames come in different designs. The commonest for touring use is 72° parallel. This means that the angle to the top tube formed by the seat and head tubes is 72° (see below).

This is the standard design and gives an excellent combination of road holding, shock absorption and power transmission. It is best for bumpy urban streets. Road and track racing frames are steeper, usually 73°, 73½°, or 74° parallel, or combinations like 74° head and 73° seat. The ride is stiffer, but more power is transmitted to the wheels. Some riders use these frames for touring and around town sprinting, but it is inadvisable for anything but very smooth roads. Out-and-out racing frames use shorter fork blades and seat and chain stays to bring the wheels in closer, and cannot be fitted with mudguards. The rake of the front fork, e.g., the distance between the front wheel axle and a line formed by extending the head tube downwards, is usually less on racing frames than touring or semi-

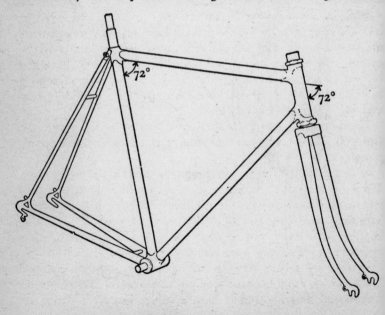

racing frames, and this also contributes to a stiffer ride and brighter handling.

Summary

One of the most satisfying and important features of a good bike is responsiveness and whip-like flex that you can feel with your whole body. The main determinants of this quality are the frame materials and construction.

In 10-speed bikes expect the following:

Under £70 – Seamed, smooth-joint frame.
£70 to £85 – Seamless, lugged-joint frame.
£85 to £100 – Seamless, lugged-joint frame, with main tubes of 531 plain gauge or equivalent.
Over £140 – Seamless, double-butted, lugged-joint, low-temperature brazed frame.

The Brakes

It is the nature of bicycling accidents that the bicyclist more often runs into something than is run into. Good, well-adjusted brakes are vital, and especially in traffic.

Pedal-operated coaster brakes are only for small children who lack the necessary strength to actuate hand levers. Although they are easy to apply, they are hard to control and can lock a wheel, causing a skid. They do not have actual stopping power. It's a skid or next to nothing. Skidding is a bad way to stop since (a) it takes too long; (b) at high speeds it is excessively exciting; and (c) wear and tear on the tyres is very high.

Hand-operated calliper brakes come in two types, centre and side-pull. These brakes give more control and hence greater stopping power.

Side-pull calliper brakes are commonly used on less costly bikes. They are somewhat inconsistent in performance, although they will work if kept in constant adjustment. Centre-pull brakes are better. Because they pull from the centre they work in balance, and are more even, precise, and powerful. They are also more reliable and require less maintenance than side-pull brakes.

Ultra-fancy racing bicycles use special lightweight side-pull brakes with a rigid design affording precise control at high speeds. Centre-pull brakes generally have a softer, less rigid design re-

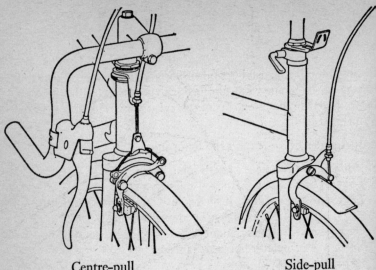

Centre-pull   Side-pull

quiring less brake lever pressure for a complete stop, but which can 'snatch' at high speeds, e.g. exert more de-acceleration than necessary or, for a racing bike, safe. Both types stop equally well; the side-pull brakes has the edge for speed control. However, good side-pull brakes run between £30 and £60 per set, and are only worth considering for bicycles costing £200 or more. For ordinary road use the much less expensive (about £12) centre-pull design is perfectly suitable, and since required force on the levers is less, even preferable for touring and utility bicycles. These distinctions are quite fine; the winning bicycle of the 1976 Tour de France was equipped with centre-pull brakes. Good brand names are Campagnolo, Shimano, Dia-Compe, Weinmann, Universal, and Mafac. Be sure that the levers on the brand you select fit your grip (see page 77 for the most often used hand position for braking).

A variant of the centre-pull is the cantilever brake, which pivots on a boss brazed on to the fork blades and seat stays (see opposite). Powerful, and less likely to 'whip' (where the whole brake assembly judders back and forth), cantilever brakes are good for the heavily laden tourist, cyclo-cross, and tandems and tricycles. There is also a saving of six ounces in weight over the conventional centre-pull. However, only cyclo-cross and custom-made frames are likely to have the requisite brazed-on bosses necessary to mount cantilevers

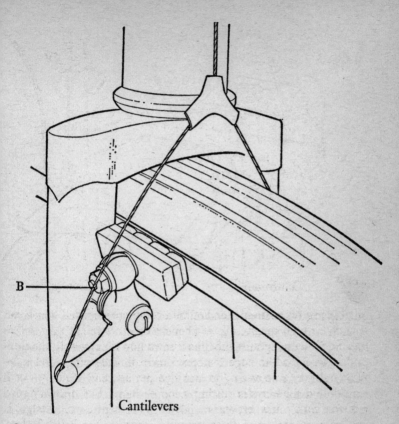

B

Cantilevers

Summary:

    Under £70 – Pedal-operated coaster or hand-operated side-pull calliper.

    Over £70 – Hand-operated centre-pull calliper.

Rims, Tyres, and Hubs

There are three types of rims. The Westwood, for use with $1\frac{1}{2}$-in tyres and roller lever brakes, is seen only on heavy roadsters and utility bikes. Modern bikes use Endrick rims, with wire-on $1\frac{3}{8}$-in to $1\frac{1}{4}$-in tyres (called 'clinchers' in the United States), or sprint rims, with tubular tyres ('sew-ups' for Americanos and 'singles' for Aussies). Wire-on tyres are the best choice for all-round urban use, as they are heavier, more durable, and easiest to repair.

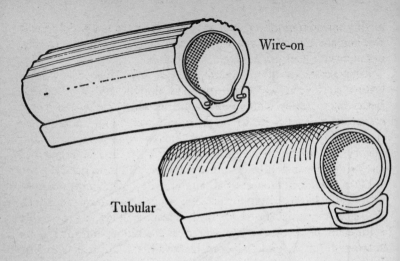

Wire-on

Tubular

Tubular tyres are lighter and offer less rolling resistance. They are common on high-quality bikes. They also cost more and get punctures more easily. Because the tube is sewn into the tyre it is impractical to repair on the road, necessitating the carrying of whole spare tyres (at £4·50 to £15·00 each) which must be glued on to the rim. While this process is quickly accomplished, it is a drag to lug a spare tyre with you wherever you go, since the spare can't be left on the bike when parked on the street. Wire-on tyres, available everywhere, are the only sensible choice.

A very lightweight high pressure wire-on (90–100 lb/sq in) has about the same performance as a heavy duty tubular. Only the lightest (and more expensive) tubulars are worth using, and then only for racing or very fast day rides. Wire-on tyres are the best choice for tours and utility riding.

Processes have been developed in America for making wire-on tyres puncture proof, at cost of greatly increased weight and harsher ride. Only riders who must regularly encounter broken glass, sharp stones, thorns, etc, on journeys short enough so that harder pedalling and a harsher ride are not important, should consider puncture proof wire-ons, and in any case these tyres are not yet available in this country.

Another development is puncture resistant tubulars. These look mighty interesting indeed, but at this writing are not widely available and are untried. If you are interested in high performance keep in touch with your dealer about this product.

Rims are either of aluminium alloy or steel. Less costly bikes feature steel rims, which are the most durable and the heaviest. Better bikes feature aluminium alloy rims which are lighter but of course more fragile. Really brutal riding over bumpy terrain may require steel rims but I have found the alloy wheels entirely satisfactory. An important consideration is that in the wet aluminium alloy rims offer much better braking power than steel rims.

Hubs also come in steel or aluminium alloy. They may use conventional bolts, requiring the use of a wrench to remove the wheel, or quick-release levers which work instantly. This is a desirable feature for bikes that will be stored in the closet, transported by automobile often, or left locked in the street. You can also buy lever-type nuts for about 50p each which are not as fast as the quick-release levers but at least don't require a wrench.

A recent development are hubs with sealed bearings which do not require lubrication or adjustment. In ordinary service these units are durable. However, very wet, muddy, or dusty conditions may make servicing a requirement, and this is difficult to do.

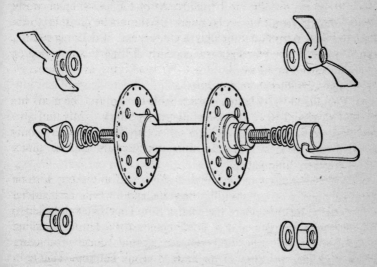

Summary

Under £70 – Steel rims and bolt-on hubs, wire-on tyres.

£70 to £85 – Alloy rims and quick-release hubs, wire-on tyres.

Over £85 – Alloy rims and quick-release hubs, choice of wire-on or tubular tyres.

Gear Changing Mechanisms, Cranks and Chainwheel, and Pedals

Nearly all 3-speed bikes use Sturmey-Archer or Shimano multi-speed hubs, no matter what price range. At the core of the design of the 10-speed bike are the derailleurs, which shift the chain from sprocket to sprocket. Differences between brands are to be found in weight, smoothness and precision of shifting, and durability. However, each manufacturer offers several different grades of derailleurs in two different categories, competition and touring. For example, the Campagnolo 'Nuovo Record' (competition) and 'Rally' are top of the line products of irreproachable beauty and performance, as well they might be with respective price tags of about £20 and £22. Campagnolo's 'Vallentino' economy model on the other hand, has not been well received, and there are plenty of other inexpensive units which are better.

Simplex is a popular brand, although a small but absolutely vital part of the main body on a brand new one I had spontaneously disintegrated, requiring replacement of the entire unit. My experience was not unique, for due to a heavy use of delrin, a plastic, the Simplex is noted for lightness, smooth shifting, a certain degree of fragility, and rapid wear.

Shimano produces a comprehensive line of derailleurs. Their low cost 'Eagle' and 'Lark' models are reliable but heavy. The medium-cost 'Titlist' and '600' series derailleurs are much lighter and give excellent performance. The Crane series derailleurs are fully competitive with the best European units, and have the edge on price. The 'Positron' automatically positions the chain correctly for any gear selected, thus avoiding missed shifts and chain grind. It is especially useful on urban utility bicycles, and for beginning riders.

Best value for money are the Madea Sun Tour series derailleurs, popular with tourists and a good choice for beginning riders. They have wide range, and positive shifting under load, e.g., when pedalling pressure is maintained while shifting. This is a common novice error, and a recurrent problem whilst climbing hills with a heavily laden touring bike. Campagnolo and Shimano units are smooth and precise when operated correctly, but can jam up and grind when shifted under load.

Gearing is a major factor to consider in the choice of derailleurs, and this subject is covered under Fitting (p 73). Read this chapter before purchasing a bike.

Cranks and chainwheel

Fine bikes use cotterless cranks and chainwheels of dural, an aluminium alloy. Campagnolo and Shimano are the top brands, with prices to £60. Best value is the Sugino 'Maxy' (about £11). Zeus, Stronglight, TA, and Williams are all good makes. Less expensive bikes use steel cotterless, or alloy cottered, cranks and chainwheels. Cheap bikes use cottered steel. A one piece design called the Ashtabula is used on many American-made bikes. A freewheeling chainwheel by Shimano which allows derailleur gear shifts without pedalling may be useful for beginning riders. However, it is mechanically complex, and of too recent development for a reliability rating.

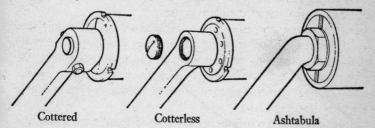

Cottered   Cotterless   Ashtabula

Pedals come in three types: (1) the classic rubber tread; (2) road racing and touring, the design you want; and (3) track racing, which has special teeth for gripping shoes.

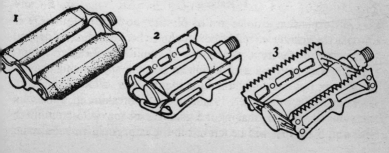

Saddle

Three-speed bikes generally have a mattress design wide saddle with coil springs. Racing bike saddles are long and narrow to minimize friction between the legs.

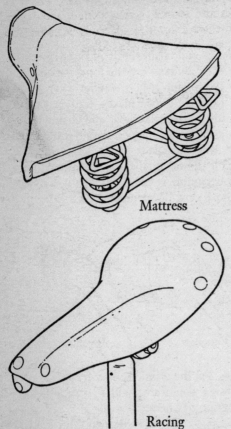

Mattress

Racing

Less expensive saddles are of plastic, the best of leather, with Brooks the acknowledged leader. A choice between the two depends somewhat on the type of riding and conditions. Leather wants a minimum of 500 miles of riding to become supple and properly broken in, but once done the fit is so good you will keep the saddle from one bike to another. Plastic needs no breaking in, and is impervious to weather, making it a good choice for cyclo-cross machines and bikes that will be left out in the rain. A plastic saddle such as the Unica (12 oz) is half the weight of the leather Brooks Pro (25 oz), and this is a decisive factor in short-distance and track-competition events. The problem with plastic is that in warm weather it has you slipping about in your own sweat. A compromise has been sought in models such as the Milremo Super de Luxe, which are plastic covered with foam and leather, softer to ride, and a good choice for riders who will cover a lot of rough roads or paths. Also popular and comfortable, are suede covered saddles.

Handlebars

Handlebars come in four standard designs:

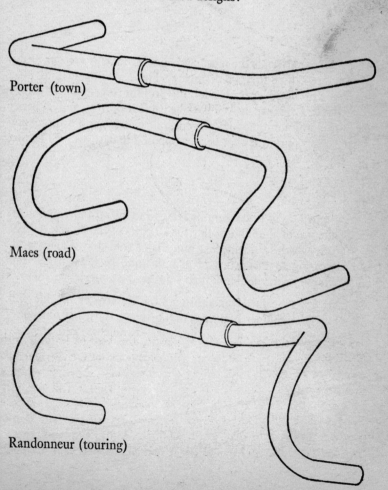

Porter (town)

Maes (road)

Randonneur (touring)

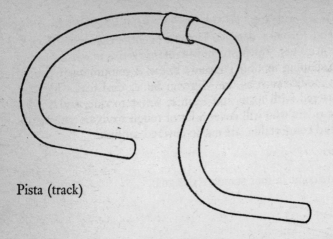

Pista (track)

The Maes pattern is the most common downswept version, and is suitable for either touring or racing. The Randonneur and Pista patterns are more specialized, and are for touring and racing respectively. On inexpensive bikes the bars are of steel, and on better bikes of aluminium alloy. For more information, and a discussion of the virtues of downswept bars as opposed to flat bars, see Fitting (p 73).

Summary

As you move up in price from under £70 to over £130 you find an increasing use of aluminium alloy for all parts of the bicycle, except the frame, which in quality machines is of cold-drawn alloy steel, and increasing sophistication of manufacture, such as lugged and brazed frame joints, double-butted frames, and cotterless cranks.

Under £70 – Seamed, smooth-joint frame; coaster or side-pull calliper brakes; wire-on tyres; rims, bolt-on hubs, cranks and chainwheels, handlebar and stem of steel.

£70–£110 – Seamless, lugged-joint frame; centre-pull calliper brakes; wire-on tyres; rims, quick-release hubs, cranks and chainwheels, handlebar and stem of aluminium alloy.

Over £130 – Seamless, double-butted, lugged-joint, low-temperature brazed frame; centre-pull calliper brakes;

choice of tubular or wire-on tyres; knurled rims, quick-release hubs, cranks and chainwheels, handlebar and stem of aluminium alloy.

There are many different brands of bicycles, and each manufacturer usually produces several grades of machine. To say 'Peugeot' means little, since the bike in question may be the utterly basic AO-8 or the very lovely competition PX-10. Major manufacturers generally offer the following categories:

(1) A basic 10-speed with steel parts throughout.

(2) A low-cost quality 10-speed racer with mostly aluminium alloy parts throughout.

(3) The same bike as (2) but equipped for touring with mudguards, chainguard, lights and rack, and sometimes 15-speeds (3 chainwheels instead of 2).

(4) Competition-grade ultra-light racing bikes.

I can't possibly cover and evaluate every available bike and therefore am going to make recommendations by category only, and largely to set standards. The bikes that I list are fair values for the money. Diligent shopping may net you a better buy. Many bike shops have one or two specials where you may compromise on colour or some other vital consideration for a good break in price or more machine for the money. In any case, apply and use the technical information I have given you. There are many, many fine bicycles which are not listed and you will be doing yourself a disservice if you pass them by.

In the standard 1- and 3-speed bicycles the large manufacturers offer good quality and value. In 10-speed racing and touring models, the products of smaller firms that specialize in this kind of bicycle are usually better. Decent 10-speed bicycles are fairly refined and exact pieces of machinery, and while the use of mass production techniques for their manufacture is far from impossible, it is difficult. Bicycle dealers, mechanics and riders report that 10-speed models from large manufacturers are sometimes poorly prepared, and are subject to breakdowns. Products of the smaller, more specialized firms are more likely to come from the factory properly assembled and ready-to-go, and give less trouble in service. They are also more likely to have quality features such as leather saddles and ball-bearing pedals.

On the other hand, there are many bicycle dealers and riders who swear by the large firms, and say their products are the best value in any model or price range. In the next chapter I tell you where and how to buy a bicycle, and extol the virtues of your friendly local bicycle shop. I suggest that you be guided by the shop owner's counsel. If he says that the product of a large manufacturer is of good quality and *he* is willing to stand behind it … that is important, and many, many, many are the miles I have gone on popular brand name bicycles. For the more esoteric touring and racing machines – say, over £75 – I personally would favour a smaller company whose main business is this sort of bike. In any case, I repeat, use the technical information I have given you. In any given model there is often little to choose between three or four manufacturers, and in fact variations in manufacturing quality control can mean that in one batch of bikes manufacturer A's is the best, while in another batch of exactly the same models, manufacturer B's is 'better'. Look for yourself.

Specifications for each bike are as complete as possible. Do not be put off however, if, for example, you find a different make of derailleur on a bike than is listed here. The desirability and/or availability of components can change rapidly. Japanese products are gaining an increased share of the market, and if quality and value are maintained, this trend should continue.

Heavy-duty Roadster

Raleigh 'Superbe'. Equipped with Sturmey-Archer 3-speed gears, brazed frame with cutaway lugs, side-pull calliper brakes, dyno lighting which functions even when the bike is stationary, roller lever brakes, 26-in special section Raleigh rims, lockable steering, enclosed transmission, rear hold-all, and prop stand. Frame sizes 21 in or 23 in, colour green. Weight 45–50 pounds. Price, approx £85, including VAT.

It is a well-made, very fully equipped bike and I wouldn't mind having one out in the shed – but not for £85. That kind of money will buy three to five similar used bikes in good nick. There is no need to pay extra for the dubious privilege of pushing 45–50 pounds around.

Sports Roadster

(1) Hercules Balmoral AW. Sturmey-Archer 3-speed gears, side-pull calliper brakes, mudguards, pump, colour green. Men's

sizes 21 in, 23 in, ladies' 21 in. Price, approx £58. Single-speed in 21 in only. Price, approx £53.

(2) Raleigh Wayfarer. Sturmey-Archer 3-speed gears, side-pull calliper brakes, mudguards, hold-all bag, pump, chainwheel protector, colour blue. Men's sizes 19½ in, 21 in, 23 in, ladies' 19½ in, 21 in. Price, approx £61. With dyno hub lights (men's 21 in, 23 in, ladies' 21 in only). Price, approx £68. Single-speed, all sizes. Price, approx £54.

(3) Puch Touring. Styria 3-speed gears, side-pull calliper brakes, mudguards, sprung rear carrier, pump, chainwheel protector. Men's sizes 20 in, 21¼ in, 22½ in, in green, ladies' 20 in, in salamander. Price, approx £65.

(4) Raleigh Esquire. Sturmey-Archer 3-speed gears, side-pull calliper brakes with self-adjusting levers, reflectorized pedals, mudguards, hold-all bag, pump, chainwheel protector, colour bronze, white-wall tyres. Men's sizes 19½, in 21 in, 23 in. Price, approx £62. With dyno hub storage (stay on when bike stops) lights. Price, approx £71.

(5) Raleigh Caprice. As Esquire above but ladies', colour mauve. Sizes 19½ in, 21 in. Single-speed. Price, approx £62. Three-speed: Price, approx £67. With dyno hub storage lights. Price, approx £71.

(6) Puch Elegance. Styria 3-speed gears, side-pull calliper brakes, chrome mudguards, reflectorized pedals, sprung rear carrier, tool bag, white-wall tyres, chainwheel protector. Men's size 21¼ in, colours red or green. Ladies' size 20 in, colours bronze or green. Price, approx £75.

All of the above with mattress saddles and 26-in × 1⅜-in tyres. Choice of bike in this category is pretty much a matter of sorting out the accessories. Your own situation and needs determine priorities here, particularly with regard to lights. See Accessories (Chapter 9) for a detailed discussion.

Semi-sports

(1) Dawes Flair. Sizes: men's 21, 22½, or 23 in; ladies' 21 in. Five-speed Huret derailleur with stem control, or 3-speed hub. Alloy flat bars, high pressure 27-in × 1¼-in tyres on steel rims, Weinmann alloy calliper brakes, semi-sports saddle (a compromise between mattress and racing), reflectorized pedals, cushion

handlebar grips. Feran or plastic mudguards sprung rear carrier, chainwheel protector. Price, approx £75.

(2) Falcon Model 88 and 89. Sizes: men's 21 in, 22 in, 23 in, 24 in or 25 in; ladies' 21 in. Frame: Reynolds 531 tubing. Shimano 5-speed derailleur gears. Sugino alloy cotterless chainset. Alloy bars and stem. High pressure 27-in tyres on alloy rims. Blemels mudguards. Colour: black. Price, approx £80, including VAT.

The Falcon is especially nice. While retaining a conventional saddle and handlebars, these bicycles offer the advantage of derailleur gears and light weight (about 25 lb). Perfect for around town use and light touring. The extra cost of £15 to £20 over a sports roadster is amply repaid in eaiser and more enjoyable cycling.

Sports

Five-speed Derailleur

(1) Eddy Merckx Tour de L'Avenir Model 118. Sizes: 19½ in, 21½ in, 22½ in, 24 in. Shimano gears. Steel chainset. Alloy: Weinmann SP brakes, S/F hubs, bars and stem. Reflector pedals. Quilted saddle. Short mudguards. Colour: orange. Price approx £66, including VAT.

(2) Coventry Eagle Supersonic Model 36. Sizes: 19½ in, 21½ in, 23 in, 24½ in. Shimano gears. Alloy: Sugino cotterless chainset, S/F hubs, Weinmann SP brakes with dual levers, bars and stem. Quilted saddle. Stainless steel full mudguards. Colours: lavender or green. Price approx £70, including VAT.

Nine-speed Bicycles

These are created by combining a 3-speed freewheel with a 3-speed hub. The complete kit for this conversion, consisting of a 3-speed freewheel, derailleur, and shift lever and cable is manufactured and sold by the Cyclo Gear Company.

The disadvantage of this system is the inherent inefficiency of the internally geared hub. The advantage is that gears can be shifted quickly and positively through a wide range whether the bike is moving or not. This can be handy for people who are fumble-fingered, and for cyclo-cross types riding through fields and woods where most of the attention goes into staying upright. Here are the gear ratios commonly obtained through this conversion. Look up the section on Gearing (p 78) if you do not understand the meaning of the numbers. A 36T front chainwheel and 26-in wheel gives:

3-*speed hub*	*freewheel*		
1st	30·5	40·7	54·3
2nd	36·9	49·3	65·7
3rd	43·9	58·5	78

and a 40T front chainwheel and a 26-in wheel gives:

3-*speed hub*	*freewheel*		
1st	33·9	45·2	60·3
2nd	41·1	54·7	73
3rd	48·7	65	86·7

Ten- and Fifteen-speed Bicycles

A word for females: a ladies' pattern frame is structurally weaker and less responsive than a men's frame. Best recommendations are the Eddy Merckx Club Special 109 (21 in., Shimano gears. Alloy: Weinmann CP brakes, Sugino chainset, bars and stem. Plastic saddle. Colour: orange); the Dawes Fleur (21 in., Huret gears. Alloy: Weinmann SP brakes, hubs, bars, and stem. Steel: chainset and rims. Quilted saddle. Colours: blue or aqua); the Falcon Black Diamond 71 (19½ in or 21½ in, specification on p. 51); the Viscount Sebring (specification on p 51); and the Peugeot UE-18 (20 in. Simplex gears. Alloy: quick release hubs, Mafac CP brakes. Steel: chainwheel, mudguards, bars and stem. Mattress saddle. Carrier rack, pump, toolkit, and dynamo lights. Colours: blue or gold). For optimum performance I suggest a men's bike, but small size ladies are limited to the Eddy Merckx 118, Coventry Eagle Supersonic, Falcon Black Diamond, and Viscount Sebring and Sport. For a high quality bike with a Reynolds 531 or 531 double butted frame you will need a custom builder. If you want to tour, I suggest specifying a slightly raked top tube. This allows adequate bottom bracket height, a comfortable straddle when stationary, and, because a longer head tube can be used, increased frame flexibility (small frames tend to be stiff).

And a word for everybody. If you have less than £70 to spend I

recommend strongly the purchase of a used machine (see next chapter). You can get an acceptable 10-speed for as little as £30, and £35 to £45 will net you something unquestionably worth riding.

I have looked at a lot of low-priced new bikes for around £60, and they are mostly junk. Here, manufacturers have given in to un-principled consumerism and cut-throat competition. Many people don't know much about bikes. They want, say, a 10-speed with chromed fork tips and quick-release wheels, and look for the bike with these features at the lowest price. They don't know if the frame is made with old lead pipe. Spotty bright paint and glitter hide the truth. Wheels are out of true. Saddles are liquid, floppy plastic. Bearings bind. Derailleurs are low grade units that either slip or jam or break quickly. Brakes are often crummy. You get on one of these machines and things are such a grinding painful tor-ment that in a short while you decide the whole idea is worthless. Where is Old Invincible Ironsides you ask, that faithful heavyweight that at least works? It doesn't always happen this way. There are some shops too proud to sell junk, that will patiently spend the hours and hours necessary to put a cheaperoo bike right from the way it came from the factory – but there is nothing they can do about low-grade components. Most reputable shops will tell you to avoid the £60 10-speed bikes as pain and grief for everybody – you and the shop, where you will spend a lot of time if you buy one of these machines.

Anyway, the problem is not to save money, but to be sure you get what you pay for. Don't get duped by avaricious manufacturers who 'give in' to market pressure and deluge you with colourful brochures filled with pictures of happy types sporting about on garbage machinery. Ignore the junk. Know the fundamentals in his chapter and buy a bicycle that really will bring you joy and pleasure.

Recommended bicycles. Prices include VAT and are approximate.

(1) Coventry Eagle Supersonic Model 36. Specifications on p 48. £75.
(2) Falcon Black Diamond Model 70 and 71. Sizes: men's 19½ in, 21½ in, 23 in, 24 in; ladies' 19½ in or 21½ in. Seamless frame. Shimano gears. Alloy: Weinmann CP brakes, Sugino cotterless chainset, bolt on hubs, bars, and stem. Stainless steel mudguards. Plastic saddle. Toe clips and straps. Colours: silver or purple. £80.

Falcon bicycles (which include the Coventry Eagle and Eddy Merckx brands) consistently offer quality features at good value for money, and careful assembly at the factory so that in-service problems are minimized.

(3) Viscount Sebring. Sizes: 19½ in, 21 in, 23 in. Seamless frame. Shimano gears. Alloy: Shimano CP brakes with dual levers, SR cotterless chainset, bolt on hubs, bars and stem. Plastic mudguards. Quilted saddle. Colours: blue or red. £85.
(4) Viscount Aerospace Sport. Sizes: 19½ in, 21½ in, 22½ in, 23½ in, 24½ in. Frame: chrome–molybdenum alloy steel cold-drawn seamless double-brazed lugless, with full chrome forks. Shimano gears. Alloy: Viscount CP brakes with dual levers, Sugino cotterless chainset, Q/R hubs, bars, and stem. Spokes: 14 gauge. Plastic saddle. Colours: blue or red. £90.

The Sport has a frame geometry suitable for both touring and club racing. The hubs and bottom bracket utilize sealed bearings which do not require adjustment or lubrication. These are durable in ordinary service, but in severe conditions may need maintenance, and this is difficult to do. The sealed bearings, dual action brakes, and strong 14 gauge spokes are of particular interest to the tourist or utility rider, and racers will find the Sport lively and responsive

Bicycle made by T. & H. King, blacksmiths,
Wimborne, Dorset, 1872

(5) Falcon Olympic Model 78 and 79. Sizes: 21 in, 22 in, 23 in, 24 in, 25 in. Frame: Reynolds 531 plain gauge. Shimano gears. All alloy components. Sugino cotterless chainset. Weinmann CP brakes. Bolt on hubs. Stainless steel mudguards. Vinyl covered saddle. Colours: blue or green. £93.

(6) British Eagle. As Olympic above, but Q/R hubs and padded saddle. £105.

(7) Dawes Galaxy Deluxe. Sizes: 21 in, 22½ in, 23½ in, 25½ in. Frame: Reynolds 531 plain gauge. Sun Tour gears. All alloy components. Cotterless chainset. Weinmann CP brakes with dual levers. Q/R hubs. Brooks B-17 saddle. Plastic mudguards. Rear pannier carrier. Toe clips and straps. Colours: brown or green, with glisten or coloured mudguards. £130.

The Galaxy is the standby favourite quality touring bicycle. Workmanship and finish are to a high standard. Handling is excellent, even on rough surfaces.

(8) Peugeot PR10L. Sizes: 20 in, 21 in, 23 in, 24 in, 25 in. Frame: Reynolds 531 plain gauge. Simplex gears. All alloy components. Stronglight 49D cotterless chainset. Mafac CP

brakes. Q/R hubs. Ideale Leather saddle. Tubular tyres. Toe clips and straps. Colour: white. £135.

A very good basic racing bike which has claimed many victories.

In the price range of £135 and up are the offerings of small manufacturers and custom shops. Several are listed on p 68. They have models for touring road racing, hill climbs, track, time trials, cyclo cross, etc, mostly in the range £135 to £250, but with the fancier bikes going to £400 and beyond. In specification, these models reflect considerable experience and are a most worthwhile investment. Often gear ratios, fittings, and colour will be done to suit your particular needs although, as I say, the recommendations of the shop are a safe bet.

For £160 and up you can also construct your own bike. A factory produced double-butted frame runs around £50, with hand-made jobs starting at roughly £70. For £80 to £100 you can have a frame built to specification. The make and quality of the rest of the components is up to you. It is grand fun but I advise against building up a fully custom bike unless you know fairly well what you are doing – it can be expensive, and leave you with a bike which is not exactly what you want.

The New Club Cripper Tandem Quadricycle Roadster.

Other Bicycles

Small-wheel Bicycles

These are mini-bikes with 16-in or 20-in wheels, available with a variety of options, including hinged, folding frames. Their virtues are: (1) easy storage; (2) good luggage capacity; (3) manoeuvrability; and (4) easy adaptation to any size rider. Their drawbacks are: (1) relatively high price, ranging from £60 to £70 depending on number of gear speeds and accessories selected; (2) a weight of 40 to 50 pounds which makes them heavy to carry and hard to pedal; (3) an unstable ride due to the small wheels so that oil slicks, manhole covers, and gravel patches are likely to throw you; and (4) poor brakes, even in the calliper versions. This last is critical, since the net effect of the mini-bike's design is to restrict it to short local trips in urban areas where good brakes are premium.

Many people who take up cycling for the second time around get a mini. It's new. They like the crisp looks and easy way it goes. But if you are in this category I want to caution you specifically that these bikes are good for some things and not for others.

For getting the groceries it is hard to beat one of the shopper versions with baskets front and rear that come off 'zip!' to carry around with you in the store. The manoeuvrability and small size of the bike make handling and parking easy. On the other hand, a conventional 10-speed with touring panniers will carry as much and more – *and* go touring. For shopping, the mini wins simply on grounds of convenience because with the 10-speed there is always a certain amount of fumbling as purchases are packed away in the panniers and/or boxes are lashed on the rack. Some of the better panniers like Karrimor's have been designed however, to go on and off the bike in seconds, so you'd better check the section on touring and luggage before opting for the mini – which won't go touring very well.

Any of the small-wheel jobs have a darting manoeuvrability that is very handy for exploring urban locales. They will U-turn and turn right and left as fast as thought. You can get on and off hundreds of times effortlessly. They encourage spontaneity – nipping down a mews to look at an old house, pulling over to study a bookshop window, even hi-jinks cutting around obstacles. The price is paid in unsteadier handling at speed and sudden dumps on slippery surfaces like oil or leaves. Running down a fast hill with a lorry breathing hard behind, an expert rider experienced with this sort of machine can keep it running true, but most people become uncomfortably aware that their slightest motion will move the bike about – and, having got the jitters, over-control and start veering. But as long as you do not intend much country running, or riding in heavy mixed traffic where predictability is premium, then the small-wheeler's snappy handling is a joy.

Many small-wheelers come with adjustable seat and handlebars. As dual person/dual purpose machines – say when Dad does the day-time shopping and in the evening Mum nips down to the local – they are mighty handy. A flicking of levers and the machine fits comfortably. Tip: use a file or some-such to mark the seat post and handlebar stem where they fit each rider best.

The braking power of the small-wheelers is a sunshine characteristic: just adequate as long as the rims and brake shoes are dry. While in the wet any bike tends to piffle out, the small-wheeler brakes go down to somewhere near zero. As a choice for steady commuting where a bit of mist is sometimes part of the game, or for habitual use by someone over 12 stone, they are just not on.

Under no circumstances get anything with less than 20-in wheels. The dodgy handling and poor brakes are a function of wheel size. And get 3-speed gears.

Modified with a suitable saddle and handlebars a small-wheeler can go touring, and adherents tout low-load placement and stability. But modern racks and panniers obviate unbalanced loads on 10-speeds, and these remain a better choice for distance work. In sum, the small-wheeler is a local-use machine with characteristics that give it the edge for light shopping, exploring areas closely, and zesty handling. It is not so good for commuting in traffic or for longer tours. Some say that you can do anything with a mini – and this is true. And two men made it around the world boating and motoring an amphibious jeep. Across oceans. Anything is possible. Sure. But comfortable?

The best – and most expensive – 20-in bikes are the Dawes Kingpin series. They are light, have just a slight edge in handling characteristics, and have quality features such as ball-bearing pedals and better grade saddles.

(1) Dawes Kingpin 500C. Sturmey-Archer 3-speed gears, side-pull calliper brakes, rustless Feran mudguards. Rear carrier bag

and prop stand, reflector pedals. Colours blue, green, brown, or purple. Price approx £70. Variant models are Kingpin Shopper as 500C but with front carrier and quick-release shopping basket. Kingpin Folder as 500C but without rear carrier bag. Dynamo lighting optional.

(2) Puch Pic-Nic. Styria 3-speed gears, side-pull calliper brakes, prop stand, chrome mudguards, sprung rear carrier, and white-wall tyres. Colour yellow. Price, approx £65 including VAT. For single-speed, price, approx £60. Variant is: Folder – as above but red. Three speed, price, approx £70.

Tall people may find the handlebar reach on the Pic-Nic more to their favour.

(3) Peugeot UNS40. Tyres 22 in. Simplex 5-speed derailleur gears. Chrome mudguards. Centre-pull calliper brakes. Adjustable seat and handlebars. Chainguard Rack. Optional: dynamo lighting and front carrier wire shopping basket. Colours blue or orange. Price, approx £70.

In folding bicycles there is only one to consider seriously: the Bickerton. Conventional folding bicycles weigh 40 to 50 pounds and are bulky and difficult to manage. The Bickerton, constructed of aluminium alloy throughout, weighs only 18 pounds and folds down in 45 seconds to an astonishing 30-in × 20-in × 9-in – about the size of a small suitcase. It is therefore genuinely portable, and you can take it on a taxi, bus, or train without fuss. It is not subject to the British Rail half-fare charge for a bicycle. In performance a Bickerton will keep up with anything short of a flat-out racing or touring bicycle. Design and materials give the frame a surprising flexibility, so that despite the use of small wheels, the ride is very comfortable. The very light weight makes for easy uphill pedalling.

The portability of the Bickerton is a great asset for touring. Hopping by train, bus, or motorcar from one interesting cycling area to another is easy. On back trails the Bickerton can be carried in a backpack when the going becomes too rough for riding.

A canvas carrier bag fits on the handlebars and will accommodate up to 40 pounds. Managing a briefcase – or even another Bickerton! – is easy. Optional extras include 3-speed gears, recommended for touring, a rear rack, saddlebags and lights. At this writing price is £90 for the single speed and £100 for the three-speed. This

s not dear for the quality of machine offered, and many users report
hat they have recovered this sum in saved transport fares in five
o six months. The Bickerton is available from cycle dealers or direct
rom

F. W. Evans Ltd
44–46 Kennington Road
London SE1

Tandem Bikes

All of my experience with tandems has convinced me that these
machines require considerably more effort than individually-
operated bikes. In addition, they are awkward and therefore dangerous in traffic. Two riders of unequal strength tend to experience
difficulties, with the stronger rider carrying the weaker. Two
equally strong riders hower, can move a tandem along at a brisk
pace, since the overall bicycle weight is less and wind resistance is
cut by half.

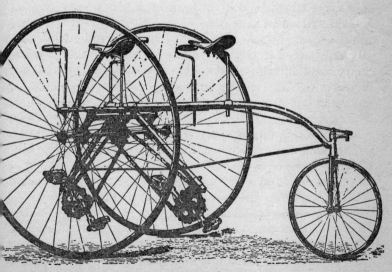

INVINCIBLE TANDEM.

This matching of strength and rhythm is rare enough so that the only practical consideration for or against a tandem is togetherness, and the value to be placed on this factor is entirely up to you. If you do opt for a tandem, get a lightweight (40 to 45 pounds) 10-speed and not a balloon heavyweight (90 pounds). Expect to spend between £180 and £400 (!) and be sure to get centre-pull calliper or cantilver brakes. A manufacturer of tandems is

Jack Taylor Cycles,
Church Road,
Stockton-on-Tees,
Teesside TS18 2LY

and adverts for used machines appear periodically in newstand publications, *Cycling* (161–66 Fleet Street, London, EC4P 4AA) and *Exchange & Mart*.

Adult Tricycles

These are popular items in retirement areas. But don't think old age automatically puts you back in the kiddie category. The last time I was in San Francisco I read in the paper that officialdom would not let a bicyclist cross the Golden Gate Bridge (they will now). The bicyclist was especially disappointed because he had just ridden across the US of A on a racing bike in 30 days (about 100 miles per day) by way of celebrating his eightieth birthday. There are a number of bicycle clubs whose members are all over seventy and who use only two-wheel machines. And I've seen plenty of over-seventy skiers having a good time on the slopes, substituting skill and grace for strength and verve. If you can do it, stick with 2-wheelers.

The manageability of a tricycle is very much a function of wheel size. Those with wheels around 20 in keep the weight down low and are quite stable as long as they are not driven briskly. Trikes with 26-in or 27-in wheels are another story, and require learning new riding skills. The trike must be steered around a corner, a distinctly odd sensation, and weight must be kept to the inside on even a moderate bend. It is quite easy to lift a wheel, and sweeping downhill bends in particular must be approached with caution. Changes in the camber of the road, throwing the balance from one side to another, are also unsettling. For a feeling of stability I much

prefer a bicycle, but of course in very wet, slippery, or icy conditions
the tricycle has an advantage. There is always some possibility of
falling off a 2-wheeler, and if you have brittle bones, poor balance
and coordination, or other problems, you should seriously consider a
tricycle.

If you live in a flat area and/or are limited in the movement of
your legs, get a fixed gear tricycle on which there is no freewheeling
and the pedals turn when the wheels turn. This has the advantage
of carrying limited motion legs through dead spots, and the tricycle
can be pedalled backwards. I have heard some wonderful stories
about people who have recovered considerable mobility of their
bodies as a result of the exercise provided by this type of machine,
which costs, new, about £90 to £100. For hilly terrain get a 3- to 10-
speed freewheel with low gearing. Expect to spend about £100 to
£125.

Tricycles are available from Jack Taylor Cycles, Church Road,
Stockton-on-Tees, Teesside TS18 2LY; and Ken G. Rogers, 71
Berkeley Avenue, Cranford, Hounslow, Middlesex, TW4 6LF.

W. R. Pashley Ltd, Masons Road, Stratford-upon-Avon, lists a small-wheel tricycle at £100 for a single-speed and £125 for a 5-speed. Accessories include: chainguard, front carrier with spring clip, PVC-coated shopping basket with handle to suit above, and white waterproof cover to suit rear luggage basket. Gearing on the single-speed is 46 or 40 front to 18 rear, and the 5-speed 46 or 40 front to 14–28 rear.

In Britain a trike is known also as a 'barrow', and there is a dedicated fraternity of adherents banded as

The Tricycle Association,
Anvil Cottage,
Sawrey,
Ambleside,
Westmorland.

Tricycles are raced, toured, and driven to market. I missed a recent opportunity to acquire a tandem tricycle, a machine that (I am told) in full cry in the wet can be *drifted* around a bend. Anyway, they are not necessarily old-age toys.

Unicycles

To my mind the unicycle is a toy in the pogo-stick category. Nothing wrong with it – in fact some day I'm going to get one. Available from

D. M. Engineering,
92 Hurn Road,
Christchurch, Hants.

for under £10·00. I've not had a chance to examine their product.

Children's Bicycles

One attitude towards buying clothes, toys, and other materials for children is something like, 'Well, the kid'll grow out of it soon, so let's not waste money. Just get him/her something good enough.' Another ploy is, 'Well, let's first see if she/he is really interested – then we'll get him/her something better.' The victim of this faulty reasoning is the helpless child, who is saddled with some worthless or even painful piece of junk and who is expected to be grateful for

it. The price difference between a good bike and a cheap one is at most £5·00. The cheap bike is difficult and unpleasant to ride, and shoddy workmanship and materials guarantee that it will grace the junkpile within a year. Result: total financial loss and total lack of stimulation for the child. The better bike is not only a pleasure to ride, thus ensuring your child's fun and interest, but will also survive for a number of years through the hands of several children. It can be passed down in the family or sold for at least half the purchase price. Result: happier *children*, and less net expenditure. If you would like to save money or are on a tight budget, check the classified adverts in local papers and put up cards advertising for what you want at newsagents, laundromats, school meetings, etc, and buy a used bike for £3 to £10.

Incidentally, the use of training wheels will only make learning to ride more prolonged and difficult for your child. He has to learn how to balance, and training wheels only postpone and make harder the inevitable. The best way to teach anybody, young or old, to ride is to let them do it themselves. Lower the seat so that they can comfortably touch the ground with their feet when mounted. All they need to do is push themselves along with their feet, like scootering. Balance and steering ability will come quickly.

Children are ready for their first two-wheel bicycle at about the age of five, depending on the development and coordination of the individual child. The first bike for a child aged five to seven should be a small-frame 20-in wheel featuring:

◎ Pneumatic tyres for a comfortable ride, easier pedalling, and effective braking. Solid rubber tyres are three times harder to pedal, provide a jolting ride, and give bad braking.

◎ Steel steering head bearings. The plastic sleeve bearings used on cheap bikes result in bad handling and steering characteristics, and wear out quickly, compounding the problem.

◎ A sturdy frame with at least two permanent members welded to the steering head. Anything less won't take the punishment kids dish out.

◎ A large seat range adjustment so the bike can grow with the child.

◎ A desirable feature is a coaster (foot-actuated) brake, as small hands sometimes experience difficulty in managing calliper brakes. Coaster brakes are rare on British kids' bicycles however, and since most children can manage a calliper brake this is not a problem – just check and make sure.

Going up to six- to nine-year-olds, the Raleigh Tempo, a 15-in cantilever frame with 20-in wheels is good, as is the Raleigh Chicco, available with either 14-in or 16-in frame and 20-in wheels. Children aged seven to nine can also manage the Raleigh Jeep, an 18-in frame with 24-in wheels and available with 3-speed gears. Athletic eight-year olds and children between the ages of nine and twelve should have a small frame 26-in wheel bicycle with 3-speed gears. Children over twelve years can use adult bikes.

I recommend increasing wheel size as quickly as possible. There are any number of children's bicycles in wheel sizes from 14 in to 20 in, and while a number are mechanically satisfactory, they are subject to the limitations of small-wheelers. On the other hand, a machine like the

Dawes Kingpin 18. Frame 14 in, tyres 18 in. Ball bearings throughout, pump, PVC-coated rear carrier with lamp bracket and fitted bag, and 3-speed gears,

has adjustable seat and handlebars so that adults under 5 ft 2 in can use it as well.

Your youngster may be the sort who is not going to instantly beat his machine to death and would like to cover some ground. In which case consider a junior racer (suitable for ages eight to twelve):

(1) Peugeot G45 CXE Junior Sports. Lugless 18-in frame. Simplex derailleurs. Steel crankset 40 × 45 to 14–16–18–20–23 freewheel. Mafac centre-pull calliper brakes with hooded levers. Steel handlebars and gooseneck. Reflectorized rat-trap pedals. Alloy large flange hubs, 24-in tyres. Leather saddle. Colours red or blue. Price, approx £70, including VAT.

(2) Dawes Red Feather. Frame 18½ in, 70° × 72°. Huret 5-speed gears, steel crankset 40T to 14-24 freewheel, steel small flange hubs, 24-in tyres. Weinmann alloy side-pull calliper brakes. Alloy gooseneck and mini-Maes pattern handlebars (all-rounder optional). Colours gold or red, with contrasting mudguards. Price, approx £70, including VAT.

A popular item with children today is the hi-riser: a 20-in or smaller wheel bike with a small frame and wheelbase, extra high handlebars, banana seat, an excess of flashy hardware, such as car-type gear shift levers, and dramatic names such as Chopper, Jet Star, Dragger, Red Line and the like. A kind of garbagy distillation of racoon-tail US of A consumerism, these bikes come in an astounding assortment of styles, colours, and equipment variations. The high handlebars, short wheelbase, and small wheels make the bikes highly manoeuvrable at low speeds, but otherwise unsafe and difficult to control.

This is reflected in bicycle accident studies published in the *British Medical Journal*. Simply put, it was found that serious accidents with head injuries, broken bones, etc, involved these bikes out of all proportion to the number in use. However, it seems that often it was a new, first bike (Christmas-time! Birthday!) or a first ride on a borrowed machine.

Kids love the whippy handling characteristics of hi-risers. With a little practice it is possible to tear off with the front wheel lifted high in the air for 5, 10 and even 20 feet (you can also go bottom over tea kettle). The tough, knobby tyres are good for off-the-road use – important with kids – but the heavy preponderance of weight aft puts the centre of gravity behind the bottom bracket axle, making them dodgy under power or climbing, and the brakes are marginal on account of the wheel size. The high handlebars mean that no weight can be supported by the arms, so that every jolt and bump is rammed up the spine. Hi-risers are really only suitable for fooling around and hanging out at the local pizza parlour.

I am not about to take an absolutist position on how people should take their fun. Indeed, since Raleigh alone has sold over 750,000 of these bikes, it would not do much good. Kid wants, kid gets. But two points, please: (1) a hi-riser is completely unsuitable as a first bike; and (2) if you do buy one for your youngster, make him/her ride it locally for a couple of weeks so that she/he can get used to the handling characteristics.

The best hi-riser on the market now is the Raleigh Chopper II (price, approx £70). The main feature of this bike is a rear seat and chain-stay design that pushes the centre of gravity forward to the bottom bracket and makes it difficult to lift the front wheel. Your youngster may find this stodgy and dull and sensibly point out that the reason he/she wants a hi-riser in the first place is for stunts and tricks, in which case the Trusty Tracker (price, approx £70) will fit the bill. The price of a hi-riser will of course also net a 10-speed, a safer bike with a much wider range of capabilities. And junior is less likely to come back with a cracked skull.

Another group of early candidates for the dustbin are the Raleigh Boxer, Strika, and Grifter bikes. These resemble the popular American MX off-road bikes and have impressive looking features such as super-knobby tyres and reinforced handlebars. Close examination reveals that items like the Strika shock absorbers are inoperative fakes, and that the bikes are deadeningly heavy, much too heavy for road work, let alone off-road riding. They are just pizza parlour bikes.

3. Buying and Keeping a Bike

New Bikes

The best place to buy a new bicycle is a bike shop. You can sometimes save money at a department or discount store, but you are virtually guaranteed disproportionate headaches and problems. In the first place, the quality of merchandise is almost always inferior. Secondly, the sad fact is that not even the finest machines are defect-free when they come from the manufacturer. Department and discount stores do not employ trained bicycle mechanics, and so the bikes they sell are often unassembled, or have been put together by some cretin who has literally done more harm than good. It takes a good bicycle mechanic to assemble a new bike without damaging anything, check all the parts, and iron out the inevitable defects. Even then, problems are not likely to be over. If a department or discount store gives a guarantee – few do – they have no mechanics to take care of after-sales problems. And if there is some totally basic defect in a machine you buy, it takes weeks for a refund or replacement.

A bike shop will assemble the machine. Although you must check their work carefully, chances are they'll do the job right. If some problem comes up later, they are available right away to fix it, and so are replacement parts. You get a guarantee, which should be for a minimum of a year, and is sometimes longer. And you will want to deal with a bike shop anyway, for servicing, parts, accessories, and advice.

The kind of bike shop makes a difference. Try to find one that deals only in bicycles. The more local a shop you can deal with, the better. Any bike shop must meet certain basic requirements in quality of bikes and in service, but convenience means a lot. A guarantee from a shop 50 miles away is useless for anything except a major disaster. If there is a local shop and they don't have what you want, talk it over with them. Perhaps they can order a bike for you. If their 'brand' of bike is not the one you had in mind take a good look at what they offer. All other things being equal, as they may

well be since many manufacturers use the same components, the convenience of a local shop is an excellent reason to switch 'brand'. Just make sure you get a fair value. Ask about servicing and parts. Don't expect however, that they will be able to offer as good a deal as a high-volume super-powered store. What you pay a little extra for is the fact that they are around the corner. Also, perhaps the general feeling and vibes are better.

At any rate, stay away from discount and department stores. I have not regaled you with horror stories about machines purchased from such sources, but they are legion, and cover everything from kids' tricycles to ultra-fancy racers. The tiny bit extra you spend in a bike shop buys an awful lot.

Taking Delivery

Anticipate that any new bike will have something wrong with it. Dealing with a good bike shop minimizes this possibility but by no means eliminates it. A couple of years ago when I picked up a new dream machine from one of NYC's finest stores I was too bedazzled to give it anything but the most cursory inspection. But as I accelerated away from the store the rear hub and freewheel exploded in a blizzard of metal flakes and chips. Most problems you are likely to encounter are not apt to be so spectacular, but the point cannot be emphasized too strongly that a thorough inspection of any new bike is necessary. The best way to learn what to look for is to read the Maintenance and Repair sections of this book. Here are the main points to watch:

◉ All nuts and bolts are secure. Every last one.

◉ Wheels should spin easily. When held off ground, weight of valve stem should pull wheel around so valve is in six o'clock position. Wheel should be centred in fork arms or chain stays. If wheel can be moved from side to side and there is a clicking sound, hub cones are out of adjustment. Check that rim is true by holding a pencil next to it and spinning the wheel. Brace the pencil on a fork arm or chain stay to keep it steady.

◉ Pluck spokes. All should be evenly tight and give the same 'twang'.

◉ Check quality of lug welds on frame. Sight down frame to check for bends.

◎ Brake blocks should hit rims squarely and not drag when released.

◎ Gears should work smoothly and with no slippage. Test first with wheels off ground and then on a ride.

◎ Pedals and chainwheel should spin easily but without side-to-side play.

◎ Ride the bike around the vicinity of the shop for a few miles.

You may think that all this is a lot of trouble to go through. I have bought a fair number of new bikes for myself, family, or friends. There was something wrong with every one of them, and a few I rejected outright. You will save yourself a lot of grief if you invest some time at the outset on a careful inspection.

Here is a list of bicycle shops noted for high-class machinery. It is of course not complete, and is just to give you a place to start.

F. W. Evans Ltd,
44–46 Kennington Road,
London SE1.

Condor Cycles,
90 Gray's Inn Road,
London WC1.

W. F. Holdsworth Ltd,
55 High Street,
Penge, London SE20.

Bob Jackson,
148 Harehills Lane,
Leeds LS8 5BD.

Jack Taylor Cycles,
Church Road,
Stockton-on-Tees,
Teesside TS18 2LY.

Roy Swinnerton,
69–71 Victoria Road,
Fenton, Stoke-on-Trent.

Harry Quinn Ltd,
7–9 Walton Road,
Liverpool 4.

David Rattray & Co Ltd,
261 Alexandra Parade,
Glasgow G31 3AD.

Tommy Godwin,
10–12 Silver Street,
King's Heath,
Birmingham 14.

Woodrup Cycles,
345 Kirkstall Road,
Leeds 4.

Fred Baker,
144 Cheltenham Road,
Bristol 6.

Major Nichols,
48 Durban Road,
Smethwick, Birmingham.

Used Bikes

Good used bikes are elusive, especially when you actually want one. But they are a good way to save money. Expect to pay about 75 per cent of list price for a machine in excellent as-new condition, and about 50 per cent of list price for one in average condition.

Sources of used bikes depend on where you live. A few bike shops sell used machines. Two excellent newsagent sources are *Exchange & Mart* and *Cycling* (161–66 Fleet Street, London EC4P 4AA). Most cities and counties have local classified publications listing all kinds of stuff – including bikes – for sale. Check also the classified ads in the regular papers. Sometimes families and people moving sell off furniture and household goods and this often includes a bicycle. Auctions are sometimes useful. A good bet in the spring are local bulletin boards at universities and colleges. Put up some cards yourself or take an ad in the student newspaper. Naturally, the more prosaic a bike you seek, the faster you will be likely to find it. But if you just put the word out something will turn up – eventually.

When buying a used machine you have to be particularly careful to avoid getting a lemon. Try to find out the history of the machine. It's best if you can talk to the owner. What does his attitude seem to be? Do you think he was interested in his bike and took care of it, or just left it out in the rain? Where did he ride it?

In inspecting the bike, cover all the points listed for a new bike. Pay particular attention to the frame. A certain number of nicks and scrapes are inevitable, but there should be no major dents or rust spots. Be suspicious of new paint. Wrinkled paint may indicate a bent frame.

It will be to your advantage to read carefully through the sections on Maintenance and Repair in this book. Often a used machine will need some work, or some component is not the one you need. You should know the cost and what is involved in replacing or repairing various parts. A £40 racer that needs £40 worth of work is no bargain. On the other hand, if you are looking for a touring bike and find a machine set up with close-ratio competition gears, it costs only about £5 to get a new wide-range gear freewheel.

A final word about used bikes related to the next problem: keeping your bike. I hope that this is not a self-fulfilling prophecy, but concurrent with the new popularity of the bicycle I expect that we shall see a growing market in stolen machines and parts. Doubtless this will not reach the giddy heights of the American Black Market, where newspapers publish articles about marketplaces for stolen machines and in some areas you can even order the type of bike you want. But in case the proposition ever seems even slightly attractive, I remind that to get a bike this way is a crime. Legally and morally. Simply put, you are helping to steal. Additionally, it is not some giant pound-greedy company's candy bar or rip-off piece of junk which you are stealing, but a possession somebody quite probably loves and cherishes.

Keeping Your Bike

As yet this is not a serious problem – at least not by American standards, where about 20 per cent of the bikes in use at any given moment will be stolen within a year. Here, in many towns you do

Carriage propelled by dogs, from France

not need to lock up your bike at all. But bicycle thefts – especially of quality machines – are steadily increasing. Precautions are a must.

Except in areas where you know everybody and everybody knows you never leave your bike unlocked. It is a temptation to impulse. While it is not serious when somebody outs of the local and staggers off around the corner on your machine, it is inconvenient. I find that for on-again/off-again type riding a cable combination lock such as sold in bicycle and ski shops is the lightest and easiest to manage.

After deterring the impulsive, locking-up procedures are a function of situation. A well-lit street is a better bet than, say, a dark alley, but in either case security counts. For day and evening use in average neighbourhoods with ordinary bikes, I use a length of chain – real chain, purchased from an ironmonger's – and a quality padlock. For night-time and/or first-class machinery I use an American lock made of case-hardened steel throughout called the Citadel. In tests conducted by police departments and cycle clubs the Citadel has withstood attack by prybar, hammer, hacksaw, and bolt cutter, while competing locks have failed. There is no reported case of bicycle theft involving a Citadel, and in America the manufacturers guarantee to replace to a value of £90 any bicycle stolen while locked with a Citadel. The Citadel is available from a few cycle shops for £13·50, and by post from F. W. Evans Ltd., 44–46 Kennington Road, London SE1, for £14·50, post included. The Citadel is expensive, but at this writing is the only absolutely secure lock made. Consider your requirements carefully and think of how you will feel if one day you find your bike – gone.

When locking up on the street you must:

◎ Lock your machine to seriously immovable objects like lamp posts, parking signs, heavy fences, etc.

◎ Run the chain through the frame and back wheel. Take the front wheel away with you, if you can, or run the chain through it too.

◎ Be selective about when and where. Slum neighbourhoods are a bad bet at any time. Even if the bike itself is not stolen, kids may make bits and pieces disappear. Business and industrial districts are OK during the day. Always try to pick a busy, well-illuminated spot.

◎ Try to enlist help. The cashier for a cinema will usually keep an eye on your bike. Newsagents and other merchants will often help, and particularly if you do business with them.

◎ Keep a written record of your bike's particulars, including the serial number stamped on the frame – most often found on the underside of the bottom bracket, but sometimes on a stay or tube.

There is another problem, not at all extensive, but perhaps new for those of you who have led sheltered lives and now astride fancy machines are meeting the world, and that is direct assault. Britain has its share of tough neighbourhoods where a good bike is an easy candidate for liberation. And there is a bit of the irrational Clockwork Orange violence which necessarily accompanies a consumer society. Happily, it is not the jungle warfare prevalent in the United States with attacks from the bushes or from behind parked cars and where, in many areas, it is just not safe to ride day or night. Things are under better control in this country. But if you are in a bad neighbourhood, stay alert, as you should in any case anywhere, and move along smartly – at 20 to 30 mph you will leave most trouble behind before it happens.

The 'Coventry Rotary'

4. Fitting and Gears

Getting the most out of your bike requires careful fitting, e.g. placement of handlebars, seat, and controls. The standard formulas for this process are the result of considerable work and study by genuine experts and will probably work the best. After you have finished setting your bike up 'according to the book' the resulting position may feel a bit odd. Give yourself at least 50 miles to get used to the new arrangement before making alterations. You may find the 'odd' position considerably more efficient and less fatiguing than a 'comfortable' position. At the same time, no two people are exactly alike, and some variation from the norm may be in order. Just give the orthodox position a fair trial, and make alterations gradually.

For how to make alterations in the position of seat, handlebars, stem, and brake levers, look up Adjustment under the relevant heading in the Maintenance and Repair sections.

Frame

Frame size is measured from the seat lug to the centre of the bottom bracket. There are two methods of calculating the proper size:

Inside length of leg from crotch bone to floor, measured in stocking feet, less 9 in, and
Height divided by 3.

Thus, a person with a 32-in inside leg measurement should have a 23-in frame, and somebody 6 ft tall would get a 24-in frame. Be sure in any event that you can straddle the frame comfortably with your feet flat on the ground. An under-sized frame can be compensated for to some degree through the use of an extra-long seat post and stem, but an over-sized frame will inevitably slam you in the crotch.

Most frames are the 72° parallel touring design (see p 34 for what this means), good for both long trips and local urban use, where the springiness of the frame softens bumpy streets. Additionally, there is no problem fitting mudguards. Racing road and track frames ordinarily use steeper seat tube angles of 73° or 74° to put the rider further forward and tighten up the bike. These frames are not usually intended for use with mudguards, although the ingenious may find a way.

Saddle

The position of the saddle determines the fitting of the rest of the bike. For most riders the correct fore-to-aft position is with the nose of the saddle $1\frac{3}{4}$ in to $2\frac{1}{2}$ in behind a vertical line through the crank hanger:

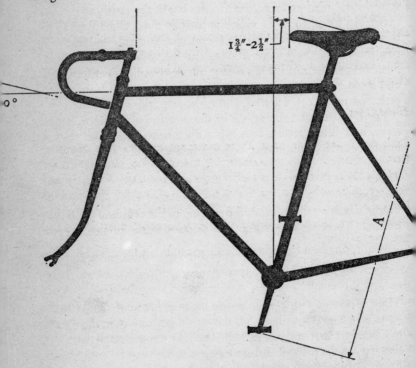

Sprint riders and traffic jammers who use brief bursts of sharp energy often use a more forward saddle position. This is the reason sprint frames come with a steeper seat tube angle. For around town use, if you are a vigorous rider, you may like a more forward saddle position. For extended going and best overall efficiency however, stick within $1\frac{3}{4}$ in to $2\frac{1}{2}$ in.

Most saddles are set too low. A rough rule of thumb is that while sitting on the bike with your heel on the pedal at its lowest point, your leg should be straight. This means that when riding with the ball of your foot on the pedal, your leg is almost but not quite fully extended at the bottom of the stroke.

A precise formula for the best saddle height has been worked out in a series of scientific tests. Measure inside length of leg from crotch bone to floor without shoes. Multiply this length (in inches) by $1 \cdot 09$. Example: 32 in $\times$ $1 \cdot 09$ equals $34 \cdot 88$, or $34\frac{7}{8}$ in. Set saddle so distance A from top of saddle to centre of pedal spindle in down position with crank parallel to seat tube is $34\frac{7}{8}$ in.

This formula has been put together by experts. They found that an alteration in saddle height of 4 per cent of inside leg measurement from the $1 \cdot 09$ setting affected power output by approximately 5 per cent. So once the saddle is set, give it a good long trial before making changes.

Handlebars

Let's settle one thing now: there are many reasons why dropped bars are more efficient and comfortable than flat bars. Here are a few:

(1) A much greater variety of positions is possible. Not only can you select the best position for conditions – like low down when headed into the wind – but being able to shift about and bring different groups of muscles into play greatly increases comfort, to say nothing of power.

(2) Because weight is supported by both the hands and seat, road shocks and bumps rock the body rather than jar it. With conventional flat bars the whole weight of the body rests on the saddle. With dropped bars, not only is weight supported by the arms, but because the body is forward, it tends to pivot at the hips going over bumps. As it happens this is also very desirable from an anatomical point of view: leaning forward stretches the spine, allowing the absorption of shocks, and increases breathing capacity. Conventional bars force the rider into a stiff-spined position where the individual vertebrae of the spine are pinched together. Further, because there is no pivoting give at the hips, each and every jolt and bump is transmitted directly up the spine, greatly increasing fatigue.

(3) The better distribution of weight allowed by dropped bars provides improved stability and steering characteristics.

Positioning of the handlebars is crucial. For conventional use they should be set so that the top bar is just level with the nose of the saddle. Sprint bikes have the bars a whole lot lower, and if you do a lot of traffic riding you may want to set yours down a bit. Mine are about $1\frac{1}{2}$ in lower than the saddle. Just remember that if you opt for short-term speed it will be at some cost to overall efficiency.

The stem should position the bars so that the distance between the nose of the saddle and the rear edge of the centre of the handlebars equals the distance from your elbow to your outstretched fingertips. Another way to determine this distance is to sit on the bike in your normal riding position while a friend holds it steady. Without changing position, remove one hand from handlebars and let arm dangle fully relaxed. Now rotate your arm in a large arc without stretching. If, as your hand comes back to the bar, it is ahead of or behind the other hand, the bars need to be moved. Stems come in increments of length, or you can buy an adjustable stem. This costs and weighs more.

The standard rake for the ends of drop bars is 10° from the horizontal:

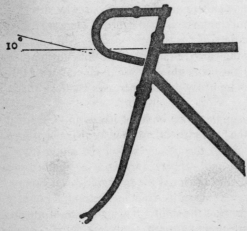

Start with this setting, which makes the tops of the bars level and thus affords the greatest variety of riding positions, and make changes as you desire.

Brakes

Do not tape new bars until you have ridden the bike enough to fully fiddle with and set the position of the brake levers. Most levers are too low. Almost all braking is done from above:

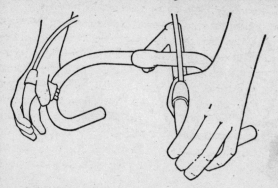

and the levers need to be high enough so that you can stop quickly and without undue effort.

Toe Clips

Use them! They virtually double your pedalling efficiency. They may be a little awkward at first, but soon you will be able to slip in and out of them without a thought (see Riding, p 89). Be sure to get the size which corresponds to your shoe size: small for ladies with small feet, medium up to size 8, and large for size 9 and up. To avoid scratching up fancy shoes, tape the fronts of the clips with a little cloth tape.

Cleats

Cleats are metal or plastic strips fastened to the soles of bicycling shoes. Used in conjunction with toe clips they hold your foot to the pedal with a vengeance, and are quite unsafe for traffic riding unless you use very loosely set straps. But they are essential for racing and great for touring. To fit cleats properly, ride your bike for a few miles without toe clips so that the soles of your shoes take an impression from the pedals. Then simply position cleats so cleat tunnel is aligned exactly with the pedal marks. Then fit toe clips.

Gearing

Fitting also includes the selection of gearing. Understanding this subject requires some knowledge of basic riding technique. Some of the information I am going to give you now is rather technical. Just use it as you need it.

When I bought my first 10-speed I was surprised to find that the gears, instead of each having a separate range like on a car, over-lapped considerably. One gear really wasn't much different from the other. The reason for this is that there is a rate of cadence – the speed with which the cranks are spun around – which is the most efficient. For most people this rate is from 65 to 85 strokes per minute. Racers run 120-130 and up. The idea behind a multitude of gears is to allow the rider to maintain the same cadence regardless of terrain.

In consequence, a racing bike will have close ratio gears, each one much the same as the next, while a touring bike will have wide-ratio gears, with much greater differences between each gear. The reason for this is that touring bikes frequently pack heavy loads up steep grades. They are also – rightly – usually the choice of the novice rider. Only expert riders in good condition can comfortably use close-ratio gears.

What determines ratio? The number of teeth on the front

sprocket divided by the number of teeth on the back sprocket. Thus a 60 front and a 15 rear give a 4 to 1 ratio. For competition a typical set-up might be a rear cluster of 23, 21, 19, 17, 15 matched to front sprockets of 49 and 52. For touring it might be 28, 24, 20, 17, 14 rear and 40 to 50 front.

To make everything a little simpler, gear ratios are expressed as a single number. The formula is:

$$\frac{\text{Number of teeth on front sprocket}}{\text{Number of teeth on back sprocket}} \times \text{wheel diameter} = \text{gear ratio}$$

A chart of commonly available gears is given on the next two pages.

In general, 100 is the top range and is hard to push, 90 is more common, and 80 the usual speed gear. 60 and 70 are the most often used, 40 and 50 are for hills. Below 40 is for extremely steep terrain and heavy loads. Most people gear too high and pedal too slowly. This increases fatigue. It is much better to pedal briskly against relatively little resistance.

There are other factors besides range to consider in setting up gears. Ease of transition from one gear to another is important. If you have to shift both front and back sprockets every time, it is laborious. For example:

		Rear				
		14	17	21	26	31
Front	52	100·2	82·3	66·9	54	45
	47	90·4	74·5	60·2	48·6	40·8

means that to run up through the gears consecutively requires continuous double shifts. On the other hand, a set up like:

		Rear				
		14	15	17	19	21
Front	54	104	97·2	85·6	76·7	69·4
	38	73·2	68	60	54	49

means that you can run up through the gears using only one shift of the front derailleur. (Never use the small front to small rear or big front to big rear. I will explain why later.)

Number of teeth on chainwheel

	24	26	28	30	32	34	36	38	40	42	44	45	46	47	48	49	50	51	52	53	54	55	56
12	54	58.3	62.9	67.5	71.8	76.4	81	85.3	89.9	94.5	98.8	101.2	103.4	105.6	108	110.2	112.3	114.7	117	119	121.5	123.7	126
13	49.7	54	58	62.1	66.4	70.5	74.5	78.8	82.9	87.2	91.3	93.4	95.3	97.5	99.6	101.5	103.7	105.8	108	110	112.1	114.2	116.1
14	46.2	49.9	54	57.8	61.6	65.3	69.4	73.2	76.9	81	84.8	86.7	88.6	90.4	92.3	94.5	96.4	98.3	100.2	102	104	106	108
15	43.2	46.7	50.2	54	57.5	61	64.8	68.3	71.8	75.6	79.1	81	82.6	84.5	86.4	88	89.9	91.8	93.6	95.3	97.2	99	100.8
16	40.5	43.7	47.2	50.5	54	57.2	60.7	64	67.5	70.7	74.2	75.9	77.5	79.1	81	82.6	84.2	85.9	87.8	89.4	91	92.1	94.5
17	38	41	44.3	47.5	50.8	54	57	60.2	63.4	66.7	69.6	71.3	72.9	74.5	76.1	77.7	79.4	81	82.6	84	85.6	87.2	88.9
18	35.9	38.9	41.8	44.8	47.8	50.8	54	57	59.9	62.9	65.8	67.5	68.8	70.5	71.8	73.4	74.8	76.4	78	79.4	81	82.3	84
19	34	36.7	39.7	42.4	45.4	48.1	51	54	56.7	59.7	62.4	63.7	65.3	66.7	68	69.4	71	72.4	73.7	75.4	76.7	78.1	79.3
20	32.4	35.1	37.8	40.5	43.2	45.9	48.6	51.3	54	56.7	59.4	60.7	62.1	63.4	64.8	66.1	67.5	68.8	70.2	71.5	72.9	74.2	75.6
21	30.8	33.2	35.9	38.3	41	43.5	46.2	48.6	51.3	54	56.4	57.8	59.1	60.2	61.6	62.9	64.3	65.3	66.9	68	69.4	70.5	72
22	29.4	31.9	34.3	36.7	39.1	41.6	44	46.4	48.9	51.3	54	55.1	56.4	57.5	58.9	59.9	61.3	62.4	63.8	65	66.2	67.5	68.6
23	28	30.5	32.7	35.1	37.5	39.7	42.1	44.5	46.7	49.1	51.6	52.6	54	55.1	56.2	57.5	58.6	59.7	61	62.1	63.2	64.5	65.6
24	27	29.2	31.3	33.7	35.9	38	40.5	42.7	44.8	47.2	49.4	50.5	51.6	52.6	54	55.1	56.2	57.2	58.5	59.4	60.7	61.8	63
25	25.9	28.1	30.2	32.4	34.6	36.7	38.9	41	43.2	45.4	47.5	48.6	49.7	50.8	51.8	52.9	54	55.1	56.2	57.2	58.3	59.4	60.4
26	24.8	27	28.9	31	33.2	35.1	37.3	39.4	41.3	43.5	45.6	46.7	47.5	48.6	49.7	50.7	51.8	52.9	54	54.8	56	57	58.1
27	23.8	25.9	27.8	30	31.9	33.7	35.9	37.8	40	41.8	43.7	44.8	45.9	47	47.8	48.8	49.9	50.7	51.8	52.9	54	54.8	55.9
28	22.9	24.8	27	28.9	30.8	32.7	34.6	36.4	38.2	40.5	42.4	43.2	44.3	45.1	46.2	47.2	48.1	49.1	50	51.1	52	53	54
29	22.1	24	25.9	27.8	29.7	31.6	33.5	35.4	37	38.9	40.8	41.8	42.6	43.7	44.5	45.4	46.4	47.2	48.3	49.1	50.2	51	52.1
30	21.6	23.2	25.1	27	28.6	30.5	32.4	34	35.9	37.8	39.4	40.5	41.3	42.1	43.2	44	44.8	45.9	46.8	47.5	48.6	49.4	50.2
31	20.8	22.4	24.3	25.9	27.8	29.4	31.3	32.9	34.8	36.4	38.1	39.1	40	40.8	41.6	42.6	43.5	44.3	45	45.9	47	47.8	48.6
32	20.2	21.9	23.5	25.1	27	28.6	30.2	31.9	33.7	35.4	37	37.8	38.6	39.4	40.5	41.3	42.1	42.9	43.7	44.5	45.4	46.2	47.2

For 27" Wheels

Number of teeth on rear sprocket

Number of teeth on chainwheel

Number of teeth on rear sprocket	24	26	28	30	32	34	36	38	40	42	44	45	46	47	48	49	50	51	52	53	54	55	56
12	52	56.2	60.6	65	69.2	73.6	78	82.2	86.6	91	95.2	97.5	99.6	101.7	104	106	108.2	110.5	112.6	114.7	117	119.1	121.2
13	47.8	52	55.9	59.8	64	67.9	71.8	75.9	79.8	84	87.9	90	91.8	93.9	95.9	97.8	99.8	101.9	104	105.8	107.9	110	111.8
14	44.5	48.1	52	55.6	59.3	62.9	66.8	70.5	74.1	78	81.6	83.5	85.3	87.1	88.9	91	92.8	94.6	96.5	98.3	100.1	101.9	104
15	41.6	45	48.4	52	55.4	58.8	62.4	65.8	69.2	72.8	76.2	78	79.6	81.4	83.2	84.8	86.6	88.4	90	91.8	93.6	95.2	97
16	39	42.1	45.5	48.6	52	55.1	58.5	61.6	65	68.1	71.5	73.1	74.6	76.2	78	79.6	81.1	82.7	84.5	86.1	87.6	89.2	91
17	36.7	39.5	42.6	45.8	48.9	52	54.9	58	61.1	64.2	67.1	68.6	70.2	71.8	73.3	74.9	76.4	78	79.3	80.9	82.4	84	85.5
18	34.6	37.4	40.3	43.2	46	48.9	52	54.9	57.7	60.6	63.4	65	66.3	67.9	69.2	70.7	72	73.6	74.9	76.4	78	79.3	80.9
19	32.8	35.4	38.2	40.8	43.7	46.3	49.1	52	54.6	57.5	60.1	61.4	62.9	64.2	65.5	66.8	68.4	69.7	71	72.3	73.8	75.1	76.4
20	31.2	33.8	36.4	39	41.6	44.2	46.8	49.4	52	54.6	57.2	58.5	59.8	61.1	62.4	63.7	65	66.3	67.6	68.9	70.2	71.5	72.8
21	29.6	32	34.6	36.9	39.5	41.9	44.5	46.8	49.4	52	54.3	55.6	56.9	58	59.3	60.6	61.9	62.9	64.2	65.5	66.8	67.9	69.2
22	28.3	30.7	33	35.4	37.7	40	42.4	44.7	47.1	49.4	52	53.1	54.3	55.4	56.7	57.7	59	60.1	61.4	62.4	63.7	65	66
23	27	29.4	31.5	33.8	36.1	38.2	40.6	42.9	45	47.3	49.7	50.7	52	53	54.1	55.4	56.4	57.5	58.8	59.8	60.8	62.1	63.2
24	26	28.1	30.2	32.5	34.6	36.7	39	41.1	43.2	45.5	47.6	48.6	49.7	50.7	52	53	54	55.1	56.2	57.2	58.5	59.5	60.6
25	25	27	29.1	31.2	33.3	35.4	37.4	39.5	41.6	43.7	45.8	46.8	47.8	48.9	49.9	51	52	53	54.1	55.1	56.2	57.2	58.2
26	23.9	26	27.8	29.9	32	33.8	35.9	38	39.8	41.9	43.9	45	45.8	46.8	47.8	48.9	49.9	51	52	52.8	53.8	54.9	55.9
27	22.9	25	26.8	28.9	30.7	32.5	34.6	36.4	38.5	40.3	42.1	43.2	44.2	45.2	46	47.1	48.1	48.9	49.9	51	52	52.8	53.8
28	22.1	23.9	26	27.8	29.7	31.5	33.3	35.1	36.9	39	40.8	41.6	42.6	43.4	44.5	45.5	46.3	47.3	48.1	49.1	49.9	51	52
29	21.3	23.1	25	26.8	28.6	30.4	32.2	34.1	35.6	37.4	39.3	40.3	41.2	42.1	42.9	43.7	44.7	45.5	46.5	47.3	48.4	49.1	50.2
30	20.8	22.4	24.2	26	27.6	29.4	31.2	32.8	34.5	36.4	38	39	39.9	40.6	41.6	42.4	43.2	44.2	45	45.8	46.8	47.6	48.4
31	20	21.6	23.4	25	26.8	28.3	30.2	31.7	33.5	35.1	36.7	37.7	38.5	39.3	40	41.1	41.9	42.6	43.4	44.2	45.2	46	46.8
32	19.5	21.1	22.6	24.2	26	27.6	29.1	30.7	32.5	34.1	35.6	36.4	37.2	38	39	39.8	40.6	41.3	42.1	42.9	43.7	44.5	45.5

For 26" wheels

Number of teeth on rear sprocket

If you use wide gaps front and rear there is almost bound to be some duplication of gears:

			Rear		
		14	17	21	26	31
Front	52	100·2	82·3	66·9	54	45
	42	81	66·7	54	43·5	36·4

and yet curiously enough, many good bikes are set up this way. It really depends on what you want the bike for, because in balancing the various factors of range, ease of shifting, and number of different gears, you are just going to have to make some compromises. For novice riders I would suggest the following:

Hilly Terrain
Competition – 45 × 52 front, 14, 16, 19, 20, 23 rear.
Touring – 36 × 52 front, 14, 16, 19, 23, 28 rear.

In Britain, which has quite steeply pitched hills, novices and heavily laden tourists may be better off with the recommendation of the Cyclists' Touring Club, 28 × 46 front, 15, 17, 19, 21, 23 rear, which gives closer ratios in a lower range, viz:

			Rear			
		15	17	19	21	23	
Front	28	50·2	44·3	39·7	35·9	32·7	27-in wheel
	46	82·6	72·9	65·3	59·1	54	

VS

			Rear			
		14	16	19	23	28	
Front	36	69·4	60·7	51	42·1	34·6	27-in wheel
	52	100·2	87·8	73·7	62	50	

Flat Terrain

Competition – 49 × 52 front, 15, 17, 19, 21, 23 rear.
Touring – 40 × 54 front, 14, 16, 19, 23, 26 rear.

Compromise

Touring – 40 × 50 front, 14, 17, 20, 24, 28 rear.

I make these recommendations with some misgivings for there is one problem or another with all of them. There always is, but these are stock gearings with which you can do quite a bit. Each person of course has his own personal preferences, and you should work out gearing to suit your own needs. I, for example, don't care a fig about competition, and am mostly interested in traffic jamming and touring. On my all-time favourite bike (stolen by an addict) I had 46 × 60 front and 13 through 30 rear, which got me incredulous and pitying regard from bike-wise friends. It suited me perfectly. The 46 front running through the 30 rear gave me a 41 gear which got me up nearly everything. When in town I used only the 60 front and the three middle gears of the back sprocket, thus minimizing shifting.

Down hills and long shallow gradients the super-heavy 60 front and 13 rear drove the bike along like a bomb. In short, it was ultra-wide range gearing also suitable for short sprints.

Such esoteric gearing is not easy to get. Most front sprockets stop at 52. A few expensive brands go to 54 or rarely, 56. The 13 rear is according to one source hard on chains. I didn't find this to be true but perhaps this is the reason why they are hard to get. Anyway, you can go a long way with conventional gearing. Since the loss of Golden Flash I've used more or less stock gearing and found it satisfactory.

If you do elect to muck around with gear ratios, you will have to take derailleur capacity into account. Besides shifting the chain from sprocket to sprocket, the rear derailleur also keeps the chain taut. A 14 to 30 rear and a 36×54 front gives a variation in chain slack (between the 36 to 14 and 54 to 30) which exceeds the capacity of some derailleurs. Derailleur capacity is a function of design: competition units do not have to cover a wide range and can therefore be much lighter; touring units are heavier and sturdier. Generally, capacity is marked on the box as, for example, 13–24–36–53. The outer figures give the high gear, the inner, the lower. Some advertised figures are as follows:

Brand	Gear Range	Front and Rear
Simplex Prestige	13–28	37
Huret Allvit	13–28	28
Campagnolo Nuovo Record	13–30	32
Campagnolo Gran Turismo	13–36	43
Sun Tour GT	13–34	40

For wide range gearing the Campagnolo Gran Turismo is a whirlaway winner. It is sturdy, beautifully made and designed – and heavy.

You will have to decide for yourself which elements in the weight v range balance are the most important. Here is the final tidbit to take into account and round out an already confusing picture: you don't need the full range of the derailleur. You should not ever run the big front sprocket to the big rear, or the small front to the small rear, because it causes the chain to cut across at too severe an angle, causing excessive wear, usually rubbing of the derailleur gates, and reduced efficiency.

So . . . the important range is between the large front sprocket to the next to largest back sprocket and the small front sprocket to the next to smallest rear sprocket. Since this is a more limited range with a little diddling you can use a competition derailleur with relatively wide-range gears. The advantage is lighter weight and improved performance.

This business of cross-angle strains on the chain bears on the subject of triple front chainwheels. These units are the choice of many experienced tourists for mountain country and packing heavy loads, as they give the most range. Because of cross-over problems however, you do not get that many extra gears. In addition, triple chainwheels are difficult to adjust and align, and the derailleur cages tend to get screwed up. Some manufacturers have simply stopped selling 15-speed bikes. Unless you really need the extra range I'd advise staying away from this combination.

Anybody can ride a bicycle. You just get aboard and pedal. Heh. Try following an experienced tourist on a 100-mile run or a competition rider around the track. Physical condition of course plays a part, but here technique counts more than anything else. Fifty-year-old grandmothers can and do run rings around fit young adults. Attention to the basics of technique will make riding easier and more enjoyable, and give you greater freedom than if you had not bothered with the subject at all.

Of course even basic technique varies somewhat with conditions. And there is a lot more to riding than technique. The following chapters on traffic jamming, and touring and racing, amplify considerably the information you need in order to cycle safely and comfortably.

Shifting

Take it easy when first learning to shift. Once you get the knack you can make smooth split-second gear changes, but let your skill develop gradually and avoid damaging 'clunk' sounding shifts.

3-Speeds: To shift up to a higher gear, ease pressure on pedals, move selector to next gear, resume pressure. Extra-fast shifts may be made by maintaining pedal pressure, moving the selector, and then pausing momentarily when the shift is desired. If done too hard, this may damage gears. Going down to 1st from 2nd or 3rd and coming to a stop, back-pedal slightly. If not stopping, use same procedure as for upshifts.

10-Speeds: Never, ever shift a 10-speed unless pedalling. To see why, hang your bike up so that the rear wheel is off the ground, rotate the cranks, and manipulate the gear shift levers so you can see how they work. Shifting a 10-speed without pedalling may result in a bent or broken chain or gear teeth. If you park your bike in the street, always give the gears a visual check to make sure passers-by have not fiddled with them. It happens often.

When going up or down through the gears, ease pedalling pressure

during shift. The shift levers do not have stops for the different gears, and you have to learn where they are by feel. Do not let the derailleur cages rub the chain. Sometimes it is necessary to make a small adjustment in the front derailleur when using a wide range of rear sprockets in order to prevent this. Do not run the big front sprocket to the big rear sprocket, or the small front to the small rear. It causes the chain to cut across at too severe an angle, greatly increasing wear and reducing efficiency. Proper shifting should also take into account the demands of cadence (see below).

Pedalling

Ride with the ball of your foot on the pedal, not the heel or arch. The fundamental technique for easy cycling is called ankling. This is where the foot pivots at the ankle with each revolution of the crank. Start at the top of the stroke (12 o'clock) with the heel slightly lower than the toes. Push with the ball of the foot and simultaneously pivot at the ankle on the downstroke so that the foot levels out between 2 and 3 o'clock, and continue this motion so that at the bottom of the stroke the toes are lower than the heel:

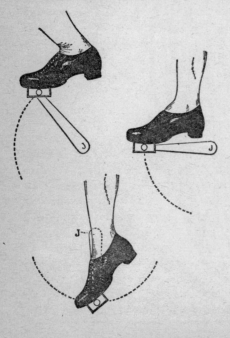

With toe clips pull up on the upstroke as well. The main thing to strive for is smoothness and steady, even pressure. Practise this slowly, in a high gear, and away from traffic so you can concentrate on watching your feet.

Toe clips are a great boon. By allowing you to pull up on the pedals as well as push down, they virtually double pedalling efficiency. They are completely safe. Smooth-soled conventional shoes can always be slipped out even when tightly strapped down. If using bicycling shoes and cleats, keep the straps loose in traffic. The technique for getting underway is simple: start with loose straps. Straddle the bike, slip a foot into a pedal at the 1 o'clock position, and tighten the strap. Push off, using the downstroke of this crank to get you underway, and simultaneously reach down with the free foot, give the pedal a light tap to spin the toe clip around to the proper position, slip foot in, bring crank around to 12 o'clock position, and tighten strap. It sounds more complicated than it is. The key is the deft, light tap to the pedal to bring the toe clip around so you can slip your foot in. Practice will soon make it second nature. When coming to a stop, reach down and loosen one strap so you can get your foot back in easily when underway again. Do not worry about being trapped by toe clips. I have made zillions of emergency stops and have always been able to get my feet free. On the other hand, do not tempt fate by riding in heavy traffic with ultra-tight straps. And if you use sneakers or other soft-soled shoes (bad – not enough support), or cleated bicycling shoes, keep the straps loose when conditions warrant.

Cadence

This subject was mentioned in connection with gearing. Briefly, human beings pedal most efficiently at a certain number of strokes per minute. The optimum cadence varies with the physical condition and technique of the individual rider. Generally, novices run from 60 to 85 strokes per minute, experienced tourists approach 100, and racers run 120–30 and up.

Most people gear too high and pedal too slowly. They don't think they are getting anywhere or getting any exercise unless they are pushing against resistance. It is precisely this pushing which creates needless fatigue. It is much better to pedal rapidly against relatively little resistance. Especially when first starting with a bike, always try to pedal as rapidly as you can without going into orbit. Soon you will find your natural cadence, and should always try to maintain this as a uniform rate of pedalling. Allow this to be one of the primary functions of the gears, and always shift up or down as necessary to maintain an even cadence. Learn to shift just before you need the new gear. Do not let a hill slow down your cadence, for example, but shift just before you hit it, and as needed going up. The way you will be able to churn along will be absolutely amazing.

Bumps

When you come to bumps, pot-holes, cables, etc, put most of your weight on the pedals and handlebars. This allows the bike to pivot underneath you, reducing shock for both you and the bike. You know how motorcycle scramble riders stand up on the pegs? Like that.

Braking

Try to use your brakes as little as possible. This will help you to 'look ahead' and know what is going to happen in advance. With

calliper brakes be careful of braking too hard and skidding. Under slippery conditions or when banked way over for a corner favour the rear brake. The rear wheel may have a slightly greater tendency to skid, but if it goes you may still be able to keep yourself upright, and at worst will land on your hip; while a front-wheel skid will pile you on your face. Going down long hills avoid overheating the brake shoes by pumping (on-off-on-off-on, etc) the brakes. In wet conditions frequently apply the brakes lightly to wipe water off the rims. And take it easy – wet brakes need four times the stopping distance of dry brakes.

THE AMERICAN STAR MACHINE

6. Traffic Jamming

Every rider must know how to ride on streets and highways shared with motor vehicles, the same way if you walk you have to know how to cross the street. Beyond this, for many people 99 per cent of their riding is in traffic, and they might as well make it as safe and enjoyable as possible. I have the worst misgivings about this chapter, for on the one hand I want you to use a bicycle as much as possible, but there is no way I can tell you that riding in traffic is safe. In plain fact, it is dangerous. Bicycle industry pundits point to the fact that cyclist casualty figures have declined since 1960, but statistics from the Annual Traffic Census indicate a decrease of two-thirds in annual mileage in the same period, so that the accident rate per mile cycled is rising. With an increasing preponderance of skilled riders and eventual segregation of motor vehicles from pedestrian and cycle traffic, this trend will reverse, but those who have been frightened away from cycling have ample justification for their fears. The other side of the coin is that taking a bath is dangerous too. There are some things one has or wants to do, accepting and attempting to prepare for attendant dangers. Each person needs to make her/his own evaluation of the amount and kind of traffic riding that suits him/her. Although the basic principles are the same, there is a considerable difference between mixing it up with heavy weekday commuter traffic and cycling a few blocks to the park on Sunday.

This chapter contains a multitude of facts and suggestions, but the most important thing I have to tell you about riding under any conditions, *and especially in traffic*, concerns psychological attitude and attentiveness. You must at all times be alert, and know everything that is going on, from the size of the pebbles on the road to the debris which might fall on you from a construction project to the number and type of vehicles before and behind you – absolutely everything. Traffic riding requires total concentration. There is no place for woolgathering here, or idyllic pastural pleasures. If you don't pay attention, you may die.

To illustrate the point: many people are fond of saying with respect to motor vehicles that 'speed kills'. Yet a few years ago when the speed limit on a major US parkway was reduced the accident rate went up. The slower travelling motorists became bored and paid less attention. Result: more accidents. People on their way to an accident will get there whether they are doing 30 or 70 mph. It is a function of attentiveness more than anything else.

Attentiveness has benefits. First of all, total engagement is refreshing. For example, I like physical challenges but spend most of my time pushing a pencil. For me the change of pace represented by traffic jamming is at times exhilarating. It does, as they say, take your mind off your troubles. Secondly, once you gain a little experience you will hopefully still be alert, but relaxed. Is crossing the street a C. B. DeMille production for you? In a more relaxed state you will appreciate the benefits of attentiveness, and see more, notice more, feel more. Getting from one place to another will be a distinctly real experience, and something *you* do.

I would like to deal with two other drawbacks to traffic jamming which unfortunately have no redeeming features:

Hyperventilation*

The inhalation of exhaust fumes and other pollutants is a serious health hazard. The automobile contributes up to 85 per cent of all air pollution in urban areas. As a cyclist not only are you at nose level with the maximum concentration of the pollution, but you are breathing harder and faster (hyperventilation). Estimating the precise degree of possible or actual damage is difficult. One statistic is that the average urbanite inhales the equivalent in particles and poisons of two packs of cigarettes a day. Does this translate for the bike rider as four packs of cigarettes a day? Five? Six?

Cars emit lead, unburnt gas, nitrogen oxides, sulphur oxides, carbon monoxide, and small quantities of grit. The worst for the cyclist are lead and carbon monoxide.

According to Dr Derek Bryce-Smith, Professor of Chemistry at Reading University, there is a good chance that airborne lead is causing real physical damage to large numbers of children today. He has also suggested that a portion of mental illness may be due to otherwise undetectable brain damage from lead pollution. Lead poisoning has been listed as a cause in the death of zoo animals. In London alone, five tons of lead pollute the air each day.

Carbon monoxide is the greatest immediate risk for the cyclist. It

*Thanks to Francis Arnold for much of the information here.

is a classic poison which interferes with the oxygen-carrying capacity of the blood. Long before it kills, this action results in decreased alertness, headaches, vague dizziness, and nausea. This dehabilitation adds to the hazard of traffic jamming.

The concentration in the air in many urban areas of both lead and carbon monoxide is already far above recommended levels. These levels are themselves suspect, for in the Soviet Union the permitted concentration of lead is 100 times lower than in the United States.

One particularly damaging type of air pollution is photochemical smog, the result of a process which occurs when sunlight and partially burned hydrocarbons interact, and for which Los Angeles, America, is famous. Until recently, owing to diffident sunlight, England was thought to be safe from photochemical smog. But the *Observer* (20-2-72) reports that scientists measured the ozone count – evidence of photochemical smog – in the south of England on thirty-five days, and on six it reached or exceeded the safety levels recommended in the United States. On two days it was above the level at which smog causes the eyes to smart, and this was *in the countryside*!

The United States standards are most certainly unrealistic, as for decades the automobile industry there resisted building pollution-free engines for reasons of profit. Considering this, and the poor performance of such engines, it is most likely that the standards are false, and tremendously minimize the real hazard. Many European cars cannot be sold in the States because they do not meet even these inadequate standards. And Great Britain is a world leader in number of cars per mile of road. You cannot draw any final conclusions from this sort of information and say, well, so and so many people are being injured. Mental illness, headaches, animal deaths, Soviet standards, two packs a day, and other tidbits of information are not readily translatable into an accurate assessment of damage, and particularly not for the cyclist, who rides through the very worst of the pollution. But the simple fact is that I get sick with headache, eye pains, nausea, and general malaise when I ride on smoggy days, and particularly the days which have a yellowish tint.

I would advise against riding at all on high air pollution count days. Try to stay clear of smoke-factory lorries and buses, and pick roundabout routes that favour parks and less travelled streets. Most gas masks will only filter out grit, but of course the sight of you using one would be wonderful guerrilla theatre.

The hazard of air pollution should not be minimized at all: the benefits you gain from the exercise of riding may well be offset by the damage caused by inhaling the chemicals, poisons, and other wondrous substances freely released into the air we breathe.

Harassment

Most often the problem with a driver of a motor vehicle is that she/he does not take sufficient notice of the cyclist, and unthinkingly drives inconsiderately or even dangerously. There are times, however, when motorists deliberately harass cyclists, passing too close at high speeds, forcing them into the kerb or off the road, or turning directly into their path and right of way. Many theories have been offered to explain this behaviour: chiefly, envy on the part of the moribund traffic-jammed motorist at the easy passage of the cyclist. From my own experience I would say that these people are unhappy and frustrated – perhaps justifiably – with their work or love lives or whatever, and – unjustifiably – are taking it out on the nearest defenceless object. Whatever the cause, there is no excuse for the inhumanity of flinging a ton or more of steel at unprotected skin and bone. If it happens to you there is little to do but move out of the way, but sometimes it is possible to communicate with the offender. Once, in London, while making a properly signalled and executed right turn from a two-way street into a one-way street, a following saloon cut around my left side and made the same turn, forcing me off the road. I remounted and caught up with the saloon farther down the street, halted it, and with polite fury informed the middle-aged gentleman driver that if he were younger he would have a bloody nose. Judging from his open-mouthed astonishment, it had never occurred to him that this was a possibility. I do not wish to recommend violence to you, but harassing drivers are bullies, meanies – and cowards who, if they encounter spirit and resistance will pick easier targets.

There are innumerable physical hazards to look out for while riding in traffic, but it is motor vehicles which are your main concern. Theory and law say that the bicycle is a vehicle which must be operated according to the rules of the road and which has the same privileges as other vehicles. Fact says otherwise. In many, many cases, the motorist is convinced that his/her vehicle gives her/him the complete right of way. Anything which obstructs her/

his forward progress – like a slow-moving bicycle – just shouldn't be there. He/she may be wrong, but it is essential for your survival to understand how she/he thinks. As a cyclist you don't really exist for him/her. As often as not she/he will cut you off, make turns in front of you, or sit right on your tail when there is no room to pass. It never even occurs to him/her to put on his brakes and give you room to manoeuvre, as she/he would for another car. Many motorists have never ridden a bicycle, and are unfamiliar with the problems of the cyclist. The Department of the Environment gives financial support to the National Cycling Proficiency Scheme, which trains cyclists in riding skills and The Highway Code, but does nothing for motorists. The Ministry of Transport's manual, *Driving*, has only a few sparse words on cycles. For most motorists, cycles are therefore not road-users of equal status, but a peripheral, obstructive nuisance.

Accordingly, riding successfully in traffic requires a blend of determination and knowing when to give in. For example, try never to block overtaking cars. At the same time if it is unsafe for you to let them pass, don't hesitate to take full possession of your lane so that they *can't* pass. Both you and the other human have exactly the same right to use the street or highway. Just because he/she has a motor vehicle confers no additional rights or privileges, and in fact the wasteful consumption of energy and vicious pollution of the environment for which her/his vehicle is responsible is a serious infringement of your rights. It is important that you understand and believe this. You have nothing to apologize for. You are not 'blocking' or 'in the way'. At the same time you have to be practical. A lot of people behind the wheel are authentic maniacs. No matter how right you are, any confrontation with a motor vehicle will wind up with you the loser.

There are enough aspects and tricks to traffic jamming so that I am simply going to run them as a list. Before doing so, a brief discussion about traffic regulations.

A cyclist must ride according to the Highway Code. If you are not familiar with the basic rules of the road, the meaning of various signs and lights (a selection is shown on the next page), and the proper techniques for turns and roundabouts, then get a copy of the Code from a post office or bookshop and study it. You can also enrol in the National Cycling Proficiency Scheme which trains and tests in the fundamentals of cycling and the Code. It takes only a few

Those with Red Circles — Mostly Prohibitive

Stop and Give Way

No Entry

Stop

No Right Turn

No Left Turn

No U Turns

No Cycling

Give Way to Traffic on Major Road

Blue Circles with no Red Border - mostly Compulsory

Ahead only

Turn Left (Right if Arrow is reversed)

Turn Left Ahead (Right if Arrow is reversed)

Keep Left (Right if Arrow is reversed)

Route for Cyclists (Compulsory)

Warning Signs mostly Triangular

Steep Hill Downwards

Level Crossing without Gate or Barrier Ahead

hours and is free. I recommended it as compulsory for children. Enquire at your police station or school.

This may all seem like a bit much to you. In my view, any user of the road whether on a lorry, bicycle, roller skates, or pogo stick should pass a test. Getting about on roads is a serious business which if it is to be done safely, and with consideration for the rights of others, requires that you know what is going on. Further, your equal status and rights are an important protection which can be maintained only by obeying the same rules as everybody else, and this is possible only if you know what the rules are.

In general, these are:

◉ that you ride as well to the left as is consistent with safety;
◉ obey traffic signs and lights;
◉ give way to pedestrians at zebra crossings;
◉ signal turns and stops. Left turn is left arm held straight out to the side, right turn ditto with the right arm, and stop a downward patting motion of the extended right arm.

I feel compelled to pass on to you the information that a cyclist can be prosecuted for endangerment of self or others, recklessness, dangerous riding, or riding under the influence of drugs or alcohol.

A knowledge of the rules is essential, but is only a bare beginning. Moreover, and especially as a relatively defenceless bicyclist, you should not rely on your 'rights' to protect you, but engage in a form of defensive riding which assumes that if there is some way for somebody to get you, they will. So . . .

◉ Hands near or on brake levers at all times. If you need to stop as quickly as possible and are not going too fast, twist the front wheel as you apply the brakes. The bike will melt into the ground in a controlled crash as the wheel and forks buckle.

◉ Be alert. There is plenty to watch for. Keep your eyes constantly moving. When looking behind don't twist your head, duck it down. Easier to do, quicker, and smoother. Do this constantly. You might have to swerve to avoid an obstacle or serious accident, and must know if you have the room or not.

◉ Be definite. Save meandering for country lanes where you can see for a long way in both directions. Ride in a straight line. Signal all turns clearly. Make right turns from right lane and left turns from left lane, if on a wide street. If you are going to do something, do it. Being definite takes the form of a certain amount of aggressiveness. Don't get bulldozed into immobility – nobody is going to give you a break. Make and take your own breaks. As far as most other drivers are concerned you either don't exist or are some alien foreign object which they want behind them. Draw attention to yourself and be super-clear about your intentions. Colourful clothing and/or a bright hat are a good idea.

◉ Be defensive. Always assume the worst. You can't see around the stopped bus? *Assume* a pregnant lady who is the sole support of 21 children is going to come prancing out. There is a car waiting to cross your lane? *Assume* it will, because *it will*. In 4 out of 5 accidents involving bicycles and motor vehicles, the motor vehicle committed a traffic violation. Always ride within a margin of control which allows you to stop or escape should absolutely everything go wrong.

◉ Look for openings in traffic, driveways, streets, garages, etc, that you can duck into should the need arise. Try to plan where you would go should you and the bike part company. The natural tendency in a collision situation is to try desperately to stop. Many

times your interests will be better served by launching yourself over an obstacle. Far better to hit the road at an angle than a car head-on.

◎ While not exceeding a speed which gives you control, try to keep moving. Within reason, avoid using brakes. This will have the effect of making you figure out well in advance what traffic situations are going to occur. There is a car double-parked in the next block. Are you going to be able to swing out? Also, a lot of the danger from other vehicles in traffic comes from differences in velocity. If you are going slow, cars bunch up behind, crowd, become impatient, etc. A racing bike can easily keep up with and pass a lot of traffic. You may find it a bit unnerving to run neck and neck with cabs and lorries at first, but it is safer than offering a stationary target. Try to *integrate* yourself with the traffic.

◎ To this end, always be in a gear low enough to give you power and acceleration. In heavy traffic an even cadence is difficult to maintain, but try to keep your feet churning away and avoid getting stuck in a 'dead' high gear. As a cyclist you have only a fraction of the power available to the motorist. To stay integrated with traffic requires that you be prepared to accelerate hard and quickly.

◎ On the other hand, do not follow the car in front too closely. Car brakes are better than bike brakes. Most bike accidents consist of the bicycle running into something. Leave plenty of room up front. This is where motorists accustomed to running bumper-to-bumper will try to pressure you from behind, even though you are moving at the same speed as the car you are following. Maintain position and if they give you the horn give them the finger.

◎ Be extra-cautious at intersections where you already have right of way. Cars coming from the opposite direction and turning right will frequently cut straight across your path. Even if the vehicle is seemingly waiting for you to pass, don't trust it, for at the last moment it will leap forward. Letting a motor vehicle precede you to clear the way is often a good tactic.

Another danger at intersections is cars coming up alongside from behind and then making a sudden left turn. One way to stop it is for you to be in the centre of the lane. However, if the intersection you are entering has a light which is going to change soon, then traffic from behind may be storming up at a breakneck pace. You'd better be out of the way.

◎ In any city anywhere in the world taxi drivers are a hazard.

All things are relative, and in London, for example, most cabbies are decent. In the US of A cabbies have the highest ulcer rate of any occupational group, as well they might considering their working conditions and how they drive. Abilities vary, but most are just no good. New York City cabbies are the bottom of the barrel.

The reason a cab driver is often a problem is that he is a professional. Driving in traffic every day, he soon knows exactly what is going on and becomes accustomed to moving ahead at every opportunity. It is second nature, and does not even require hostile intent on his part. It is just something that he does. Every day. As long as you ride clearly and decisively a cabby will present you with few difficulties; but if you start to fumble and wonder what to do, then he will quickly become impatient, and shut you in behind a bus, or cut you off, or submit you to some other unpleasantry about which you can do nothing.

◎ Very often you will be riding next to parked cars. Be especially careful of motorists opening doors in your path. Exhaust smoke and faces in rear-view mirrors are tips. Even if a motorist looks right at you and is seemingly waiting for you to pass, give her/him a wide berth. Believe it or not, you may not register on his/her consciousness, and she/he may open the door in your face.

◎ Keep an eye on the road surface. Watch out for broken glass, stones, potholes, etc. Plenty of bumps and potholes are big enough to destroy a bike – and you. Going over bumps, cables, etc, get off the saddle and keep your weight on the pedals and handlebars.

◎ Quite a few things can dump a bike:

Oil slicks in the centre of traffic lanes at busy intersections and on sharp curves. When cars stop or turn hard, a little oil drops off. The resulting slick can send you off the road or sliding out into the middle of a busy intersection.

Newly wet streets. There is a light film of oil which until it is washed away mixes with the water to make a very slippery surface. Wet manhole covers and steel plates can dump you in a hurry. I have seen this happen often.

Wet cobblestones.

Wet autumn leaves.

Gravel and sand.

Storm sewers. Many storm sewers are just the right size to swallow up a bicycle wheel.

◎ Ride with the traffic. Sometimes when there is no traffic coming the other way, it is better to ride in the opposite lane.

◎ The velocity of traffic on free-way style streets which have no parking is usually too high to permit safe cycling. If you run in the centre of the lane, you block traffic. If you go to the side, cars whiz by you at high speeds with only inches to spare. Stick to streets with parked cars and look out for opening doors.

◎ Cars and lorries pulling out. They do it unexpectedly and without signalling. Look out for driveways, building entrances, construction projects, cab ranks, and any other possible source of a vehicle. Remember, you don't exist for many drivers. They look right at you, the image is flashed on their brain, but they don't comprehend. They don't *see* you.

And perhaps some do. One time in New York City I had the lights in my favour at an intersection with a police car waiting on the cross street. The eyes of the driver fixed steadily on me and he waited until I was just going through the intersection before pulling through a red light and right in front of me. Expect the unexpected.

◎ Pedestrians are another unreliable bunch. They don't think 200 pounds of bike and rider coming towards them at 30 mph means anything, and will frequently jaywalk right in your path. Your odds are much better here than when mixing it up with a car, but even so any collision is going to hurt you, the pedestrian, and your bike. Use a horn, yell – and give them the right of way if you have to.

◎ Kids. As much of a hazard to the cyclist as to the motorist. Any child has the potential to race out suddenly into the street.

◎ Other cyclists. I don't know why, but many cyclists and especially children cyclists are erratic. Give them a wide berth.

◎ Yellow glasses are good for city riding to keep the dirt out of your eyes.

◎ Lights are a legal requirement at night. You must have a white front light, and a red rear light marked BS 3648 mounted on the centre line or offside of the bike not more than 20 in from the rear-most point, and between 15 in and 42 in off the ground. For around-town use, generator lights have the advantage that they can be left on the bike when you park, and the disadvantage that they only work when the bike is in motion. Battery lights stay lit at all times, but unless you modify the mounting bracket with a screw or other locking device, you should not leave them with the bike. See under

Accessories, p 149, and Touring, p 125, for other discussions about lights. I like a large, permanently-mounted rear reflector. Lights have a habit of failing.

⊙ Alcohol and cannabis. In a recent experiment a group of motorists were tested for driving ability. Then half the group was stoked up on booze, the other half stoned out on hash or grass, and driving ability measured again. The booze group became more belligerent and aggressive, for example, passing more often, and demonstrated slowed reaction times, while the dope contingent slowed down, became easy going and accommodating, but showed no diminishment of reaction time to emergency situations.

All these endless cautions are depressing. It seems that riding in traffic involves girding yourself for battle and inducing a constant state of morbid apprehension for your life. This is true. The idea of mixing cars and bicycles together is crazy. Cars themselves are an atavistic idiocy responsible for millions of deaths and injuries. It is entirely logical to want to have nothing to do with them.

On the other hand you can get used to it. If you are an alert, defensive rider you are reasonably safe. In return for the risks there are many benefits and it is up to you to decide how they balance. It isn't all bad by any means, but never deny the stark reality: in traffic there is a chance that you will be killed.

Accordingly, if you can avoid traffic, do so. In Great Britain it is illegal to ride on the footpaths. However, a cyclist is closer to a pedestrian than a car is to a cyclist. Mixing pedestrians and cyclists together on footpaths is not only much safer than mixing cars and cycles on roads, it is not even dangerous, as the accident statistics from Stevenage where the two have mixed for twenty years, bear out. A number of factors make this so, but the simplest is that the cyclist, like the pedestrian, is vulnerable and exposed, and has every interest in avoiding conflicts.

Riding on footpaths must be done with discretion – dashes through Sunday parks filled with strollers are inconsiderate – and you must give way to pedestrians, dismounting if necessary. But many footpaths are little used and offer a more sensible transit than running with the road traffic. Just remember that however rational your case, to ride on a footpath makes you liable to infringement of the law, an alternative you may prefer to risking your life.

Touring is the real joy in biking. The only better way to see the country is to walk or roller skate. A bike has advantages in mobility and luggage-carrying however, and the aesthetic sacrifice is not too great. Touring can be done in a tremendous variety of ways. You can go for an afternoon's jaunt or spend a summer or more travelling thousands of miles. You can go as a self-contained unit with your own camping gear, or ultra-light and stay in inns, guest houses, hostels, and hotels. You can count the miles travelled, or concentrate on the scenery (yeah!). Your journey can include transit by auto, bus, train, boat, and plane, so that you can hop from one interesting place to another. You can have a plan, or absolutely none at all. Touring is a call to adventure, beauty, new sights and experiences.

There's a lot to touring, and plenty for you to think about. At the same time it can be kept simple. Any bike headed for the sticks should have a tool kit, unless you don't mind pushing your bike a few miles to a garage and/or the possibility of an overnight

'A merry heart goes all the way,
Your sad tires in a mile, a.'—*Shakespeare*.

stay until it opens. Equipment makes a difference, but the main thing is to get out there. My greatest, happiest tour was on a battered 1935 BSA whose vital parts shed like water.

Part of the fun of touring is figuring it out and planning or not planning for yourself. Some people insist that the only way to tour is with a meticulous and detailed plan; others heave map and compass into the bushes and go wherever fancy takes them. For some the fun and relaxation comes as a result of planned and concentrated effort; for others it is through not thinking about anything. There is no 'right' way to tour. Each to his own. Accordingly, this chapter tries simply to give basic information about touring. It is not a step-by-step guide. It's up to you to decide where and when you want to go, and what sort of equipment you expect to need.

You can cover a lot of ground touring – right around the world. First, and while covering the basics of technique and equipment, let us do Great Britain. Then we will spread out to the Continent, Africa, Asia, Australia, and the Americas.

Great Britain
Where

One source of information is books. *Explore the Cotswolds by Bicycle*, by Suzanne Ebel and Doreen Impey (50p, published for the British Cycling Bureau by Ward Lock Ltd, 116 Baker Street, London W1M 2BB), lists a number of detailed, relatively traffic-free tours, with historical background and notes on places and events of interest. Written with the cyclist in mind is *The Roadfaring Guide*, *South-West England*, by Reginald Wellby (5p, Cyclists' Touring Club, 69 Meadrow, Godalming, Surrey, GU7 3HS).

Another source of information is

British Cycling Bureau,
Greater London House,
Hampstead Road,
London, NW1.

which distributes leaflets on various aspects of cycling, a list of equipment-hire shops throughout Great Britain, detailed itineraries for a number of tours, and comments on good touring areas. The

British Tourist Authority,
239 Old Marylebone Road,
London NW1.

publishes *Inns of Britain, Egon Ronay's Pubs and Tourist Sights in Great Britain* (£1·75), and *Britain: 100 Historic Inns* (free). General information on touring, brochures, accommodation lists, etc, can be obtained from tourist authorities:

British Tourist Authority

Tourist Information Centre, 64 St James's St, London SW1, tel 01-629 9191.

England

English Tourist Board and London Tourist Board, 4 Grosvenor Gdns, London SW1, tel 01-730 0791.
East Anglian Tourist Board, 14 Museum St, Ipswich, Suffolk, tel (0473) 21411.
East Midlands Tourist Board, Bailgate, Lincoln, tel (0522) 31521.
English Lakes Counties Tourist Board, Ellerthwaite, Windermere, tel 4444, Westmorland.
Isle of Man Tourist Board, 13 Victoria St, Douglas, tel (0624) 4323.
Isle of Wight Tourist Board, 21 High St, Newport, tel (0983-81) 4343.
Northumbria Tourist Board, 8 Eldon Sq, Newcastle/Tyne, tel (0632) 28795.
North-West Tourist Board, 119 The Piazza, Piccadilly Plaza, Manchester 1, tel (061) 236 0393.
South-East England Tourist Board, 4–6 Monsoon Rd, Tunbridge Wells, Kent, tel (0892) 33066.
West Country Tourist Board, Trinity Ct, Southernhay East, Exeter, Devon, tel (0392) 76351.
West Midlands Tourist Board, 1 Shaw St, Worcester, tel (0905) 29511.
Yorkshire Tourist Board, 312 Tadcaster Rd, York, tel (0904) 67961.

Wales

Wales Tourist Board, Welcome Hse, High St, Llandaff, Cardiff,
tel (0222) 566133.
Mid-Wales Tourism Council, 3 China St, Llanidloes, tel 664, Mont.
North Wales Tourism Council, Civic Centre, Colwyn Bay,
Denbighs, tel (0492) 55222.
South Wales Tourism Council, Darkgate, Carmarthen, tel 7557.

Scotland

Scottish Tourist Board, 23 Ravelston Terr, Edinburgh 4, tel
(031)-332 2433.
The Borders Tourist Association, 66 Woodmarket, Kelso, tel 2125,
Rox.
Clyde Tourist Association, c/o Information Centre, George Sq,
Glasgow, tel (041) 221 9600.
Grampian Tourist Association, 17 High St, Elgin, Moray, tel
(0343) 3451.
Highlands and Islands Development Board, Bridge Hse, Bank St,
Inverness, tel (0463) 34171.
South-West Scotland Tourist Association, Douglas Hse, Newton
Stewart, tel 549, Wigtowns.

Northern Ireland

Northern Ireland Tourist Board, 48 High St, Belfast, tel (0232)
31221.

Probably the best way to get into touring is to join a society or
organization. You get a variety of planning and insurance services,
and riding with fellow members you receive a planned tour, the
benefit of a group leader who will set a pace within your capacity,
and lots of free friendly help and advice. First and foremost is:

Cyclists' Touring Club,
69 Meadrow,
Godalming, Surrey GU7 3HS.

I recommend this organization to every cyclist, tourist or not. The largest and oldest (1878) national cycling association, it not only provides an extraordinary range of services, but also safeguards and champions the cyclist's rights at every level of government and municipal authority. Membership (£5·00 for one year) includes the Cyclists' Touring Club Handbook, a thick list of 3,000 recommended accommodation addresses, places to eat, cycle repairers, and CTC local information officers for Great Britain; a list of overseas touring correspondents; information about touring areas, equipment, and travel by air, rail, and sea, including ferries, tunnels, and bridges; a catalogue of the books and maps for Great Britain, the Continent, and Morocco available through the bookshop; and a complete exposition of club services. For the tourist, the most important of these is the Touring Department, which not only has available a large library of comprehensive, personally researched tours, complete with maps (see overleaf) but which will also plan and suggest tours for routes and areas you request, as well as advising on cycle and personal equipment, gears, maps, and travel books. In addition, the CTC London office,

CTC Travel Ltd,
13 Spring Street,
London W2 3RA.

will make bookings for all air, sea, and rail journeys abroad, and has information sheets on most European countries. In this connection, CTC is a founder member of the Alliance Internationale de Tourisme, linking touring clubs (see list pp 133–43) all over the world, and provides on request an AIT cycletouring card as introduction for requests for advice and assistance. There is an International Camping Carnet, and CTC members are allowed to take cycles via cross-channel hovercraft, which you normally cannot do from April to September. Membership includes subscription to the bimonthly *Cycle Touring*, filled with news of interest to the cyclist, articles on touring and tours, equipment tests, letters, adverts, and useful information. Insurance services include free third-party liability anywhere in the world up to £50,000 and policies are available for personal accident, damage or theft to cycle, cameras, luggage; and inclusive, which takes in all the foregoing, cancellation and curtailment, and personal liability up to £250,000. Membership is worth it for the third party £50,000 cover alone, even for the

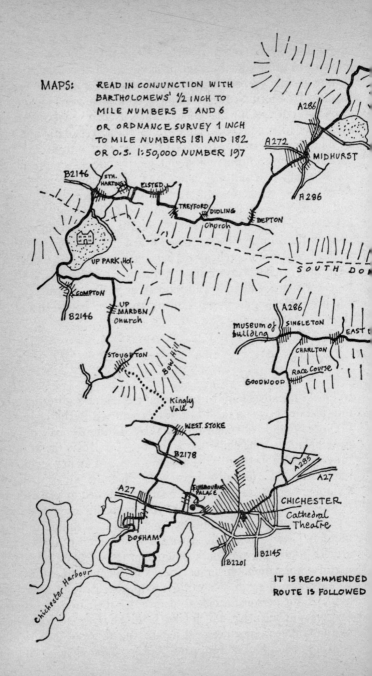

MAPS: READ IN CONJUNCTION WITH
        BARTHOLOMEWS' ½ INCH TO
        MILE NUMBERS 5 AND 6
        OR ORDNANCE SURVEY 1 INCH
        TO MILE NUMBERS 181 AND 182
        OR O.S. 1:50,000 NUMBER 197

A286

A272   MIDHURST

A286

B2146   STH.
        HARTING   ELSTED
                    TREYFORD   DIDLING
                               Church   BEPTON

SOUTH DO

UP PARK Ho.

COMPTON

UP
MARDEN   A286
Church

B2146   museum of   SINGLETON
                building   EAST

STOUGHTON   CHARLTON

            Bow Hill   Race Course
                  GOODWOOD

            Kingly
            Vale

                    WEST STOKE

B2178

                                            A285
                                                   A27
A27
            FISHBOURNE
            PALACE   CHICHESTER
                                      Cathedral
                                      Theatre
      BOSHAM

                              B2145
                    B2201

                        IT IS RECOMMENDED
Chichester Harbour   ROUTE IS FOLLOWED

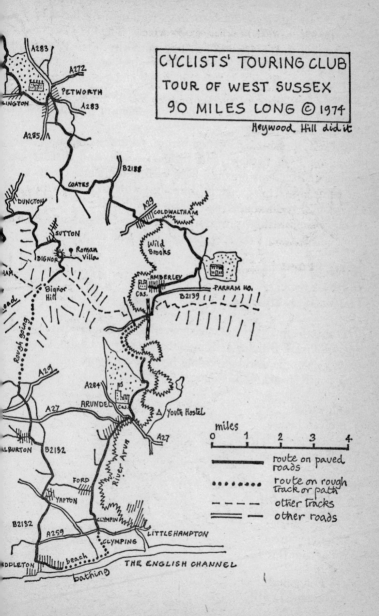

cyclist who goes only to the station and back. The CTC also provides free legal aid in obtaining compensation for members in road accidents ranging from encounters with motor vehicles to dog bites to damages caused by bad road surfaces. The CTC will make representation to the appropriate local authority or to Parliament in regard to any justified complaint by members on such matters as dangerous road surfaces, traffic difficulties and unfair restrictions on the use of cycles; discourtesy and poor service in the conveyance of cycles by public transport; and misinformed or biased Press or public criticism of cyclists.

The CTC organizes any number of rallies, tours, and competitions on both national and regional levels, and district associations and sections organize local cycling tours and events and social occasions. Tours vary in difficulty, with accommodation at youth hostels, guest houses, and inexpensive hotels.

Another organization providing an accommodations handbook, touring and insurance services for members, and maps, is

British Cycling Federation,
26 Park Crescent,
London W1N 4BL.

This is also the internationally recognized controlling body for cycle racing in Great Britain, and is affiliated to the Union Cycliste Internationale, the world governing body of the sport.

The Youth Hostel Associations:

Headquarters:
Trevelyan House,
8 St Stephen's Hill,
St Albans, Hertfordshire.

offices and shops:
29 John Adam Street,
London WC2 N6JE.

14, SOUTHAMPTON ST.,
L - WC2E 7HY
01 - 836 - 8541

35 Cannon Street,
Birmingham B25 EE.

36/38 Fountain Street,
Manchester M2 2BE.

166, DEANSGATE,
M - M3 3FE
061 - 834 7119

Scottish Youth Hostels Association,
7 Glebe Crescent,
Stirling, Stirlingshire,
Scotland SK8 2AJ.

Irish Youth Hostels Association,
39 Mountjoy Square,
Dublin,
Eire.

Youth Hostel Association of Northern Ireland,
Bryson House,
Belfast BT 27FE.
Northern Ireland.

The Youth Hostel Associations are a somewhat strait-laced but nevertheless very good outfit with over 4,000 hostels in forty-seven countries, many in beautiful and/or historic areas. Hostels are sometimes spartan, but always serviceable. You provide your own sleeping bag, and help a bit with the chores. Inexpensive, and you can cook your own food. The Association stores sell camping and touring equipment and have a tourist service, as well as running guided tours. An essential organization for the economy-minded.

So. Where you go depends on your own temperament, interests, physical condition, and equipment. If you favour back roads off the beaten track and camping, you are going to have to deal with equipment for both you and the bike; touring on better roads and sleeping in inns means less and lighter equipment. I would suggest that you make your initial rides about 20 miles or so, and work up to longer tours and overnight stays as you get used to it. Until you are quite experienced, do not target over 50 to 60 miles a day, and try to balance hard runs with days of relaxation and shorter jaunts. Excess zeal will turn you into a basket case. Start easy and finish strong.

Riding

I recommend taking the smallest, least travelled roads practically possible. These are B class roads and smaller. Not only are they almost always more interesting, but the fewer cars there are around the more comfortable you will be. Motor vehicles in the country are a serious hazard for the cyclist. Fewer cyclists ride in the country than in the cities, but more are killed in the country. The speed differences between cycles and cars are much greater. On the dual-lane carriageways, for example, the vehicles run at 70 mph plus, often bunched so tightly together that drivers' vision is limited by the vehicle they are following, and hence they do not see the cyclist until the moment of overtaking, when they no longer have the time to swing out and give room. This danger is acute at night-time. Often there are footpaths adjoining such roads, little-used and a sensible alternative, but keep a keen eye out for broken glass and other litter. On the two-way A and B class roads many vehicles move smartly, particularly if the driver 'knows the road', and hare around tight corners at 40 to 60 mph. With an up to 50 mph difference in speed between the motor vehicle and the cyclist, and limited space for manoeuvring, a bad situation can develop much faster than the many drivers who over-rate themselves think is possible. You, the naked, exposed, defenceless cyclist are utterly dependent on the abilities and emotional maturity of drivers. Even acceding to the insanity which states that rapid motoring is permissible when executed with requisite skill, there is still the odd (these days?) exception, for whatever reason simply incompetent. And however odd, for dying, once is sufficient.

The best bet for the cyclist are small roads which keep vehicle speeds down to about 30 mph, at which rate there is almost always enough room and time to prevent serious accidents. These roads meander and take longer, but are usually more interesting. The point of cycling in the first place is to savour and enjoy, and so for reaching somewhere in a hurry use other transport, or take you and your cycle by rail or air.

An alternative to roads are bridlepaths (which the cyclist is legally entitled to use) and footpaths (which he is not). These honeycomb Britain and I have taken many long tours touching road for only a mile or so. The scenery is usually fantastic, and the riding often demanding. Most bikes will stand up to this sort of use well enough, although tubular tyres are pretty much out. An exception of sorts are the special cyclo-cross lugged tyres, but while these provide excellent traction the casings are not as strong as for wire-on tyres (see the equipment discussion on p 124 for further information). As far as the legality of footpaths is concerned I again suggest common sense (I hear the hounds now!). A popular walking area filled with Sunday strollers is a poor choice and you should dismount and walk. But most times there is nobody around and you will have the outdoors to yourself.

Safe country road riding is largely a matter of common sense. Most of the rules for traffic riding apply here also.

◎ The cardinal rule is 'what if?' Look and think ahead. Don't, for example, time your riding so that you and an overtaking car reach a curve at the same time. If a car – or worse yet a lorry – comes the other way there just isn't going to be enough room.

◎ Bear in mind the tremendous relative velocity of cars. In traffic you can pretty much keep up, but in the country cars will have up to 70 mph over your 5 to 15. If you crest a hill, for example, and there is no oncoming traffic, move over into the opposite lane for a while. This avoids the hazard of overtaking cars who cannot see you over the crest.

◎ Try to have a hole to duck into should everything go wrong. Where will you go if that tractor pulls out? If a car comes around the corner on your side of the road, are you going to try for the ditch or a tree? You may wreck a bike going off into a field, but this is a lot better than colliding with a car. Think about this as much as you can and try to make it an automatic process. This way, when an emergency arises, instead of freezing in panic you may be able to save your life.

◎ Be particularly wary, when you have speed up, of people doing odd things. Cannonballing down a hill you may be doing 30–50 mph, a fact that many motorists and pedestrians do not comprehend. They see a bicycle, and automatically class it as slow and unimportant, dismissing it from mind (as you can be sure they would not do for a large lorry), and step or pull out on to the road, or pass, or whatever. This capacity for visual recognition with no subsequent cognitive comprehension may seem bizarre, but I assure you it is so. Never trust other road users – you cannot afford to do so.

◎ Mind your brakes. After running through puddles or wet grass, dry off by applying them lightly as you ride. When running down steep hills, do not hold the brakes steady, which causes heat build-up and fade, but pump on and off. This also tells you if you have something in reserve – which you always should.

◎ Run well to the left (or right, on the Continent) but leave yourself a little bit of room to manoeuvre. There are all sorts of broken pavement, sewers, and odd bits of litter which crop up unexpectedly at the road's edge.

◉ Rural farm traffic is a law unto itself. Many farmers operate machinery on local public roads as if they were in the middle of a field.

◉ Watch for loose gravel, dirt, or sand, and especially at driveway and side road entrances.

◉ Bridge gratings, cattle guards, railway tracks, etc, can all swallow up a bicycle wheel and send you flying.

◉ Dogs. Dogs and other creatures of the field and air are a menace to the cyclist. I was once attacked by a determined and large goose. Dogs are the main problem though, and you need to keep a constant look-out for old Towser.

This is not such a problem in England, and I have been advised that what I have to say next is offensive. I do not think so. I offer a variety of techniques for dealing with a threatening or attacking dog designed to resolve the situation without harm to either you or the dog. These failing, and assuming you are under meaningful attack and must defend yourself, I tell you how to kill a dog. If this is too stark, then skip this section.

There are many theories about why dogs attack two-wheeled vehicles. I think that the spokes make a noise which drives them nuts. There are also a number of dog owners who take a not-so-secret pleasure in having vicious attack-prone animals, and others who should not even try to take responsibility for a cockroach. One couple expressed puzzlement to me after their dog bit my riding companion: every time the dog was disobedient they said, they beat it until their arms hurt. Why wouldn't it obey? With treatment like that, any dog will become vicious and irrational.

If you can do it, the best thing by far is to outrun an attacking dog. Often this is not possible, but 99 times out of a 100 there is still no serious problem. Many cyclists become hysterical on the subject of dog defence, and recommend whips, car aerials, clubs, and other weapons that will really hurt a dog. This is not necessary. It really isn't the dog's fault. Nine times out of ten he is normally friendly. All you have to do is stop, dismount, and face him directly. That's all. Simply stop. Often he will come up wagging his tail. When you leave, walk away like all 'normal' (to the dog) people do, and the matter will be forgotten.

The tenth time, when a dog still threatens attack: the main thing when dealing with a vicious dog is to have *confidence*. As a human being you are one of the largest mammals on earth and a formidable

contender in a fight. Suppress your fears and radiate the notion that any dog that messes with you will regret it for the rest of his days, if he lives that long. It is only the rarest of dogs that will attack a human obviously prepared for self-defence. Speak to the dog in firm tones, keep your bike between you, and slowly walk away.

If a dog attacks: an effective defence is the aerosol pepper sprays made for exactly this purpose. They have a range of about ten feet and are light enough to clip to the handlebars or to your belt. Or a water/ammonia solution can be sprayed with a squeeze out of a small plastic container such as is used for detergent or hair shampoo. Even an ammonia-filled water pistol will work. If you have neither of these and can't or won't climb a tree, get a stick or large rock. No? The bicycle pump. Try to ram it down his throat. In any event, don't cower or cover up, because the dog will only chew you to ribbons. *Attack*. Any small dog can simply be hoisted up by the hind legs and his brains dashed out. With a big dog you are fighting for your life. If you are weaponless try to tangle him up in your bike and then strangle him. Kicks to the genitals and which break ribs are effective. If worst comes to worst, ram your entire arm down his throat. He will choke and die. Better your arm than your throat. You can avoid this problem by carrying pepper spray or an ammonia solution.

If you are bitten and the dog gets away, make every effort to find the dog and owner. If the dog cannot be quarantined you will have to get a long series of painful rabies shots. Ask around the area, check with local petrol stations, stores, etc. In any event, get immediate medical treatment, even for a light bite. Then notify the police or the dog owner of the incident. If the dog owner is uncooperative, just find a solicitor. The law is completely and absolutely on your side.

If you successfully fend off an attack, notify the dog owner or police. This is a very real responsibility because the next person might not be as well prepared as you. A little girl, for example, like the one who lived down the road from my parents' place; several summers ago she was pulled down and killed by three dogs.

Technique

Cadence (see pp 89–90 for basics) plays an extremely significant part in the technique of long-distance touring. In a short sprint you can drain your body's resources and strength, but on a long tour output must not exceed ability to continuously replenish fuel and oxygen. Which makes it sound simple: just take it easy and have something in reserve. Not quite.

If you are interested in covering a lot of ground (not everybody is) and in feeling comfortable, then you must strive for an exact balance between energy output and the body's ability to synthesize and store energy. There is a *pace* which works best. Go too fast and the result will be fatigue and possibly strained muscles that will dog you throughout the tour. But go too slow, and you will become sluggish and lethargic, and mistake this for genuine tiredness.

A rough indicator of pace is respiration and heartbeat. You simply cannot sustain for long periods effort which noticeably increases either. Thus, the exact pace you can maintain depends on your physical condition, not on your strength.

I particularly recommend that you take it easy at first, sticking to the lower gears and not pushing hard against the pedals. This will help you to find your own cadence and pace, and perhaps avoid

excessive initial effort. Most people tend to lean into it hard the first day. The result is strained and sore muscles, and the next day they can hardly move. You'll go farther and faster if you take it easy at the start.

Riding position can make a tremendous difference. Going into the wind try to get low down. With a strong tail wind, straighten up and get a free push. In Europe many riders use home-made 'sails' resembling kites strapped to their backs. These are effective even with a quartering wind. Position determines the muscle groups in use: hands high on the bars eases the back, stomach, arms, and hands; down positions do exactly the opposite and are best for hill climbing.

Equipment

Bike: Touring can be done on a 3-speed but don't try to cover a lot of ground. You'll be packing an extra 15–20 pounds and working through an inefficient gear train. A 10-speed is the best choice by far. Experienced tourists sometimes prefer 15-speed bikes, but for the tyro these have mechanical problems which offset the advantage of extra gears. Be sure to gear for the terrain you will encounter and weight of luggage. Although not alpine, many hills in Britain are sharply pitched. For a 5-speed, the Cyclists' Touring Club recommends 13-15-18-23-31 to 40 front, and for a 10-speed, 15-17-19-21-23 to 28 × 46 front (if you don't understand these numbers, see pp 78–84). I myself prefer to have a little more top end, and to get low gears by running a large back sprocket, 14-16-19-23-28 rear to 36 × 52 front, for example, and would gear a very heavily-laden bike with a still larger rear sprocket, 30 or even 32, and/or go down a bit on the front sprockets, say 34 × 50. Age, weight, physical condition, all play a part and what is sauce for the goose, etc, but the recommendations above, and on pp 78–84, will not let you down.

Most 10-speed bikes can be altered for touring, and the discussions of luggage, lights, etc, below will suggest what bits and pieces are necessary for your needs. A touring frame, 72° parallel (see pp 73–74 for what this means), is the most desirable. There are only a few off-the-shelf touring bikes available. Two are the Dawes Galaxy (approx £130) and Falcon Olympic (approx £93) (see pp 51, 53 for specifications). The Cyclists' Touring Club has tested the Galaxy extensively and reports that the roadholding is good, even on rough surfaces, and this is a prime feature. The demanding should substitute alloy mudguards for the plastic which will eventually warp and spray water about. Workmanship and finish are good.

Other bicycles to consider are the Falcon Black Diamond (specifications on page 51), which wants only the addition of a luggage rack, and the Viscount Areospace Sport (specifications on page 51), which wants mudguards and a luggage rack. The Viscount is of especial interest, as it comes with sealed bottom bracket and hubs requiring no maintenance, heavy duty 14 gauge spokes, and dual-action touring brakes.

Most manufacturers of lightweights will build a touring model to order, and have stock 'bespoke' deluxe touring models with either Reynolds 531 plain or double-butted tubing throughout, and high-grade components. Prices range from £160 and up, most with a ceiling of about £225. Any of the shops listed on p 68 can supply, and firms with considerable experience are:

Jack Taylor Cycles,
Church Road,
Stockton-on-Tees,
Teesside TS18 2LY.

Condor Cycles,
90 Gray's Inn Road,
London WC1.

F. W. Evans,
44–46 Kennington Road,
London SE1.

W. F. Holdsworth Ltd,
55 High Street,
Penge, London SE20

Off-road Woods Bicycles

One excellent form of sport/touring is along trails and bridlepaths and cross-country. The going can get muddy and rough, and even on smooth sections there are concealed rocks, limbs, and other debris. Machines for this sort of use need heavy-duty tyres with the widest and roughest tread possible, and should have a minimum of equipment to rattle off or get damaged. Mudguards will be found to be both a curse and a boon, protecting against water spray and flying stones, but also jamming up tight with mud and litter. Riding technique calls for sensitivity and control. On bumpy sections keep the weight on the pedals. Not only easier on the bike, and you, but aids balance. Be relaxed. To a certain extent let the bike find its own way.

Machines made especially for this sort of riding are called cyclo-cross. They feature extra clearance for the wheels, and lugged, tubular tyres. Since they are competition bikes, the rims are typically alloy and if used hard, sooner or later bend. Also, as they are 5- or 10-speeds, the derailleurs constantly need soaking and cleaning. All worth it if you are particularly keen on the sport, but otherwise I suggest simply equipping an old beat-up 3-speed with a small front sprocket and lugged tyres.

Tyres (we're back to regular road bikes now): Tubular tyres are fragile and fast. Although on the road a tubular can be changed quickly, they are time-consuming to repair. In the hands of an expert they will give reasonable service and fast running, but tyros should start out on wire-ons. These are more durable, easy to repair, and only fractionally slower. Tubulars for point to point speed runs, wire-ons for back road meandering, and heavy-duty in either case.

Tool Kit
Tyre tools (wire-ons)
Tyre repair kit
6-in adjustable spanner
Screwdriver
Chain tool
Spoke spanner
Spare spokes
Spare chain links
Brake pads
Valve stem
Brake cable
Derailleur cable
Lubricant
Pump
Snip pliers

Sounds like a lot, but it all packs into a very compact bundle. If you are two or more, cut down on the number of spare parts, and share one set of tools. And on longer runs, for mending you, I suggest a small first-aid kit.

Lights: A requirement at night. The majority of tourists prefer dynamo lights as they are bright, consistent (batteries fade), and less expensive. However, some people do not care to pedal against the additional resistance of the dynamo. If this is a properly tuned hub unit, then the drag will be minimal, but of course it is constant night *and* day, which is when most people ride. With battery lights, if you are trying for speed on a daytime run, then they can be left off. If you are camping, then having a battery light gives you a free flashlight. Why carry two? Map-reading is also facilitated with battery lights. For very rough off-the-road work a battery light is pretty much a requirement. Going fast enough to keep a dynamo light functioning is sometimes dicey.

It's a never ending debate with pros and cons on each side and you will just have to make your own choice. Some people take both, running a dynamo set and carrying a lightweight battery light to be used as needed and as a spare in case the main system fails. For more discussion, see Accessories, pp 149–51.

Mudguards: These are pretty much a requirement for British and Continental touring. The plastic models are light and easily removed when not needed, but eventually warp and allow water to spray. The alloy and stainless steel models are sturdier and heavier, and offer mounting points for lights and other knick-knacks. They have an annoying characteristic of transmitting sound, but this can be prevented by using undercoating paint, available at motorists' accessories shops.

Bicycle shoes and cleats: Used in conjunction with toe clips these are essential for any long-distance travelling, unless you plan to be on and off the bike frequently. Pack shoes for walking as bicycle shoes are very unsuitable for this.

Baggage: Loading a touring bike is an art. There are two cardinal principles: load low and load evenly. Piling gear up in a high stack or all in one place creates tremendous instability for the bike. Bicycle carriers are designed to distribute loads properly. There are three basic kinds: handlebar bags, saddlebags, and panniers. People travelling light can get by with a saddlebag. These fasten to the seat and seat post and can hold a lot of gear. The next addition would be a handlebar bag. This makes for good fore and aft weight distribution, and is handy for food, cameras, and other things you often need. Get one with a transparent map case and that opens forward for easy accessibility. Campers will want rear panniers hung on special frames alongside the wheel. Panniers both front and rear are just too much baggage. Front panniers also stiffen steering and do not have the carrying capacity of rear panniers.

Excellent lines of cycling and camping baggage equipment are manufactured by:

Karrimor Products Ltd,   Carradice of Nelson Ltd,
Avenue Parade,   North Street,
Accrington, Lancashire   Nelson, Lancashire BB9 7NF
(catalogue on request)

and sold in bike shops and there is really no need to go further as this is first-rate equipment. The Youth Hostel Association stores (addresses p 114) also carry this sort of gear.

Whatever you use, load evenly and low. Put heavy gear at the bottom, light bulky stuff like sleeping bags at the top. Give yourself a few local shakedown trial runs. The extra weight takes getting used to, and nothing is quite so irritating as rebuilding a broken luggage rack with inadequate tools in the middle of a tour.

Maps: A compass is not only useful in conjunction with a map, but can itself guide you in the general direction you want to go without strict routing. Sometimes it is fun to dispose of maps altogether. Just go where fancy takes you, and ask directions on the way. You get to meet people, and often they can suggest really interesting routes, scenic attractions, swimming places, and the like. But have a map in reserve.

As well as keeping you on a desired route, maps have the vital function of keeping you off main arterial roads and out of industrial areas. Petrol station maps are inadequate. Excellent are the Ordnance Survey maps, a catalogue of which is available from:

Director General,
Ordnance Survey,
Romsey Road,
Maybush, Southampton SO9 4DH.

The maps are obtainable in many bookshops, and from Ordnance Survey Agents, a list of which is obtainable from:

Cook, Hammond & Kell Ltd,
22–24 Caxton Street,   for England and Wales
London SW1.

Thomas Nelson & Sons,
18 Dalkeith Road,   for Scotland
Edinburgh EH16 5BS.

The 1 : 25,000 scale maps are extremely detailed, showing individual buildings, walls, tiny streams, and the like, and give an endless amount of information about the area covered. They are wonderful for detailed exploring, but for overall route planning $\frac{1}{2}$-in or 1-in scale maps are better. These still show virtually all roads, footpaths, villages, rivers, and other stuff like youth hostels, inns, National Trust properties, windmills, public rights of way and more. There are also a number of tourist maps made up especially for popular and scenic areas, and archaeological and historical maps.

Bartholomew's $\frac{1}{2}$-in series, probably the most useful size, is obtainable in bookstores or from:

John Bartholomew,
12 Duncan Street,
Edinburgh, Scotland.

Both Ordnance and Bartholomew's maps are available from the Cyclists' Touring Club at a reduced price for members.

Clothing: Shorts are pretty much universal garb. Morning chill evaporates after two or three miles. Wash and wear is a must for long jaunts. A nylon windcheater is very useful, as are cycling jerseys with big pockets for stashing gear. A poncho will serve also as a groundsheet and/or a tent, but most people use cycling capes, which have an annoying habit of flapping about, and do not really protect the legs. The alternative, a proper rainsuit, means that one gets drenched from within by perspiration, and hence the cape is the preferred choice. Sweaters, suits, morning dress, according to climate and the preferences of the cyclist, but I suggest minimizing your load wherever possible.

Camping:

The Camping Club of Great Britain and Ireland Ltd,
11 Lower Grosvenor Place,
London SW1.

Membership includes an International Camping Carnet, insurance services, a handbook on camping, and a guide to 1,500 sites in Great Britain and Ireland. Another organization is:

Cycling Section,
Association of Cycling and Lightweight Campers,
30 Napier Road,
Wembley, Middlesex.

and site lists are also available from

British Tourist Authority,
239 Old Marylebone Road,
London NW1.

Camping gear: Personal preferences and abilities can completely determine choices here. Some people need a tent and a prepared campsite with running water. Others insist on portable stoves, radios, etc. There are many good books on camping equipment and woods lore, and if you are unfamiliar with this craft you should get one. There is space here for only the most generalized suggestions.

1. Sleeping bag. Tents and stoves, etc, can always be improvised with fair success, but only the most skilled can keep warm in a bad bag. A poor bag weighs more, and if you freeze and can't sleep, this will give you ample time to brood on the economic and practical merits of having got something that would do the job in the first place. Get the best bag you can afford. Also, although your bike has carrying capacity and most of your touring is apt to be in warm weather, I suggest you keep other possibilities such as camping, or tours in the autumn (fantastic!) in mind.

The best bags, pound-for-pound, are of down. Down has the greatest range (temperatures at which the bag will work), resiliency (bag packs small), recovery (gets body back when unpacked), wicking properties (carries moisture away from body), and moral character. Down bags run from £30 to £60 and the less expensive, lighter (filled with $1\frac{1}{2}$–$2\frac{1}{2}$ pounds of down) models are OK for warm weather. I suggest a multi-layered and/or openable bag that will also take a flannel insert. This gives optimum range and comfort.

An interesting new insulative material is poly foam, used in Ocaté bags. These are only fractionally heavier ($4\frac{1}{2}$ pounds overall) than lightweight down bags ($3\frac{1}{2}$ pounds), and the manufacturer claims a degree range down to —5°, about that of a middleweight down bag (4–4½ pounds). The advantage is that it will keep you warm, wet or dry.

The least expensive bags contain synthetic fillers such as 'Dacron 88' and 'Astrofill'. These run from £6 to £15, weigh about 6 pounds, and are OK for warm weather and low altitudes.

2. A ground sheet such as a triple-purpose (raincape, tent) poncho.

The remaining equipment listed here can always be improvised. The trouble with this is that garnering boughs for a bed or building fires is rather wasteful and ecologically unsound. There are enough campers now so that the total destruction can be devastating. In many areas you are not allowed to do these things. So, drag that it may be, it is both practical and considerate to be as self-sufficient as possible.

3. Sleeping mattress or pad. Air mattresses (avoid plastic ones) are comfortable but bulky. Pads such as ensolite are fine.

4. Tents come in all shapes, sizes and grades. Conditions and personal preference dictate choice. Tents are good for protection against bugs, rain, and to ensure privacy. For myself I see no point in hieing to the Great Outdoors and then sleeping in a dark hole. Polyethylene fly sheets can be rigged into a decent shelter with only a little effort and are extremely cheap and light. A poncho is just as good. In tents, the Gerry 'Pioneer' is well thought of by everybody. This makes up as a one-man tent with floor and mosquito netting, or as a two-man tent without a floor.

Gerry,
5450 North Valley Highway,
Denver, Colorado 80216, USA.

For a two-man tent the Itisa Senior is rugged but heavy:

Blacks of Greenock Ltd,
22 Gray's Inn Road,
London WC1.
and
53 Rathbone Place,
London W1.

5. Cooking stove and utensils. You should have, but I don't know anything about them. Four skewers can be used to form a grid for a pot, a grill, to skewer food, or as tent pegs. Heavy-duty aluminium foil will make a flat-folding re-usable pot.

6. Food. Dried lightweight foods are extremely convenient and quite palatable. I suggest carrying enough for emergencies only however, and trying for fresh food along the route. Stock up on breakfast and supper at about 4 o'clock. Mixtures of dried fruit, nuts, grains, dried milk, yeast, etc, are nourishing, tasty, and easy to carry.

Nearly every city or town has a camping equipment store. The Youth Hostel Association stores (p 114) always offer good value. If you have a bit more money to burn, and would really prefer the lightest possible equipment, then your best bet may be an alpine outfitter such as:

Robert Lawrie Ltd,
54 Seymour Street,
London W1.

Camping equipment can be hired from:

Crystal Palace Camping,
5 Church Road,
London SE19.

Eaton's Outdoor Centre,
100 Haydons Road,
London SW19.

Getting There

Other forms of locomotion complement bicycles very well.
Cars: A 10-speed with the wheels off will fit in the boot of many economy cars and certainly on the back seat. For carrying several bikes you can buy or make a car carrier. There are two types, rear end and top. The rear end version holds two bikes and is easy to load. It is hard to get at the boot however, and the bikes get a lot of road grit and scratch each other. Top-mounted carriers hold four to five bikes, and require each to be strapped down. But machines are kept clean, separate, and out of harm's way. They are available from bike shops, but I have always found an ordinary luggage rack such a

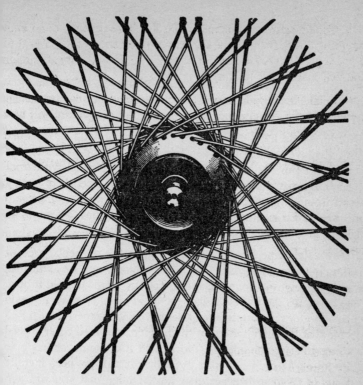

NEW RAPID TANGENT WHEEL.

sold in car accessory stores entirely suitable, sometimes with the addition of a thin board on which saddles rest. Or you can make your own, and have something exactly suited for the job. *Bicycle Camping and Touring* (Tolby Publishing Co, Box 428, New Canaan, Conn 06840 USA, $3·00) has plans, and so does:

Bicycle Institute of America,
122 East 42nd Street,
New York, NY 10017,
USA.
(free)

When loading, alternate direction for three or more bikes. Seat on one cross-bar, handlebars on the other. Careful of brake and shift cables. Lash down with toe straps or elastic luggage straps at contact points, and especially the handlebars, since these hold the bike upright. Guying, i.e. running, straps from the side of the car to high points on the bike (as with a sailing mast), is a *good idea*.

Mixing up a tour with public transport, or even just complementing a trip with a bicycle, is a great way to travel. You have the benefits of mobility and covering a lot of ground, but at the same time a bike lets you examine interesting areas in detail. Preparation of your bike for travel depends on the kind of carrier you will use.

Airlines: These handle bikes well and some provide special bike boxes. Remove the rear derailleur (pp 302–11) if you have one, and loosen stem (pp 211–12) and twist handlebars parallel with front wheel. They may ask you to remove or reverse the pedals (p 247). I myself would protect the frame and chainwheel with a broken-up cardboard box. Deflate tyres to half pressure. Airlines sometimes let bikes on free, and sometimes charge.

Railways: Really perfect for speeding you on to a particular area, or for skipping over uninteresting sections on a long tour. Load the bike into the luggage van yourself, and use elastic straps to hold it firm. The charge for the bicycle is half the adult fare. There is no good explanation for this. Continental rates are *much* cheaper. British Rail tells me that the justification for the high charges is to cover special handling and accommodation. No British Rail employee has ever had to (or will) handle my bikes. And there has always been literally vanloads of room in baggage/mail vans. I hope that you will join me in urging British Rail to carry bicycles free of charge and to provide overnight locking facilities at stations. The bicycle stimulates economic benefits to the community which far outweigh any profit accrued to British Rail by their inhibiting fares. See also the last Chapter for a fuller discussion of this issue.

A special note: do not ever ship a bicycle by itself by British Rail unless it is insured against any possible disaster. I had a bike shipped to me which was mangled into a worthless pile of junk – frame, forks, and even the cranksets bent beyond repair – and did not get a penny of compensation. Insure – and be prepared for the worst.

The Continent

Cycle touring is a particularly satisfying way of travelling around the Continent, allowing you to explore and savour to a degree not otherwise possible. People are exceptionally friendly and helpful to cyclists. You really 'get into' the country. And for uninteresting or arduous sections of the journey, you simply take a train, boat, or plane.

There is no end of information available. An excellent book is *Bicycle Touring in Europe* by Karen and Gary Hawkins (Pantheon Books, 201 East 50th Street, New York, NY, USA, $2·95), which, while written for Americanos, has much useful information on technique and places to go, including nine complete, mapped tours. There are cycling clubs, associations, federations, and organizations to which you can write for information. Those marked * are specifically concerned with touring; others sometimes operate touring services, and will usually assist with information:

Albania
   Federata Sportive Shgiptare-Bruga, Abdi Toptani, 3, Tirana.

Austria
   Osterreichische Radsport Kommission, Prinz Eugenstrasse 12, Vienna IV.
   *Osterreichischer Automobil, Motorrad und Touring Club, Schubertring 3, Vienna I.

Belgium
   *Touring Club Royal de Belgique, Rue de la Loi 44, Brussels.
   *Royale Ligue Vélocipédique Belge, 49 Avenue du Globe, 1190 Brussels.
   Ligue Vélocipédique Belge, 8 Place des Martyrs, Brussels.

Bulgaria
   Fédération Bulgare de Cyclisme, Boulevard Tolbouk hine 18, Sofia.
   *Automobil and Touring Club, Rue Sv Sofia 6, Sofia.

Czechoslovakia
   *Ustredni Automotoklub, CSSR, Opletalova 29, Prague 1.
   Ceskoslovenska Sekce Cyklistiky, Na Porici 12, Prague 1.

Denmark
   Danmarks Cykle Union, Gronneraenge 21, 2920 Charlottenlund, Copenhagen.
   Danmarks Professionelt Cykle Forbund, Grambyvei 56, 2610 Rodovre.
   *Dansk Cyklist Forbund, Avedøre Tvaervej 15, 2650 Hvidovre.

East Germany
  Deutscher Radsport Verband, Kochhannstrasse 1, 1034 Berlin.

Finland
  Suomen Pyorailyliitto, Yrjonkato 21b, Helsinki.
  *Suomi Touring Club, Unioninkatu 45H, Helsinki 17.

France
  *Touring Club de France (TCF), 65 Avenue de la Grande-Armée,
  Paris 16.
  *Fédération Française de Cyclotourisme (FFCT), 66 Rue René
  Boulanger, Paris 10.

Germany
  *Allgemeiner Deutscher Automobil-Club (ADAC), Königinstrasse
  9–11a, Munich 22.

Greece
  *Automobil et Touring Club de Grèce, 6 rue Amerikis, Athens.
  Hellenic Amateur Athletic Association, 4 rue Kapsali, Athens.

Hungary
  Magyar Kerekparos Szoveteg Millenaris Sporttelep, Szabo
  Jozsef u3, Budapest XIV.

Iceland
  *Felag Islenzkra Bifreidaegenda (FIB), Eiriksgata 5, Reykjavik.

Irish Republic
  Irish Cycling Federation, 72 Prospect Avenue, Glasnevin, Dublin 9.

Italy
  Federazione Ciclistica Italiana, Palazzo delle Federazione Viale
  Tiziano 70, Rome.
  *Touring Club Italiano (TCI), Corso Italia 10, Milan.

Japan
  Japanese Cycling Federation, Kishi Memorial Hall, 25 Kannami-
  Cho-Shipuyaku, Tokyo.

Luxembourg
  Fédération du Sport Cycliste Luxembourgeois, Case Postale 145,
  Luxembourg City.

Netherlands

*Koninklijke Nederlandse Toeristenbond (ANWB), Wasse-
naarseweg 220, The Hague.
Koninklijke Nederlandse Wielren Unie, 15 Nieuwe Uitleg, The
Hague.
*Stichting Fiets, Europaplein 2, Amsterdam.
*Netherlands Cycletouring Union (NRTU), Ambachtsherenlaan
487, Zoetermeer, Alphen-a-d-Rijn.

New Zealand

New Zealand Amateur Cycling Association, CPO Box 30459,
Lower Hutt.

Northern Ireland

Northern Ireland Cycling Federation, S. Martin, 13 Premier Drive,
Belfast 15.

Norway

Norges Cykleforbund, Youngstorget, 1 Oslo.
*Norges Automobil-Forbund (NAF), Bertrand Narvesens Vei 2,
Etterstad, Oslo 6.

Philippines

Philippine Cycling Association, Rizal Memorial Track-Football
Stadium, Dakota Street, Manila.

Poland

Polska Zwiazek Kolarska, 1 Plac Xelaznej Bramy, Warsaw.
*Polskie Towarzystwo Turystyczno-Krajoznawcze (PTTK),
Senatorska II, Warsaw 40.

Portugal

Federacao Portuguesa de Ciclismo, Rua Barros Queiroz 29–1,
Lisbon.
*Automovel Club de Portugal (ACP), Rua Rosa Araujo 24 & 26,
Lisbon.

Romania

Federatia Romina de Ciclismo, Vasile Conta, Bucharest 16.
*Association des Automobilistes (AAR), Stradan Beloianis 27,
Bucharest 1.

Russia

Fédération Cycliste USSR, Skatertnyi Pereoulok 4, Moscow 69.

Spain
  Federaciòn Española de Ciclismo, Alfonso XII 36, 1st Dacha,
  Madrid 14.
*Real Automobil Club de España (RACE), General Sanjurjo 10,
  Madrid 3.

Sweden
  Svenska Cykelforbundet, Stora Nygatan 41–43, Stockholm C.
*Svenska Turistföreningen (STF), Stureplan 2, Stockholm 7.

Switzerland (German-speaking Cantons)
  Schweiz Radfahrer-u-Motofahrer-Bund, Schaffhauserstrasse 272,
  Zurich 57.
                    (French-speaking Cantons)
  Union Cycliste Suisse, 4 rue du Vieux-College, 1211 Geneva 3.
*Touring Club Suisse (TCS), rue Pierre-Fatio 9, Geneva.

Turkey
*Turkiye Turing ve Otomobil Kurumu, Sisli Meydani 364,
  Istanbul.

West Germany
  Bund Deutscher Radfahrer, Westanlage 56,BP 263, Giessen-Lahn
  (Hessen).

Yugoslavia
  Fédération Yougoslave de Cyclisme, Hilendarska 6, Belgrade.
*Auto-Moto Savez Jugoslavije, Ruzveltova 18, Belgrade.

Many national tourist offices have developed information especially for the cyclist, with pre-planned tours, information on
roads, places to rent bicycles, cycling areas, and other relevant data.

The best source of information is the Cyclists' Touring Club,
whose membership benefits are chronicled on pp 110–14. They have
information sheets, pre-planned tours, maps, and insurance and
travel services which make them unbeatable value for the tourist.
They also conduct tours. So do the Youth Hostel Associations
(pp 114–15), and membership includes a number of useful guides
and handbooks. The British Cycling Federation (p 114) does not
conduct tours, but does offer insurance services and some 50-odd
pre-planned tours. The

  International Bicycle Touring Society,
  846 Prospect Street,
  La Jolla, California 92037, USA.

also runs tours in Europe. These tend to be at an easy pace, with a following 'sag wagon' car for carrying all but members' personal clothing, and accommodation in inexpensive hotels and meals in restaurants. Higher in cost than hostelling of course, but pre-selection of hotels keeps expenses moderate.

And then there are always the traditional aids to travel – the Michelin Guides and various sight-seeing tomes. One of the nicest things about cycle touring is that you are not obliged to make a plan and stick to a schedule. Even in crowded holiday areas you should not have much difficulty in finding accommodation if you just veer off the beaten track – which a bike makes easy.

Africa

Bicycles are a common form of transport in Africa, and their machines are of course extremely stout and sturdy, as often there is simply no road at all. But this depends on where you are. Off-hand I would say that the prospects for an interesting tour are good. In Morocco, for example, the roads are quite negotiable and there are not many cars – but when one comes you are expected to give way and move off the road if necessary. Parts are a problem, and in many areas so is theft, so that often you will of necessity be married to your bike. On the other hand a lot depends on your attitude and how you get on with people. As a cycle tourist you will be an object of intense curiosity and interest and I suspect that you might have a uniquely excellent time. In any case, few enough people have done it so there is little annotated information. If you go, it will be as a pioneer. The Cyclists' Touring Club has correspondents in Africa, and if you are seriously interested you might try corresponding with Walter Stolle, c/o POB 728, Lagos, Nigeria, who in 1973 chalked up 23,700 miles cycling through Chad, Ruanda, Bahrain, Saudi Arabia, and Uganda, to name just a few of the many countries he saw.

Asia

An epic list of cycling conditions in Asia is to be found in *Sting in the Tail*, Peter Duker's account of his around the world ride (Pelham Books, 52 Bedford Square, London WC1; £2·60). Duker battled sandstorms and government officials, crashed, ran endless gauntlets of rock-throwing men and boys, was clouted viciously by three men who tore limbs off a tree and attacked him, and in general had a Hard Time. By his own account Duker seems a unique enough individual so that his experience is not necessarily the norm, but it would be foolish not to anticipate some difficulties. Both the Cyclists' Touring Club and the Youth Hostels have information on Asia.

Australia

Duker's ride covers this area, and you should be able to get information from

Amateur Cyclists' Association of Australia,
W. S. Young,
34 Wardell Road,
Earlswood,
Sydney, New South Wales.

Australian Cycling Council,
153 The Ringway,
Cronulla, 2230,
Sydney, New South Wales.

as well as the Cyclists' Touring Club and the Youth Hostels.

United States

Bicycle touring is a fine way to see the United States. Unless you are extraordinarily perverse you will not find ghetto areas such as New York's Lower East Side or Harlem attractive, and so do not need to worry overmuch about personal safety. Most of your riding will probably be in the countryside where you are relatively safe. But be warned: the level of violence in many urban areas is considerably greater – shockingly so – than most people from civilized countries are prepared for. Americans no longer say in parting, 'Have a nice day', but 'Have a safe day'.

Another problem is that American drivers have not fully caught on to the bicycle boom. The idea that motor vehicles take precedence over any other road-users is much more prevalent than in Britain, and the problem of motorists not really noticing or thinking about cyclists is much worse. Most American cars are large, softly sprung, and do not handle well. Roads are wider and straighter. Accordingly, American drivers have not developed the same level of skill and expertise as their British counterparts, who have to cope with narrow, twisting roads. In terms of road safety cycling in America is, overall, more dangerous than here.

These nasty things said, I am sure that if you go touring the

States, you will have an excellent time. Although it is more dangerous than Great Britain, it is not so unsafe as to be inadvisable. And
Americans are warm, open, friendly people.

Bicycle Camping and Touring (Tobey Publishing Company, Box
428 New Canaan, Conn 06480, USA; $3.00) has a lot of inform-
ation on techniques and equipment. *The North American Bicycle
Atlas* (American Youth Hostels, 20 West 17th Street, New York,
NY 10011, USA; $2.25) gives detailed, mapped tours throughout
the country.

Once again the bicycling organizations are especially useful.
Tours are run by

American Youth Hostels,
20 West 17th Street,
New York, NY 10011.

whose hostels are sometimes spartan but always serviceable, with
fees up to $2.00, and the

International Bicycle Touring Society,
846 Prospect Street,
La Jolla, California.

which is an easy-going outfit for adults only. Tours are volunteer-
organized and fairly luxurious. A trailer follows each tour and
carries baggage and repair parts. Overnight stays at inns and motels
at about $5 to $10.

Information about routes can be got from the:

League of American Wheelmen,
5118 Foster Avenue,
Chicago, Illinois 60630.

whose nation-wide members will give you information about local
conditions to aid in planning a tour. The

Bicycle Institute of America,
122 East 42nd Street,
New York, NY 10017.

is a trade organization which gives out a lot of free information on
all aspects of cycling. If you send

Clifford L. Franz,
36 Grand Boulevard,
San Mateo, California 94401.

your favourite local tour, mapped, and tell him where you want to go, he will provide you with recommended mapped routes together with information on campgrounds and/or motels and an assortment of checklists.

Of petrol station maps I have found Esso's to be the most detailed, but even these do not meet the needs of the cyclist. The best source is the US Geological Service, who publish contour maps for each state. If you know the exact area you'll be in, they also have local maps down to 1:24,000, a scale which shows walls, footpaths, tiny streams, etc. These are too detailed for any but the most local use, but are extremely interesting. Many map stores carry the USGS maps, or you can order them direct (for local maps ask first for free state index map):

East of the Mississippi,
US Geologic Survey,
Washington District Section,
1200 South Eads Street,
Arlington, Virginia 22202.

West of the Mississippi,
US Geologic Survey,
District Section,
Federal Center,
Denver, Colorado 80225.

If you plan a tour which includes travel by rail, be chary of baggage handlers. The make-work contingent has rigged it so that a baggage handler must load the bike aboard the train – badly. Stories of bikes mangled into oblivion by these clods are legion. Insist on personally supervising loading or don't travel by rail at all. Hang the bike from the ceiling or side of the luggage van if possible, and in any case see that it is lashed down securely and that no heavy objects can fall on it.

Take your own bike over with you. British bikes are expensive in America. Japanese bikes in America are good value, but frames tend to be less flexible. And incidentally, if you buy a bike here and remove it from the country within three months you get a refund on purchase tax. Between the price difference and the tax refund, if you sell your bike in the States at the finish of your tour you should at least break even. But a more important reason for taking your own bike is that it allows you to sort it out before going, and not waste vacation time hanging about a bike shop making adjustments and screwing on bits and pieces.

You may wish to purchase Stateside regardless, or need repairs.

Bicycle shops now litter the landscape but, just in case, here are a few of the better known:

Lifecycle,
1005 Massachusetts Avenue,
Cambridge, Mass 02139.

Wheel Goods,
2737 Hennepin Avenue,
Minneapolis, Minnesota, 55408,
Catalogue $2.

Big Wheel Ltd,
Dept K,
310 Holly Street,
Denver, Colorado 80220,
Catalogue $2.

Pleasant Valley Shop,
PO Box 293,
Livingston, New Jersey 07039.

Turin Bicycle Co-op,
2112 North Clark Street,
Chicago, Illinois 60614.

Thomas Avenia,
131 East 119th Street,
New York, NY 10035.

Thomas Avenia,
10205 Rio Hondo Parkway,
El Monte, California.

Cyclo-Pedia,
311 N Mitchell,
Cadillac, Michigan, 49601,
Catalogue $1.

Stuyvesant Distributors,
10 East 13th Street,
New York, NY 10003,
Catalogue $.75.

Cupertino Bike Shop,
10080 Randy Lane,
Cupertino, California 95014.

Hans Ohrt Lightweight Bikes,
9544 Santa Monica Boulevard,
Beverly Hills, California 90210.

Velo-Sport Cyclery,
1650 Grove Street,
Berkeley, California.

John's Custom Bike Center,
741 East Dixie Drive,
West Carrolton, Ohio.

Bikecology,
3006 Wilshire Boulevard,
Santa Monica, California.

Twenty per cent of the bicycles in use in the United States are stolen every year, so you must have a lock, and a serious one. The latest, best, and lightest that I know about is the Citadel, manufactured by Bike Security Systems, 177 Tosca Drive, Stroughton, Mass 02072, USA, and available in the UK by post from F. W. Evans Ltd, 44–46 Kennington Road, London SE1 for £14·50 post included.

The Citadel costs about $25·00, which is cheap. Case-hardened chain and a meaningful padlock will run $30·00–$40·00 and are not as good. A truly marvellous convulsion of heavy steel bar which fully encloses the padlock called the Kryptonite had its day, but thieves can now defeat it with ease. Other than keeping one hand firmly on the bike at all times, the Citadel (available also from Lifecycle, address above) is the answer.

There is some first-rate cycle-touring and camping equipment available in the States. Panniers, saddlebags, and the like are available from

Cannondale Corporation,
35 Pulaski Street,
Stamford, Connecticut 06902.

I especially like Cannondale's line, but also excellent are:

Gerry,
5450 North Valley Highway,
Denver, Colorado 80216.

Bellweather,
1161 Mission Street,
San Francisco, California 94103.

Touring Cyclist Shop,
Box 378,
Boulder, Colorado 80302.

Bikecology,
3006 Wilshire Boulevard,
Santa Monica, California.

Camping equipment can be had by mail from:

L. L. Bean,
Freeport, Maine 04032.
(catalogue free).

Herter's,
Route 1,
Waseca, Minnesota 56093.
(catalogue $1·00).

Sierra Designs,
4th and Addison Streets,
Berkeley, California 94710.

Recreational Co-op,
1525 11th Street,
Seattle, Washington 98122.

Gerry,
5450 North Valley Highway,
Denver, Colorado 80216.

Colorado Outdoor Sports,
PO Box 5544,
Denver, Colorado 80217.

Canada

The Canadian Bicycle Book (D. C. Heath Ltd, Toronto; $3·95) is mostly an introduction to cycling but has some touring information. Organizations are:

Canadian Cycling Association,
3737 rue Monselet,
Montreal Nord, PQ.
also at
333 River Road,
Vanier, Ontario.

Canadian Youth Hostels Association,
268 First Avenue,
Ottawa, Ontario.

Mexico

Federacion Mexicana de Ciclismo,
Confederation Sportive Mexicaine,
Avenue Juarez Num 64-311,
Mexico City 1.

The Cyclists' Touring Club has correspondents in Mexico.

South America

Organizations are:

Federacion Ciclista Argentina,
Ave Pte Figueroa,
Alcoeta 4600,
Buenos Aires, Argentina.

Brazilian Confederation of Sports,
Rue da Quitanda 3,
2nd Andar,
Case Postale 1078,
Rio de Janeiro, Brazil.

The Cyclists' Touring Club and Youth Hostels may have information. I'm headed that way myself with a boat and bicycles and will be happy to let you know how it goes, but this won't be for a while yet.

8. Racing

For me cycling as a sport is personal, a way of being with myself, and while an interest in going fast has necessarily involved me with competition machinery, the only race I have ever seen was by accident, and I did not see the finish. Information here has been gleaned from books and talking to people. I suggest *Cycling*, edited by David Saunders (Wolfe Publications Ltd; 30p; available from Foyles, 119 Charing Cross Road, London WC2), *Cycle Racing* by Bowden and Mathews (Maurice Temple Smith Ltd, 42 Russell Square, London WC1), and *The Book of the Bicycle* by Roger St Pierre (Ward Lock Ltd, 116 Baker Street, London W1M 2BB; £1·50) for further information than you will read here. The flavour of the sport is contained in books such as *Continental Cycle Racing* by N. G. Henderson (history and results of major continental tours and one-day classics) and *Cycling Crazy* by Charles Messenger (a British team manager's reminiscences of three decades of racing), both published by Pelham Books, London at £1·75 each. The psyche of the racer and the all-out effort that attends serious competition is suggested in a novel, *The Yellow Jersey* by Ralph Hurne (Weidenfeld and Nicolson, London; £2·25). The periodicals *Cycling* (161-66 Fleet Street, London EC4 – weekly) and *International Cycle Sport* (Kennedy Brothers Publishing Ltd, St John Street, Silsden, near Keighley, Yorks – monthly) offer comprehensive coverage of the sport.

To race, you will have to belong to one or even two organizations, depending on the type of event(s) in which you compete. There are basically four types of events: time trial, road race, track, and cyclo-cross. Here are the addresses of the national organizations:

Maurice Cumberworth, General Secretary,
British Professional Cycle Racing Association,
Hebden Travel Lodge,
Mill Lane,
Hebden, Yorkshire.
Pro racing under BCF rules.

British Cycling Federation,
26 Park Crescent,
London, W1.
International, affiliated to Union Cycliste International.

R. J. Richards, General Secretary,
British Cyclo Cross Association,
5 Copstone Drive,
Dorridge, Solihull,
Warwickshire.

E. G. Kings, Secretary,
Road Time Trials Association,
210 Devonshire Hill Lane,
London N17 7NR.

Irish Cycling Federation,
155 Shanliss Road,
Shantry,
Dublin 9, Eire.
Also known as the CRE, supervises organized cycle racing in
Irish Republic. Many races are held under the National Cycling
Association, which is not internationally recognized.

J. E. Fletcher, Secretary,
Northern Ireland Cycling Federation,
144 Princes Way,
Portadown,
County Armagh,
Northern Ireland.
Ulster sport, but the NCA operates here also.

The appropriate national organization above will supply you
with the name and address of a local club for you to join. Time-
trialists need only be a member of a club affiliated to the Road Time
Trials Council, but competitors in other events must also take out
membership with the British Cycling Federation.

Time-trials

This is the premier type of event in Britain, in which each rider is
timed separately over 10, 25, 30, 50 and 100 mile courses, or rides

The 'xtraordinary bicycle

as far as possible in 12 or 24 hours. Riders are dispatched at regular intervals and must ride alone. The season is February to October, with a predominance of 10 and 25 mile events to start, then the 50 and 100 mile and 12 and 24 hour events at the height of summer, and ending with hill climbs. An advantage is that anybody can participate, racing themselves against a record. British courses are easier than those on the Continent.

Road Racing

Everybody starts together, first human over the finish line wins. Most single-day events are between 50 and 100 miles for amateurs, and 80 to 180 for professionals. Stage races are run over a number of days and can be as large as 2,600 miles (Tour de France). In road racing riders are pitted against each other, and the resulting shenannigans are sometimes incredible. Teams work together to launch a strong teammate ahead of the pack to victory and simultaneously block opposition riders. In big races like the Tour de France bicycles collide and pedals jam into spokes.

Cyclo-cross

Cross-country races from point to point or around a course, from 1 to 16 miles in length, run either as a time trial or with a massed start. These are typically through steep climbs and descents, mud, thick woods, streams, and hurdles. Some sections have to be negotiated on foot. It is a rough sport, with plenty of spills.

Track

The machine common to a wide variety of track events is the greyhound of bikes: an ultra-light frame with a short wheelbase; a fierce position with the saddle high and handlebars low; a single wheel fixed gear, with no brakes; and tyres bonded to the rims with shellac, to withstand the stresses of violent track manoeuvres. There are no quick-release hubs, gears, pumps, cables, etc, making these among the most lovely and functional of bikes.

There are many kinds of track events. Here are a few:

Sprint – Usually a 1,000 metre course with only the last 200 metres timed. Involves all kinds of tricky tactics and scheming. There are times when racers hold their bikes stock still while jockeying for position. Behind the leader and in his slipstream until the final dash is the favoured winning position.

Pursuit – Two riders or teams start on opposite sides of the track and try to catch each other. Usually 4,000 to 5,000 metres or for ten minutes.

Handicap Races – Riders are given a start over the scratchman in accordance with previously demonstrated abilities. Varying distances.

Scratch Races – Massed start races commonly over 3, 5, and 10 miles and 20 kilometres.

Devil-take-the-hindmost – Last man over the line every two or three laps is out.

Paced Racing – Motorcycles are used as pace-setters for the riders, who stay as close as possible to the pacer's rear wheel so as to minimize wind resistance. Speeds up to 60 mph.

Madison – Two-man teams run in relays. Events run from 50 kilometres or one hour to six-day races. Each team member runs one or two laps and then hands over to a teammate, literally throwing him in by the seat of his pants or by a hand-sling. A very spectacular form of racing.

Speedway – Run on dirt track ovals with stripped-down bikes using low gearing and studded track tyres, this is a grass roots sport as yet unrecognized by any 'official' organization. Fast action, with lots of broadside skids and spills. About 100 clubs in Great Britain under

Cycle Speedway Council,
W. F. Gill, Secretary,
67 St Francis Way,
Chadwell St Mary,
Grays, Essex RM16 4RB.

Conditioning

The demands of racing are rigorous, and it is rated by many as the most arduous sport. Most racers are not interested in touring because it is not hard enough exercise. Any serious racer has to keep fit with a year-round physical conditioning programme which is best worked out individually. A great deal of information on training, as well as all aspects of technique and equipment, are contained in the encyclopedic *Cycling* published by the CONI Central Sports School of Rome (available from Condor, 90 Gray's Inn Road, London WC1; £2·75).

THE FINISH

Most accessories are unnecessary. Whenever possible try to peel weight off your bike. Streamers, doodads, and various decorative garb are out, unless they are of such incredibly redeeming character as to make them worth carrying at any cost. I had a Bombay Taxi Driver's Horn like that once, a great gleaming diesel-like trumpet, but it went with the Golden Flash.

Pump – A necessity for tubular tyres, an excellent idea for wire-ons. Pumps left on a locked bike tend to be pinched. A pocket size pump will do for an emergency.

Toe Clips – These nearly double pedalling efficiency and with smooth-soled shoes the feet can be slipped out easily in an emergency. See Riding, p 89, and Fitting, p 77.

Bicycle Shoes and Cleats – These are cut for ankling and have a steel shank for even foot pressure on the pedal. Cleats will give you tremendous get up and go and are a must for long tours and racing.

Lights – A peculiar problem. You must have them. They are even useful at times.

There are two kinds of lighting systems: battery and generator. Generator types take power off the wheel and this is precisely the problem. Plus they work only when you are under way, there is more hardware, wires, etc. Battery types all tend to be of the cheapest possible manufacture. There isn't one to recommend. Sorry, but you will have to fight into working condition whatever lights you acquire.

I prefer a portable battery light which slides on to a clip mounted on the handlebars or stem. This way there's no dead weight to lug around during the day, nothing for sticky fingers to dismember, and a free flashlight. But in weighing up pros and cons, it is your own needs and situation which are important. If cost is a consideration, dynamo lights are cheaper to run. If pilferage is a problem, then dynamo lights are better because they are securely bolted to the bike. You can do this of course with battery lights, but then you lose the advantage of portability. If it is dynamo lights for a bike that will be used mostly at night, then some preference goes for the dyno hub type as it has much less drag than the spring dynamo, which rides against the side of the tyre. Of course, for a bike that will be used mostly in the daytime, a spring dynamo offers the feature of no drag at all except when in use. There are also dynamo systems which provide light even when the bike stops. In the country, trying to go fast enough with a dynamo unit on a bumpy path or lane so that you can see where you are going can sometimes be unnerving and even dangerous. In towns there is generally enough light at intersections and the like so that having the lights go out when you stop is not a serious handicap. But technically, it should affect how you ride. For a right-hand turn on a bike where lights extinguish when the machine is stationary, the Highway Code says you must stop by the left kerb, and pull away when other traffic clears. I've never seen this happen. See also Touring, p 125 for additional discussion.

Bikes that will get rough use in the woods are better off with battery lights carried only when necessary. This way there are no wires to snag and fewer things to get jounced off. A useful accessory no matter which system you use is a French flashlight, Matex, with a white front and red back that straps to the arm or leg. It weighs only five ounces and the resulting show is pretty good. Available from:

Ron Kitching,
Cycling Centre,
Hookstone Park,
Harrogate, Yorkshire.

Often it will appear pointless to have lights. Most times you can see better without them. Lights are not so much that you see, as that you are seen. A moonlit road in the middle of nowhere is a perfect place for a *car* to run without lights. As I found out. Have some kind of a light. Use it.

Carrier – The best sort of carrier depends on your needs. A cloth rucksack can go with you on and off the bike and is handy while shopping. For around town use and carrying the odd parcel or briefcase the light aluminium Swiss jobs fitting over the rear wheel and clamping on to the back seat stays are excellent (bike shops). For lots of shopping get a quick-release hold-all (ditto). For heavy-going, a steel rack designed for use with panniers is probably best (ditto again). See pp 125–26 for additional information.

Nail-pullers – Half-ounce gizmos that ride along above the tyre and brush off shards of broken glass, pebbles, etc. For tubulars only.

Baby-seats – The only kind worth considering put the child behind the rider and have full leg shields to prevent toes from bloodying spokes. The greatest protection is afforded by adapting a baby's fibreglass-shell safety seat sold for use in cars.

Mudguards – A requirement for tourists and people living in rain forests. If you want to go like the clappers and don't mind getting dirty once in a while, leave them off. Plastic mudguards are light and easy to get on and off (weekend racers, note), but eventually warp and fail. Stainless steel and aluminium are more durable, and offer a mounting point for lights and other gear, but are slightly heavier and make a noise. This last can be cured with a coat of undersealing paint (motor accessory shops).

Locks – See Keeping your Bike, pp 70–71, and pp 141–42.

Horns – Yelling is the quickest, most reliable, and colourful. Little bells and squeeze horns are forever failing or being vandalized. Freon horns are wonderfully loud – excessively so.

Helmet – In most fatal bicycle accidents the injury is to the head. Even a drop of two feet on to a hard surface is enough to fracture the skull. Racing, training, or just riding to work, a helmet is a good idea. It's inconvenient. So is not being able to think or talk because your head has been pounded into jelly.

Feeder Bottle – If you're worried about a drink . . .

Kickstands, odometers, speedometers, chain guards – no.

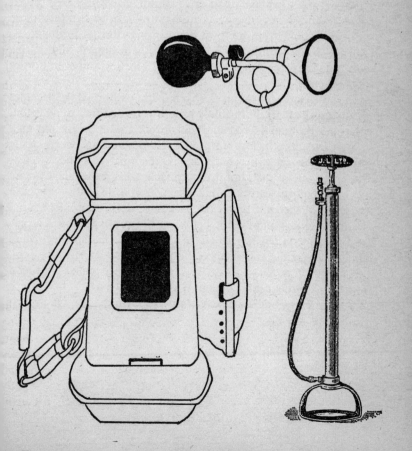

If you have a little spare space, antique cycles are a dandy item to collect and restore. Early models were largely a blacksmith's creation, and bringing them 'up to snuff' is well within the capacity of a competent handyman. The last part of the nineteenth century was the heyday of innovation and experimentation in cycles, and many wacky and wonderful machines were produced. Some are illustrated in this book. Because they are unique they can command high prices, and even a plain ordinary (penny-farthing) in good nick can fetch £300 to £400. By about 1910 cycle designs had fairly well settled down, and machines from this date onwards can be had for a more reasonable sum. From my own point of view this is fortunate, as I collect (when I can) on the basis of aesthetic appeal, and on this count find the machines of the Twenties, Thirties, and even Forties very attractive.

The best source for old bikes is Grandfather's attic. Most machines already on the market are wildly expensive. The thing to do is find some old wreck mouldering in a field or root around in the old junk shed of friendly Uncle Fred the bicycle-dealer who unexpectedly kicked the bucket two decades ago. Often what you find is a disheartening pile of rust, but it is surprising what some elbow grease and rust remover can do. And, listen, if you do know of such a wreck or old shed and aren't interested . . . drop me a line, hm?

There are any number of books on old cycles, and a nice inexpensive one is *Discovering Old Bicycles* by T. E. Crowley (Shire Publications, Ltd, 12B Temple Square, Aylesbury, Bucks; 35p). A real winner is *King of the Road* by Andrew Ritchie (Wildwood House, 1 Wardour St London W1V 3HE; £2·95). There are a number of clubs but some have restricted membership. One which does not is:

Southern Veteran Cycle Club,
Iain Cowan,
Woodbine Cottage,
8 Shrubbery Road,
Gravesend, Kent.

Others are

National Association of Veteran Cycle Clubs,
Ray Heeley,
124 Southfields Avenue,
Stanground, Peterborough.

Benson Veteran Cycle Club,
C. N. Passey,
61 The Bungalow,
Brook Street,
Benson, Oxfordshire.

Boston Veteran Cycle Club,
P. Bates,
15 Rosebery Avenue,
Boston, Lincolnshire.

Bygone Bikes Yorkshire Club,
J. W. Auty,
85 Priory Road,
Featherstone,
Pontefract, Yorkshire.

Long Sutton and District Veteran Cycle Club,
P. Shirtcliffe,
Hillcrest,
Crowhall,
Denver,
Downham Market, Norfolk.

Peterborough Vintage Cycle Club,
Ms Young,
48 Newark Avenue,
Peterborough.

Roadfarers Veteran Cycle Club,
A. C. Mundy,
22 High Street,
Caister, Peterborough.

Enthusiasts headed for the United States
may want to get in touch with:

Antique Bicycle Club of America,
Roland C. Geist,
260 West 260th Street,
New York, NY.

Veteran Wheelmen's Association,
Franklin Institute,
Philadelphia, Pennsylvania.

The Wheelmen,
Robert McNair,
32 Dartmouth Circle,
Swarthmore, Pennsylvania 19801.

The Wheelmen Antique Bicycle Club,
214 Maywinn Road,
Defiance, Ohio.

The Wheelmen Newsletter, (has ads)
Keith Larzelere,
PO Box 38,
Petersburg, Michigan 49270.

ELLIOTT QUADRICYCLE.

Contents

Maintenance Programme

The subject of maintenance and repair of bicycles is usually clouded with negative feelings. It is regarded as something in the 'must be done' category and approached as a chore. Bicycle repair books are fond of saying that any cretin can understand how to fix his machine, or that the book itself has the answer to any problem that might conceivably come up. Both approaches underestimate the reader's intelligence and compartmentalize maintenance and repair, keeping it separate from 'riding'. This is a basic mistake. The extent to which you get involved in working on your bike should be a direct function of how you ride. One follows the other like night and day. The awareness that riding a bike precipitates usually includes an awareness and interest in the bike itself. How the bike responds is very much a function of maintenance. Ideally, you are going to work on your own bike because you want a to-gether, tight machine under you, i.e., you will do it because *you want to*.

As with all things, you get back in proportion to what you put in. It is essentially a question of fineness. It is the nature of bikes that they are at their best when well-lubricated and carefully adjusted. A sensitivity to this sort of refinement does not happen the instant you mount a bike. Give it time. As you ride you will become increasingly aware of your bike's mechanical characteristics. A well set-up bike fits you like a suit of clothes, and you will soon develop an 'ear' for the sound of bearings and a 'feel' for other parts, such as the brakes. The development of this sensitivity – the result of personal and direct participation – is part of the reason for owning a bike in the first place. Eventually, you will find that increased riding pleasure is not just a reward for doing your own maintenance, the mechanical sensitivity itself becomes part of the riding pleasure.

As I say, this is all something that you should grow into. The idea of having a bike is to have fun. A fair amount of latitude is possible in servicing bikes and you have hopefully chosen a machine suited to your level of interest. So you can minimize or maximize maintenance as per your own inclinations. But bear in mind that most machines, and certainly bicycles, need a certain amount of lubrication and adjustment if they are to function at all. Without it, they rust away, and because the parts are unlubricated and out of kilter, they slowly chew themselves to bits when ridden. I have seen 'old dependables' that have been left out in the rain for years and have never seen an oil can or a mechanic. They make it for years – and then snap a chain in the middle of a tour or a brake cable at the start of a long hill. Or eventually the rust destroys them. There is on need for this. A properly maintained bike will easily last a lifetime and more. For reasons of simple economy and safety, if you can't be bothered to do routine maintenance then take your machine to a bike shop for servicing at least twice a year.

An excellent reason for doing your own work is that you are apt to do a better and quicker job than the shop. No matter if the shop is good or bad, you can't expect the mechanic to have as much interest in getting things just right as you do. Once you learn the drill you will almost always do a better job. Also, it is time-consuming to leave your bike at the shop for three days for work that takes ten minutes to do.

Another important reason for doing your own work is that it makes preventive maintenance almost automatic. Preventive maintenance is replacing parts before they wear out and break, usually at an inopportune time and miles from any bike shop. If you are paying attention to the various parts of your bike and keeping it in tune, this is pretty much going to happen as a matter of course. In turn, breakdowns and repairs will also be fairly well obviated.

I think this approach is the easiest and the most efficient. I have studied every repair manual I could find. Most stress fixing something *after* it has broken. Even though I know how to fix bicycles, most of them lose me right away. Either they are filled with long passages of incomprehensible jargon, or they have computer-programming style directions ('If A, go to page 28 C; if not A, go to B, page 34, then to page 28 D.') designed to reduce you to a mindless automaton.

Here is my approach: each major component system of the bicycle such as brakes, wheels, gears, etc, is broken down into four areas –

How it Works
Routine Adjustments
Replacing Parts
Trouble-shooting

The idea is to give you a basic understanding of what is happening – and make you a mechanic! How it Works for each section is required reading. It does no good for you to diddle with this or adjust that if you have no idea of how it works. And if something is broken, it is impossible for you to fix unless you know how it works in the first place.

It will help a lot if as you read, you look at and feel the corresponding parts on your bike.

I don't cover everything. One wheel is pretty much the same as another. I have tried to include representative types of equipment currently in use but there are bound to be exceptions. If this happens to you, try to find the item in this book which most closely resembles the part you are servicing or fixing. Pay particular attention to *function* and then analyse your own part the same way. This should get you through most anything.

There are also some tasks which are just not worth doing. Delving into the innards of a coaster brake multi-speed hub is one of these. It takes a long, long time and isn't fun at all. Some people may resent these omissions. They want to do everything for themselves. Well, the point of diminishing returns is reached with attempts to service the coaster brake 3-speed hubs. Even most bike shops refuse to overhaul these units and simply replace them – it's actually cheaper this way. If you insist on doing this sort of work, detailed instructions are available from the bicycle manufacturer or from the hub manufacturer.

Tools

You can get by with amazingly little in the way of tools. However, for some kinds of work there are a few you will just have to get. Also, what you need depends on what kind of bike you have.

Before going into particulars a word on tool quality: do yourself a favour and buy good ones. Cheap shops, supermarkets, and even hardware stores carry cheap bargains like 10p screwdrivers and 40p wrenches. These are a false economy, for they are made of inferior metals that will break or bend under stress, or they are made badly enough so that they don't even work. You do not need many tools, and the total investment should be between £5 and £10. In the long run it is worth it. I have had the same 8-in adjustable end wrench for 26 years.

For both 3- and 10-speed bikes:
Hardware shop
8-in or 6-in adjustable end wrench.
Pliers.
Hammer.
$\frac{1}{4}$-in tip, 4–5 in shank screwdriver.
$\frac{1}{8}$-in tip, 2–3 in shank screwdriver.
Wire clippers.
6-in file, mill bastard.
Bike shop
Mafac tool kit – contains tyre irons, wrenches, other gear, including tyre patching kit.
All-purpose tool like Raleigh give-away.
Thin hub wrenches, 13 × 14 and 15 × 16.
Spoke wrench.
Pedal wingnut wrench (for pedals with outside dustcap only).
Tyre gauge: for Schrader valve if you have clip-on tyres.
for Presta valve if you have tubulars.
Tyre patch kit for your tyres.

10-speed bikes:
Bike shop
Chain rivet remover.
Freewheel remover.
There are two kinds:

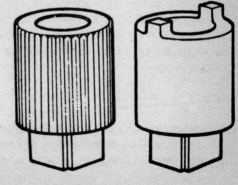

Look at your freewheel and see if it is splined or not on the interior to see what kind you need.

Set metric allen wrenches.

If you have a Campagnolo derailleur, a special Campagnolo combination allen and socket wrench.

If you have cotterless cranks you will need a special crank-removing tool as per your brand of crank.

Other useful tools:
Set of wrenches.
Vice-grip pliers.
Channel lock pliers.
Small portable vice.

As you can see from studying the list, many of the tools are for specialized jobs so you do not have to acquire them all at once. Absolutely essential, and especially for trips, is the Mafac toolkit, a screwdriver, and an all-purpose combination tool like the Raleigh give-away.

You will need some means of holding the bike upright with one wheel off the ground. A nail driven into the doorjamb with a rope to hang the bike by will do. So will more elaborate arrangements of supporting arms and clamps. Your situation will be the main determinant here – garage, basement, flat, or whatever – but you will want something.

Lubrication

This is a general discussion of lubrication. For details look under the system in question, e.g., brakes, gears, wheels, etc.

There are three basic types of lubricants:

1. Aerosol can sprays such as WD-40 or LPS. These can be used as a substitute for oil, are easy to apply, and most importantly, are clean.

2. Oil. Use only a good grade, non-gumming, such as Sturmey-Archer, or gun oil. Do not use household oils.

3. Bearing grease. Lubriplate and Gold Medal are good brands. Or save money and buy it in a motor accessory shop.

Your bicycle has upwards of 200 ball bearings held in place by cups and cones:

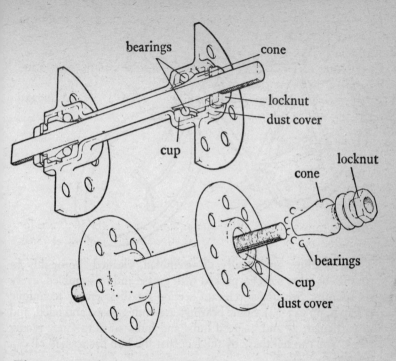

bearings

cone

locknut

dust cover

cup

locknut

cone

bearings

cup

dust cover

The cone remains stationary while the cup, and whatever part is attached to it – in this example it would be a wheel – rides on the ball bearings and spins around. The distance between the cone and the cup is adjustable and must not be too tight or too loose. Sometimes the ball bearings are held in a clip called a *race*:

Typically, this is positioned so that the open side through which the balls stick is against the cup. You will find bearings at the headset, bottom bracket, wheels, and pedals:

These bearings are usually disassembled, cleaned thoroughly in paraffin or other solvent, packed with grease and reassembled, every six months. See under relevant section for disassembly technique (Chap 2, pp 243–44). Some bearings are both greased and oiled, and in particular, 2- and 3-speed hubs and hubs on ultra-fancy racing bikes. You can tell these by the fact that the hub has a small oil cap or clip:

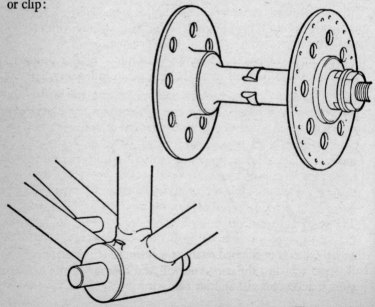

These need oil once a month: multi-speed internal gear hubs a table-spoonful, regular hubs about half a teaspoonful, and coaster brake hubs two tablespoonfuls. Some bottom brackets are set up to use oil. A teaspoonful once a month. Use oil wherever you find oil caps or clips. Do not use spray on these parts as it dissolves the grease.

I greatly prefer the use of an aerosol can spray like WD-40 or LPS-3 for the chain, freewheel, derailleur, brake pivots, cables, and any other parts which do not use grease:

The spray is easy to apply with pin-point accuracy, displaces water, and dries clean. This last is really important. The trouble with oil is that it attracts dirt which then mixes with the oil to form a gooey abrasive mixture. In the case of the chain, for example, this means that once a month you have to remove it, soak it in paraffin or other solvent, and then oil and install. It's time-consuming and messy. If you use spray, you need do this job only once every two or three months or even longer if you do not use your bike much. Since the spray goes on in seconds, you can lubricate the chain every two weeks. The same rationale applies for the freewheel and derailleur. The spray is particularly useful for the brake pivots and all cables. Oil has a tendency to leak out on to the brake levers and handlebars, and brake shoes. Once a month is sufficient.

If you are doing this on the cheap, paraffin wax makes a good sub-stitute, and you can buy it at hardware shops. Clean your chain in the conventional manner with paraffin or other solvent. Melt the wax in a coffee can over the stove. Dump the chain in and then hang to dry so that drippings fall back into can. Use oil or spray for the brake pivot points, freewheel and derailleur. The wax will not work well on these parts because it cools and hardens too quickly on contact with the metal to penetrate effectively. It is excellent for brake cables, however. Just run the cable through a block of wax a few times until it is well impregnated. Save and re-use the old wax. Wax, like spray, does not attract dirt.

Note : New bikes fresh from the dealer and bikes that have been standing around for a long time may be dry as a bone. *Oil Evaporates!* Be sure to lubricate such machines before using.

General Words

There are a number of things to keep in mind when servicing bikes:

1. Do not use a great deal of force when assembling or disassembling parts. Bicycle components are frequently made of alloys for light weight. These are not as strong as steel and it is not hard to strip threads or otherwise damage parts. Always be sure that things fit. Be careful and delicate. Snug down bolts, nuts, and screws firmly, not with all your might.

2. Most parts tighten *clockwise* and come apart turning *counter-clockwise*. This is called a right-hand thread. A left-hand thread tightens *counter-clockwise*, and loosens *clockwise*. Left-hand threads are not used often.

3. When fitting together threaded parts, hold them as perfectly aligned as you can, and turn one backwards (loosen) until you hear and feel a slight click. Then reverse and tighten. If this is new to you, practise on a nut and bolt until you have the feel of it perfectly.

4. If you get stuck with a rust-frozen bolt or nut, soak it in penetrating oil, give it a few light taps to help the oil work in, and then try to undo it again with a tool that fits exactly. If this fails, try a cold chisel and hammer:

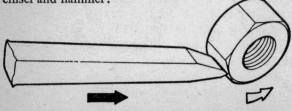

Go at this carefully since if you slip you may gouge a chunk out of your bicycle. If this fails, hacksaw or file the nut or bolt off. How did it get this rusty in the first place?

5. When assembling or disassembling try to be neat and organized. Lay parts out in the order which they came apart or go together. Put tiny parts in boxes or jars.

6. There are a number of little nuts and bolts on your bike for cable clamps, racks, brake lever mounts, gear shift lever mounts, and the like. These tend to get loose and need tightening about once a month.

7. The left side of the bike is as if you and the bike both point forward.

8. Solvents: paraffin and paint thinner are good. Petrol is very dangerous.

9. Finish: a good-quality auto paste wax will preserve your paint job and make it easier to keep clean. Wipe the bike down once a week and after major journeys. Do not wax wheel rims where brake shoes contact.

Contents

General

Bicycle brakes come in three basic types: coaster, or pedal–operated,
and roller lever and calliper, both hand-operated. The coaster brake
is inferior, because under conditions requiring a quick stop it tends
to lock the rear wheel, causing the bike to skid rather than slow
down.* It is also extremely difficult to service, and is for the rear
wheel only, cutting braking efficiency below 50 per cent, since it is a

* A screeching tyre-smoking stop is not the quickest. When the wheel is
locked, the rubber literally melts into the road, providing a *liquid* point of
contact between the tyre and road surface, and greatly increasing stopping
distance. The quickest stops are done by slowing the wheel to the point just
before locking. Skidding also means a loss of directional control and often
results in a fall.

the front wheel that the greatest braking power can be attained. In fact, on dry roads it is difficult to lock up a front wheel. This is because braking throws the weight forward, increasing traction. If you have a bike which has only a coaster brake at least equip it with a calliper brake for the front wheel. Only children without the necessary strength to operate calliper brakes should have a coaster brake, and they should not ride in any situation requiring quick stops or sustained braking. Lots of the small-wheel hi-riser handle-bar banana-seat chopper jobs feature coaster brakes. Kids are fond of diving these bikes into a tight corner, jamming on the brake, and pivoting on the front wheel to come around in a tight, flashy skid. Each to his own, but the same effect can be achieved with a well-adjusted centre-pull calliper brake.

If something goes wrong with your coaster brake, simply remove the entire rear wheel (p 224) and take it to a bicycle shop for over-haul or replacement. It is much too complicated to attempt to fix it yourself and infinitely more trouble than it is worth.

How Brakes Work

Calliper brake systems all work on the same basic principle. There is a hollow, flexible tube called a cable housing between the brake lever mount and the cable hanger:

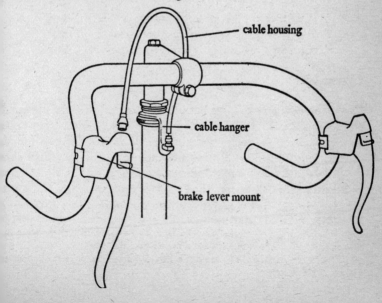

The cable housing is flexible so that the handlebars can turn back and forth. Through the cable housing passes a cable which is attached to the brake lever at one end:

And to the brake mechanism at the other. This is in turn attached to the bicycle frame and functions like a pair of complicated ice tongs with double pivot joints. When the brake lever is operated, it pulls the cable through the cable housing and pinches together the arms (called *yokes*) of the brake mechanism, causing the two rubber brake shoes attached to the yokes to press against the wheel rim and stop the wheel:

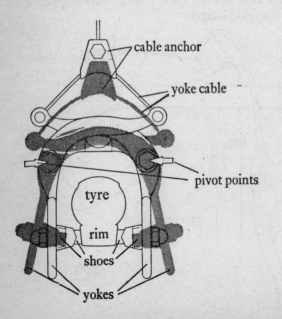

When the lever is released, a spring forces the yoke arms away from the wheel rim:

This in turn returns the brake lever to an off position, and keeps continuous tension on the entire brake assembly. This is the basic centre-pull mechanism.

A variation is the cantilever brake:

B

in which the brake yokes are bolted directly onto the fork or seat stays.

The side-pull brake uses only one pivot point, with the cable housing attached directly to one yoke, and the cable to the other. The effect is the same:

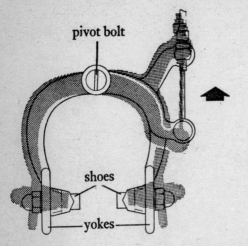

pivot bolt

shoes

yokes

All calliper brake systems have an adjusting screw (called a *barrel adjustor*) for changing the relationship of the cable housing length to the length of the brake cable. On the side-pull brake this is almost always found on the yoke to which the cable housing is attached (A), while on the centre-pull brake it is usually at the brake lever (B) or the cable hanger (C):

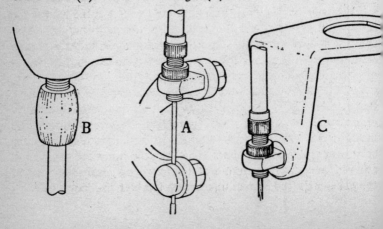

Properly adjusted brake shoes are so close to the wheel rim that the tyre will not slide between them when removing the wheel. Accordingly, better-grade brake systems have a means for creating a little extra slack in the brake cable. This is usually a small button which allows the brake lever to open more:

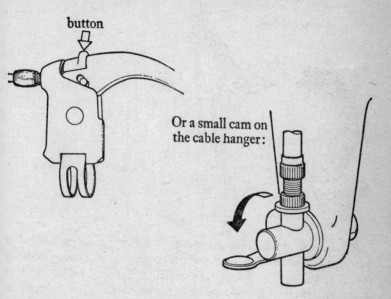

button

Or a small cam on the cable hanger:

These are the basics of any calliper brake system: a brake lever, a brake cable and housing with adjustor barrel, a cable hanger for centre-pull systems, and the brake mechanism, including yokes, springs, and brake shoes. Better systems include either a button or cam to provide extra slack in the cable when removing the wheel or servicing the brakes (see next two pages).

Roller lever brakes are found on older bikes and on utility bikes. Brake levers on the handlebars transmit motion through a series of steel rods, and brake shoes are pulled up directly against the inside of the rim. As with the calliper brake system, there are springs to pull the brake shoes away from the rim when the lever is released, and these are found at the handlebar, and sometimes at the joint in the rod system underneath the bottom bracket axle.

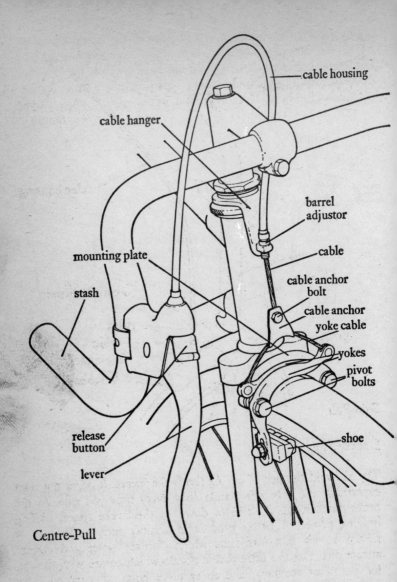

cable housing

cable hanger

barrel adjustor

cable

cable anchor bolt

cable anchor

yoke cable

mounting plate

stash

yokes

pivot bolts

release button

shoe

lever

Centre-Pull

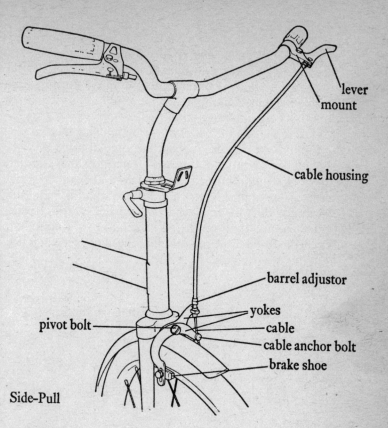

lever
mount

cable housing

barrel adjustor

yokes

cable

pivot bolt

cable anchor bolt

brake shoe

Side-Pull

Lubrication

Try to avoid the use of oil. At the brake levers, it oozes out over everything and gets your hands dirty every time you ride. At the brake mechanism, it dribbles down to the brake shoes, cutting braking power. A better product is a spray such as WD-40 or LPSW-1, dry film lubricants which displace water and do not attract dirt. Use the little plastic nozzle which comes with the can for pin-point accuracy, and spray pivot bolts, all exposed cable (use a piece of paper or cardboard as a backstop to prevent the spray from going all over the bike), yoke cable anchor points, brake lever pivots, and inside the cable housings. Machines used once or twice a week need lubrication every two months, those in daily use, monthly. More often on tours.

Routine Adjustments

Whatever kind of calliper brake system you have, there are two basic kinds of adjustments: (1) seeing that the brake shoe hits the wheel rim properly, and (2) keeping slack out of the cable between the brake lever and mechanism, so that the lever travels the shortest possible distance when putting on the brakes.

First check to see that the wheel is true by spinning it and seeing that the rim, not the tyre, stays about the same distance from the brake shoe all the way around. If play is greater than approximately $\frac{1}{8}$ in the wheel should be trued (see pp 238–39) before any brake adjustments are attempted. Check also that the wheel is reasonably centred between the fork arms, and that the rim is free of major dents and abrasions. If off-centre, take the bike to a shop to have the forks checked, and if the rim is badly banged up, get a new one.

Calliper Brakes
Brake Shoes

These need to be aligned so that the shoe hits the rim squarely:

Wrong   Wrong   Right

Brake shoes are held on either by a conventional bolt:

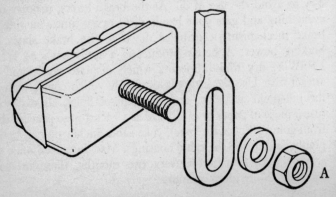

A

or an eyebolt:

In either case, loosen nut A, adjust brake shoe to meet rim, and tighten. One method is to loosen nut A just a little bit and gently tap the shoe into the proper position with the wrench handle. With conventional bolts you'll find that the brake shoe twists to the right when you tighten the nut back down. A good trick is to set it slightly counter-clockwise so that the final tightening brings it perfectly into position. Do not use too much force. Brake bolt screws strip easily.

Eyebolt-type shoes are easy to adjust so that the face of the shoe is flush with the rim. Achieving this effect with a conventional-bolt brake shoe sometimes requires bending the yoke. Remove the brake shoe altogether and fit an adjustable end wrench snugly over the end of the yoke:

If the yoke needs to be bent outward, simply pull on the handle of the wrench. *Go Slow* – if you break or mangle the yoke you will probably have to get a whole new (expensive) brake mechanism. If the yoke needs to be bent inward, provide a pivot point by wedging another wrench, screwdriver handle, or other object between the yoke and tyre, and push on the wrench handle:

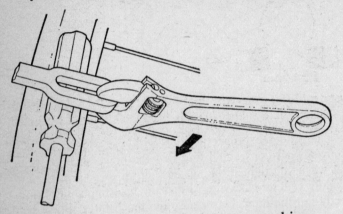

If you don't have a suitable wrench, use a screwdriver:

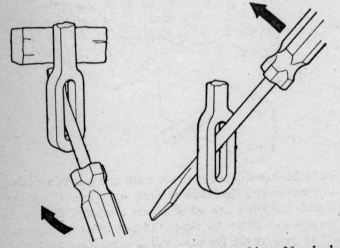

Do not be especially keen to start bending things. New brake shoes, for example, will frequently wear into correct alignment with a few days' use:

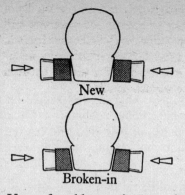

New

Broken-in

Use soft rubber racing-type brake shoes (usually coloured red) rather than the hard rubber (usually black) kind typically supplied with side-pull brakes. The soft shoes wear out faster but work a lot better and cost only a few pence each. You can buy the shoes separately from the metal holder and bolt. The holder is open at one end. Slide the old shoe out and the new one in:

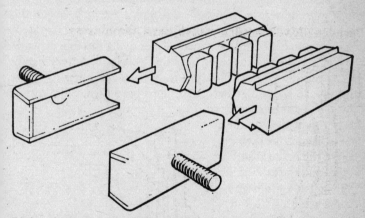

If the old brake shoe will not come out easily and you do not have access to a vice to grip the holder securely while you tap out the shoe, forget it and buy a new set of holders and shoes. Be sure to install the new units so that the closed end faces forward (the direction the bike goes), or else the shoes will slide out when the brakes are applied.

Some people consider it good practice to toe-in the fronts of the brake shoes. This is done by twisting the yoke with a wrench or screwdriver so that the front of the shoe hits the rim $\frac{1}{32}$ in before the back. Under hard braking, however, the whole shoe is flush to the rim. If you have squealing brakes this may cure the problem.

Cables

Once the brake shoes have been properly aligned, they should be placed as close to the rim as possible without rubbing when the wheel is spun, $\frac{1}{8}$ in or less. This is done, for both side- and centre-pull brakes, with the barrel adjustor and locknut, and the cable anchor nut and bolt:

Barrel adjustor

Cable Anchor Bolt

The idea is to screw in the barrel adjustor, take up as much slack as possible at the anchor nut, and then use the barrel adjustor to take up slack every few days. The cable is always stretching. When the barrel adjustor reaches the limit of its travel, the process is repeated. There are a number of different methods for doing this job, depending on the number and type of tools that you have. A very handy gadget is called a 'third hand' and is a spring-like affair for compressing brake shoes together. Bike shops have them. The reason for this tool, or substitute, is that if you just loosen the anchor cable nut the spring tension of the brake yoke arms will pull the cable through and you will have a hard time getting it back in. With or without a third hand, undo locknut and screw adjustor barrel all the way in:

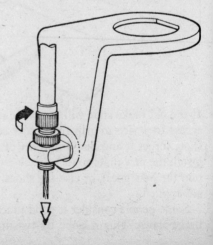

Check and see that the brake release button or cam is set for normal operation (not on all bikes). If you have a third hand, mount it. Or use a C-clamp. Or even string. If you have none of these things, squeeze the brake yoke arms together with your hand. With the other hand, pull the cable at the brake mechanism out so the brake lever is fully home, as it would be if the brakes were not on. Make sure the cable housing has not caught on the outside lip of the barrel adjustor. Now look at the amount of slack in the cable. For centre-pull brakes this is the distance between the yoke cable and the cable anchor A:

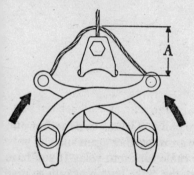

And for side-pull systems, it is the amount of new cable protruding beneath the yoke A:

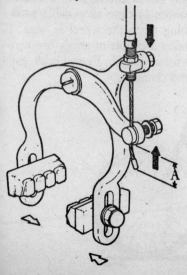

Estimate the amount of slack to be taken up with a ruler, tool handle, or finger. Disengage the yoke cable from the cable anchor (centre-pulls) or the cable end from the yoke (side-pulls). Eliminate this step if you have a third hand or similar device. Use two wrenches to slacken the cable anchor nut. Avoid twisting the cable. Pass the cable the required distance through the hole in the cable anchor bolt:

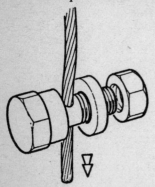

If it is sticky, use a pair of pliers to pull it. Tighten cable anchor nut. If no third hand, hold brake yoke arms together again and slip yoke cable back over cable anchor, or cable back into yoke. If you have the feature, now is the time to use the brake button or cam to give you that little bit of extra slack you need. Release the second or third hand, as the case may be. Only one or two turns of the barrel adjustor should bring the brake shoes as close as possible to the wheel rim without actually touching when the wheel is spun. If you have got it right (it usually takes a couple of tries), use wire-cutters to snip off the excess cable for a neat job. Frayed cable ends have a habit of snagging fingers and clothing.

SANGER RACER.   AAP

Side-pull brakes:

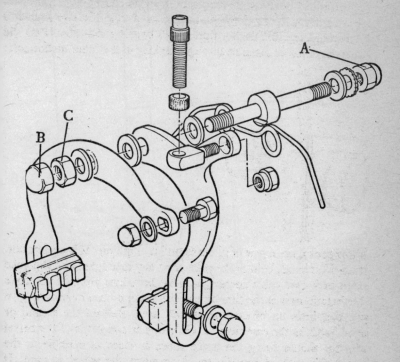

Make sure nut A is tight. Turn in locknut C one half-turn while holding acorn adjusting nut B still with another wrench. Turn both B and C in flush against brake yoke arm. Back B off one half-turn, hold in place, and lock locknut C against it.

Centre-pull brakes: see pp 199–201

Roller Lever Brakes

As with calliper brakes, roller lever brake shoes must be aligned to hit the inside of the rim squarely. This is done by means of a metal guide (A) clamped to the fork blade or chainstay (see over page).

Loosen the bolt B and move the guide as necessary so that when the brakes are applied, the shoes hit the inside of the rim.

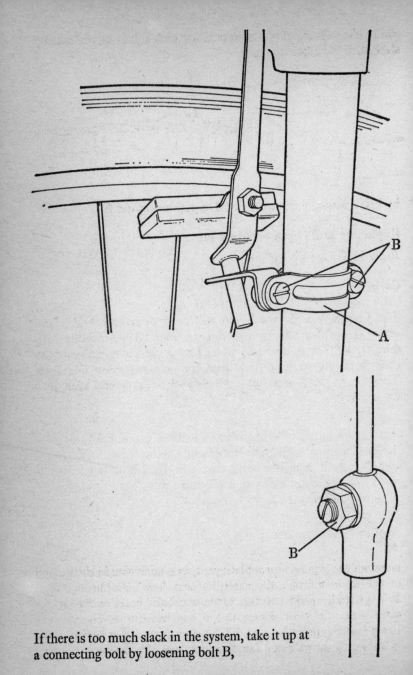

If there is too much slack in the system, take it up at
a connecting bolt by loosening bolt B,

sliding the rods together, and resecuring with bolt B, and/or take up slack with the adjusting bolt:

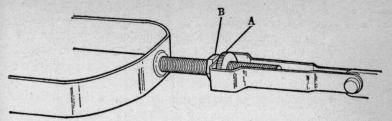

by first undoing locknut B, and then tightening nut A.

Replacing and Disassembling Parts

Brake shoes: see pp 178–82

Cables

The frequency with which you will need to replace brake (and other) cables depends on how you use your bike. Machines consistently left out in the rain, or used hard every day, are going to need them sooner than well-cared-for or average-use machines. There is no hard and fast rule. Any obvious defect, such as a frayed cable:

is immediate grounds for replacement, as is stickiness in the motion of the cable through the cable housing (see Trouble-shooting). It is generally good practice to replace both brake cables at the same time. They are cheap, and if one has run its course, it is likely that the other has too. The inconvenience of a broken cable is not worth the gain of a month's extra use. If you have purchased a used bike, I would replace cables all around unless you know they are relatively new and obviously in good condition. Good condition means they are clean, have no kinks or frayed spots, and pass easily through the cable housings.

Unless you can specify the brand and model of brake, take your bike or old cable to the shop. Cables come in different shapes, lengths, and thicknesses. It is very irritating to discover in the middle of things that you have the wrong part.

I recommend using the left hand brake lever for the rear brake. This follows standard practice, and since the rear brake is generally more favoured for routine braking, leaves the right hand free for cross-traffic signals.

For any calliper brake system, first screw home the barrel adjustor:

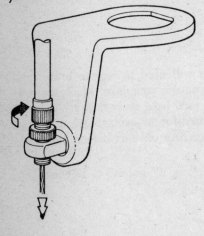

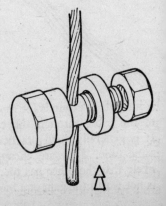

Centre-pulls : push together brake yoke arms (use third hand or similar device if available) and slip yoke cable off brake anchor. Undo cable anchor bolt and nut and slide same off cable:

Side-pulls: One kind of side-pull brake uses a cable anchor bolt and nut at the yoke. Slack it off and pull out the cable the same way as with a centre-pull. Another type of unit has a ball or nipple on the cable which slips into a slot on the brake yoke arm. You will have to replace both the cable and cable housing as a single unit. Compress brake yoke arms and release ball or nipple from yoke:

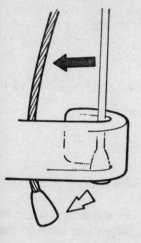

Centre-pulls and Side-pulls

Front brakes: Slide the cable housing off the cable. If yours has ferrules:

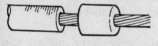

keep track of where they go.

Rear brakes: Leave the housing attached to the frame and pull the cable out of the housing. If you have a one-piece cable and housing (nipples on both ends of the cable), loosen the clamps on the frame and draw the unit through. Examine the cable housings to see if they need replacement. Are they kinked or broken?

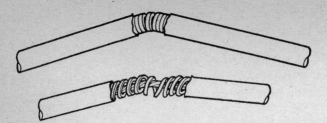

Are the ends free from burrs?

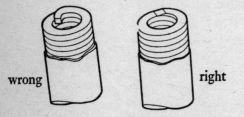

wrong   right

You can eliminate a burr by
    (1) Snipping off the cable housing end with a strong pair of wire cutters (pliers are not good enough);
    (2) clamping the cable housing end in a vice and filing it down; or
    (3) by using a tool called a taper ream, which you insert in the cable housing end and twist until the burr is gone.

When installing the new cable, save any cutting for last. Cutting invariably frays the cable end and makes it hard to slide through the housing and cable anchor bolt. Installation is the reverse of removal, and for clarification look at the illustrations for that section.

One-nipple cable: Slip cable through brake lever mount and attach to brake lever. Front brakes: including ferrules where used, slip housing on cable. Rear brakes: slide cable into housing. Twist the cable or housing as you do this to avoid catching the cable:

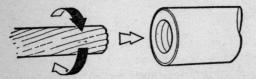

and be sure to do it in the right direction or the cable will unravel. Push free cable end through cable hanger (centre-pulls), or through barrel adjustor at yoke (side-pulls), and then through cable anchor bolt hole. To adjust see pp 182–84.

Two-nipple cable (one-piece housing and cable): Attach to brake lever. For rear brakes, slide housing through clamps on frame. Front and rear, pass cable end through barrel adjustor on brake yoke arm and fix to opposite brake yoke arm by slipping ball or nipple into slot. Take up slack with barrel adjustor. Rear brakes, tighten housing clamps on frame, and take care that they are set so clothing will not snag on the screws when riding.

Handles
Outside bolt type:

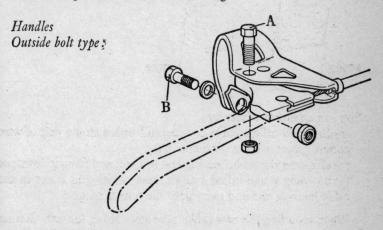

To adjust, slacken A and move. To remove, take off bolt B. May have to be slid back off handlebar in which case grip must be removed. If your brake lever mount has a slot in the bottom:

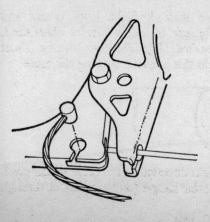

or if the cable ball or nipple will pass through the hole in the mount, then create enough slack by screwing home the barrel adjustor and clamping together the brake shoes, and disconnect the cable from the lever. If this is not possible, then disconnect the cable anchor bolt at the brake mechanism and take the cable out altogether.

Inside bolt type:

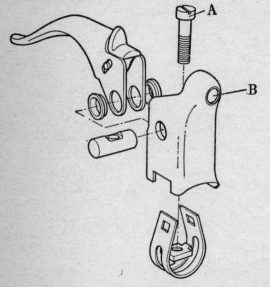

Disconnect yoke cable from cable anchor. Fully depress brake lever and use screwdriver or socket wrench on bolt A. If you are replacing the brake lever, you may need to take out the brake cable (see pp 188–89). On some systems such as Weinmann the cable end will pass directly through the hole B in the brake mount.

Brake Mechanism

First disconnect brake cable.

Side-pull systems:

To remove entire brake from bike, undo nut A. Disassembly: should be done only to replace a specific part if it won't work.

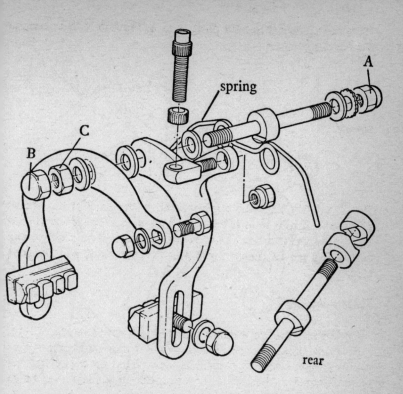

spring

A

C

B

rear

Start with brake mechanism on bike. Undo the brake spring by prising it off with a screwdriver. Careful of fingers. Separate nut B from nut C, and take them both off the pivot bolt. Then the rest of the stuff. Keep the parts lined up in the order in which you remove them. If you are replacing the pivot bolt, undo nut A and take off bolt. Reverse procedure for reassembly.

Centre-pull systems :

To remove unit from bike, undo nut A, remove washers and seating pads, and then brake mechanism (see overleaf). Disassembly: there's no good reason for this. Any badly busted-up parts needing replacement probably cannot be obtained, and you will need a new mechanism. You insist? See pp 199–201.

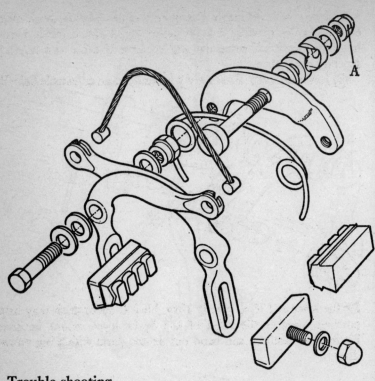

A

Trouble-shooting

Before using this section please read How it Works and Adjustments. You have to know how it works in the first place in order to figure out what's wrong. Brake problems come in three broad categories. In each category there are three possible areas in which the trouble may be: brake lever, cable or rods, or mechanism. The first thing is to find in which of these the problem originates, and this is done by isolating and actuating each unit separately.

Category 1 – No, or Very Weak Brakes.

◉ Is rim oily?
◉ Are shoes hitting rim?
◉ Will brake mechanism compress when you squeeze it with your hand? If no, go to Category 3, sticky brakes, below. If yes,
◉ Does lever move freely? Yes? Broken cable. Replace.

◉ Lever will not move. Disconnect cable at brake mechanism end. Will cable housing slide off cable? No? Cable is frozen inside housing. Get it off somehow and replace. If cable and housing separate easily then,

◉ Lever is frozen. First see if your unit has an adjustable bolt (B)

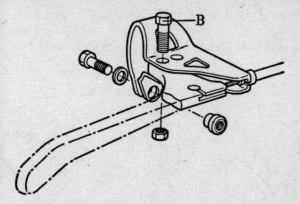

for the lever and if so give it a try. No? A major bash may have pinched together the sides of the brake lever mount housing. Examine it carefully and bend out dented parts with a big screwdriver:

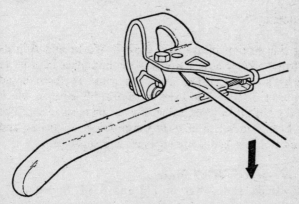

Or the lever itself may be bent. Bend it back. If the bend has been severe, replace the lever or unit. Metal which has been bent a lot may look perfectly OK but is fatigued and weak, and may well snap under the pressure of an emergency stop.

◉ Juddering. Can be caused by a loose brake mechanism, uneven rims, or sometimes by a very loose headset. To fix the brake mechanism:

Side-pulls. Make sure nut A is tight. Undo locknut C from acorn adjusting nut B and screw both in flush against brake yoke arm. Back off B one half turn and lock in place with locknut C (see opposite page).

Centre-pulls. Tighten up nut A on the mounting bolt.

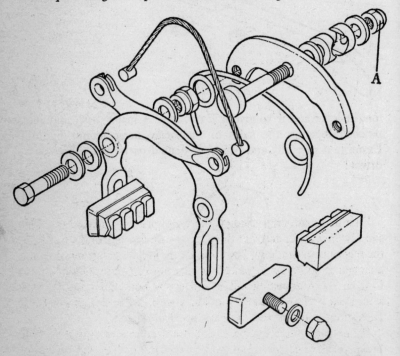

A

◉ Squealing. Brake shoes may be old and hard. Sometimes rubber from shoes has streaked rim. Clean with a strong solvent like benzene or cleaning fluid in a WELL VENTILATED AREA. Squealing brakes can sometimes be fixed by toeing in the brake shoes (see pp 181–82), and sometimes this problem just can't be eliminated.

Category 3 – Sticky or dragging brakes.

This is the most common problem. First determine if it is the lever, cable, or mechanism which is at fault.

- ◉ If it is the lever, see Frozen lever p 195.
- ◉ If it is the cable, replace it (pp 187–91).
- ◉ Brake mechanism.

Side-pulls :

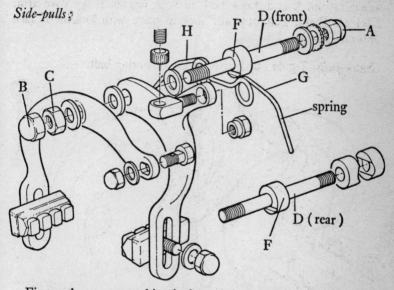

First make sure everything is there and properly hooked up. This sounds simple-minded, but there is a reason for each of the parts and the mechanism won't work without them. Is the spring complete and attached to both yoke arms? Make sure nut A is tight. Undo locknut C from acorn adjusting nut B and screw both flush against yoke arm. Back B off one half turn and lock with C. Check that pivot bolt D is straight and replace if necessary. Lubricate.

If one shoe drags against rim: loosen the mounting nut A, hold brake yokes in correct position, and re-tighten. No soap? Examine brake seating pad F. If it has a slot for the spring you will have to try bending the spring. There are two ways to do this. One is to prise the spring arm off the brake yoke which is dragging and bend it outward using pliers or similar tool. The second is to take a big screwdriver and poise the end against point G or H, whichever is *opposite* the dragging shoe, and give it a sharp bash with a hammer.

This second method is quicker, but of course a little riskier.

Still no soap? Check to see that the brake yokes are not rubbing against each other. If so, bend them apart with a screwdriver:

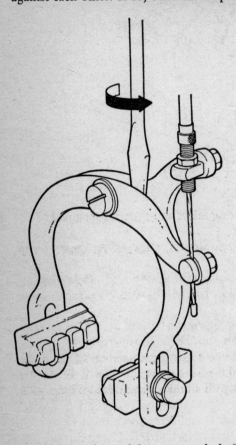

or slide in a piece of fine emery cloth (like sandpaper) and file it down.

If this is not the problem and you have tried everything else a complete disassembly (see pp 192–93) is necessary. Study each part to see if it obviously needs replacing (like a washer bent out of shape). It may be that the yokes cannot rotate on the pivot bolt. File down and polish the bolt, or enlarge the holes in the yokes (with a taper ream, or emery cloth wrapped around a nail). If none of these things work get a new brake mechanism.

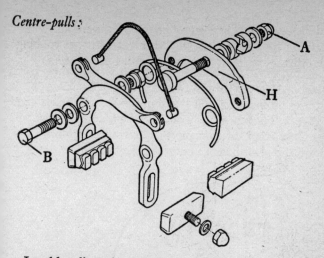

Is cable adjusted correctly?

Are all parts there? Is spring intact and properly mounted?

Is mounting nut A tight?

If one shoe is dragging against rim, slack off A, centre brake mechanism, and re-tighten A.

If both shoes stick try lubricating the pivot bolts B while wiggling the yokes back and forth. No? You will have to get into the pivot bolts.

First disconnect the spring. Study the bolts to see if they are type 1, where the pivot bolt screws into the brake arm bridge H; type 2, where the pivot bolt screws into a post which comes off the brake arm bridge and on which the yoke rotates; or type 3, where the pivot bolt simply goes through the brake arm bridge and the yoke rotates on a bushing.

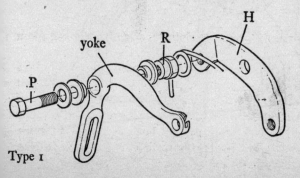

Type 1

Type 1 : First try slacking off the locknut R and undoing the pivot bolt P one quarter to one half turn. On some models the locknut R is on the other side of the brake arm bridge H. If yoke will now pivot, retighten locknut R. If not, remove pivot bolt P altogether. Keep track of all the washers. Is the pivot bolt P straight? Look for dirt or scarred surfaces on the pivot bolt P and inside the yoke. Clean and polish. If yoke will not turn freely on pivot bolt, enlarge yoke hole with a taper file or ream, drill, or emery cloth wrapped around a nail. Or sand down the pivot bolt. Lubricate and reassemble.

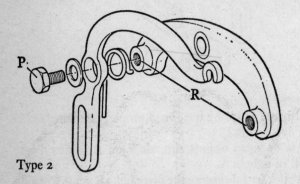

Type 2

Type 2 : Undo spring and remove pivot bolt P. Remove yoke and keep track of washers. Check for grit and clean. Is post R scarred? Polish with fine sandpaper or steel wool until yoke will rotate freely on it. Lubricate and reassemble.

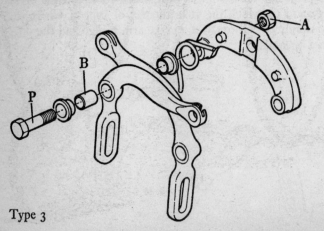

Type 3

Type 3 : Undo nut A and remove pivot bolt P. Keep track of bushings and washers. Is pivot bolt straight ? Is bushing B in good condition ? Check for grit and clean. If yoke still sticks, try polishing pivot bolt with steel wool. Lubricate and reassemble.

Contents

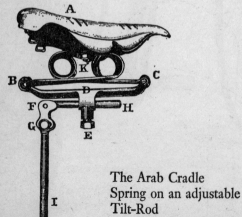

The Arab Cradle
Spring on an adjustable
Tilt-Rod

Saddle

There are two important factors in bicycle saddle design: supporting weight, and reducing friction between the legs. The mattress saddle used on bikes with level handlebars has to support all of the weight of the rider, and is therefore usually wide, and equipped with coil springs:

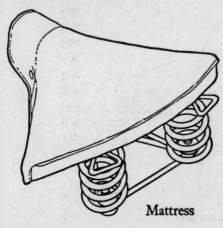

Mattress

Bikes with dropped handlebars support part of the rider's weight on the bars, and can use a long, narrow seat which minimizes friction between the legs:

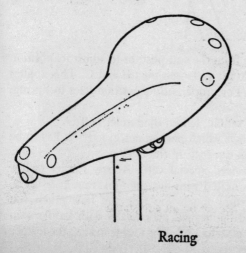

Racing

Springiness in the narrow racing saddle should be kept to a comfortable minimum as it adversely affects pedalling power. If yours is too tight or loose, adjust it by turning nut A:

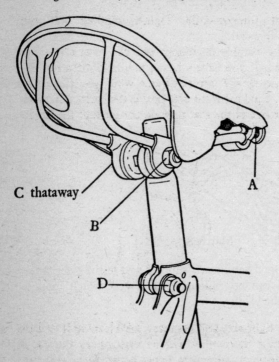

C thataway

B

A

D

To remove the saddle from the seat post, or to adjust its position backward, forward, or to tilt it, loosen nuts B and C. This applies also to mattress saddles. For proper saddle position refer to Fitting, PP 74–75.

To raise or lower the saddle, loosen the binder bolt D.

Be sure to use a wrench which fits the nut exactly. It has to be tight, and the wrong tool can tear up the nut.

Only leather saddles need special care. A new leather saddle should be thoroughly saturated with neatsfoot oil from *underneath*.

Then, depending on how much you ride and how much you sweat, the saddle should be cleaned periodically with saddle soap and lightly dressed with neatsfoot oil. The idea is to keep the leather clean, nourished, and comfortably pliable. Once a year should be enough. You can avoid this bother by using a plastic saddle, but in warm weather you will slide about in your own sweat.

Trouble-shooting

Seat tilts or swivels unnecessarily. Tighten binding bolt nuts B and C (see opposite page).

If the seat bottoms harshly on bumps and you have a mattress type saddle – too bad. If you have a racing saddle, tighten nut A.

The seat post sinks slowly into the frame while you ride. This can be a real stinker. First see if the seat post is the correct diameter by checking that the lips of the seat tube do not meet at the binder bolt:

right   wrong

If the post is the right size and is greasy, try cleaning it and the inside of the seat tube thoroughly. On no account try the use of shims or abrasive material like emery paper between the seat tube and the seat post. The chances are excellent that some of the material will fall down the seat tube and get into the bottom bracket, where it will make mincemeat of your crankset bearings (thought seats were simple, hah?). The only sure-fire solution is to install a thin bolt through the seat post and seat tube at point P:

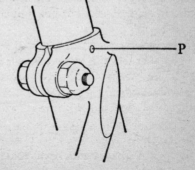

To do this you need a drill, hand or electric, a bolt, nut, and washer, and a drill bit. *Do all drilling with the bike upside down so that shavings do not fall down the seat tube into the bottom bracket.* If you are having a shop do the job make sure that they do this. Position seat at desired height. Make an initial dent with a centre punch or with a hammer and sharp nail at point P. Then put a couple of drops of oil on the end of the drill bit and drill through. Go slowly to avoid heat build-up. Use single-speed electric drills in short bursts. You will want more than one saddle-height position. To do this, loosen the binder bolt and rotate the seat post one-eighth of a turn at the same time that you raise or lower it a little bit. Now use the already existing holes in the seat tube as a guide for drilling a new set of holes in the seat post. Repeat 3 or 4 times. The idea is to be able to make fine adjustments in saddle height without weakening the seat post. At the finish, the job should look like this:

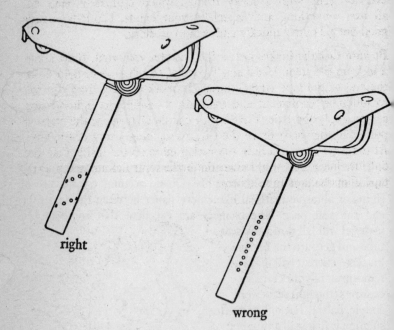

right

wrong

Be sure to clean up all shavings and filings so that they do not fall down into the bottom bracket.

Handlebars
Adjustments

To change
handlebar
position
loosen binder
bolt A on
stem and reset
bars:

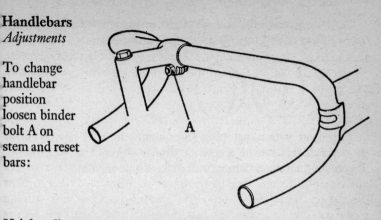

A

Height adjustments are made with the *stem* (pp 211–12).

Taping: I prefer non-adhesive plastic tape. Adhesive tapes gum everything up with a sticky residue which ultimately leaks out all over everything and especially your hands. Cloth tape feels good but gets dirty quickly and is hard to clean.

Be sure that the brakes are in the position you want. Start about 2 in from the stem. Use a small piece of scotch tape to hold down the end of the tape where you start. Work directly from the roll to minimize confusion, and maintain a continuous light tension as you apply the tape. First take a couple of turns at the starting point and then start down the bar, overlapping $\frac{1}{2}$ to $\frac{1}{3}$ of the tape. At the bends you will have to overlap more on the inside than the outside. For a neat job, loosen the brake lever mount (see p 171), tape underneath, and retighten:

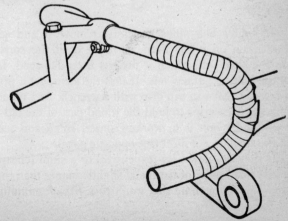

When you reach the end of the bar leave an extra 2–3 in of tape. Fold this over and push it inside the handlebar:

Finish off with a bar plug (bike shops) to hold tape securely. In a pinch this can be a cork or similar object. Use something – if you spill, an open bar end can make a hole in you.

Trouble-shooting

⊙ Bar spins around on stem: tighten binder bolt A:

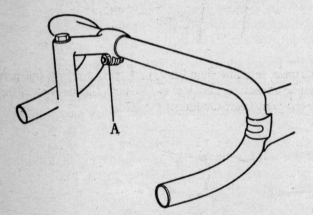

If binder bolt spins uselessly, remove it and see if the little protrusion on it has been worn off, or if the corresponding slot on the stem into which it fits has been damaged. If the problem is the bolt, get a new one. If it is the stem, get a proper bolt with a hex nut that you can grip with a wrench. At a pinch, you can use pliers or vice-grips to hold the round part of the old bolt.

If binder bolt is in working order, check and see that the lips of the stem do not meet (see opposite page).

If they do, new bars (expensive) or a shim (cheap). Shimming: find a small piece of flat metal slightly longer than the width of the stem lips. Something that won't rust, like aluminium, is preferable

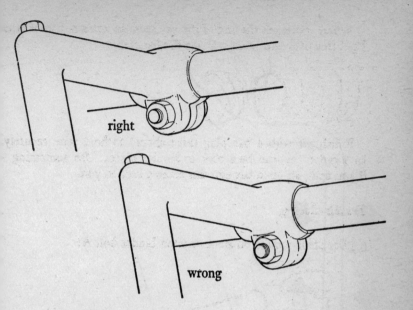

right

wrong

(hardware stores, machine shop litter, junk lying around), but part
of a tin can or a finishing nail will do. Remove binder bolt. Using
a screwdriver, prise apart the lips of the stem:

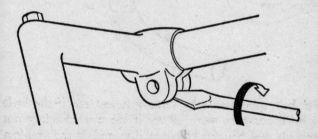

Slip the shim into the gap between the handlebar and the stem,
and reinstall binder bolt.

◉ Bent bars: steel ones are hard to bend, alloy a lot easier. Lay
the bike on its side. If the ends of the handlebars have been bent in,
place your foot on the end resting on the ground (watch out for
the brake lever) and pull up on the other end. If the ends have
been bent out, lean your weight on the upright bar:

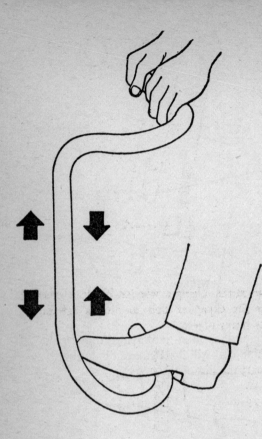

Stem
How It Works

The stem is a tube which holds the handlebar in position, and fits down inside the headset. The tube is split at the end, and down its length runs a bolt, called an expander bolt, which is attached to a wedge nut (A, see opposite page).

When the expander bolt is tightened, it draws the wedge nut into the tube, and this in turn forces apart the split sides of the stem, pressing them against the sides of the headset and holding everything in place.

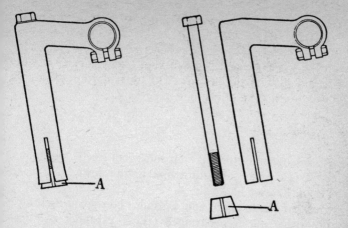

Adjust or Remove

Undo expander bolt two turns. Using a wooden block or piece of cardboard held against the expander bolt to protect the finish, tap it with a hammer or heavy object:

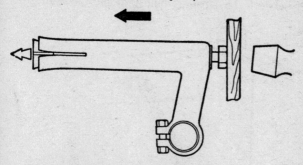

Repeat as necessary to get stem loose. Adjust height or remove. If you remove altogether and reassemble, take note: some wedge nuts have a dog guide which must fit into a corresponding slot on the stem:

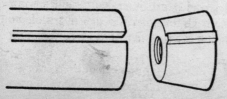

Keep at least $2\frac{1}{2}$ in of the stem tube in the headset.

Retighten expander bolt so that when you stand in front of the bike with the wheel clasped between your legs you can twist the handlebar and stem in the headset. This way, if you take a spill the bars will give instead of bending or breaking.

Trouble-shooting

◎ Stem is loose and expander bolt comes out freely: wedge nut has come off. Take out stem, turn bike upside down, and shake wedge nut out. Reassemble.

◎ Stem is frozen in place and expander bolt spins uselessly: threads on wedge nut have stripped (1), or expander bolt has snapped (2).

(1) Separate expander bolt from wedge nut by grasping it with pliers or vice-grips and maintaining a continuous upward pressure while twisting it. If it is obstinate, help it along by wedging a screwdriver between the expander bolt head and the stem:

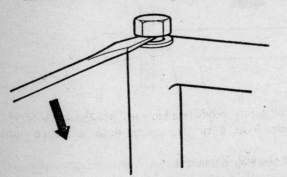

Once the expander bolt is free of wedge nut leave it inside the stem.

(2) Remove top-half of snapped expander bolt. Find a rod or bolt which will fit inside stem and touch wedge nut while still protruding an inch or two above the stem.

(1) and (2): Use a hammer to lightly tap the expander bolt or rod, working the end inside the stem around the edges of the wedge nut:

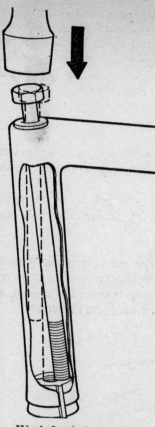

Work firmly but gently; too hard a blow will jam the whole thing. When stem comes loose, turn bike upside down and shake out wedge nut.

◎ Stem tube cracked. Replace it.

Headset
How It Works

The headset connects the front forks to the head tube of the bicycle frame and, through the stem, to the handlebars. The fork is held solidly to the bicycle but allowed to turn freely by using ball bearing sets at the top and bottom of the head tube. Starting at the bottom, the crown of the fork has a fork crown bearing race (A), then come the ball bearings (B),

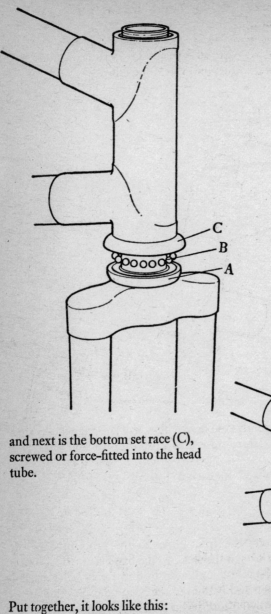

and next is the bottom set race (C), screwed or force-fitted into the head tube.

Put together, it looks like this:

To keep the forks inside the head tube and evenly positioned, a second set of races is used at the top of the head tube. There is a top set race, screwed or force-fitted into the head tube, more ball bearings, and what actually keeps the forks in position is the top race, which is threaded on to the fork tube:

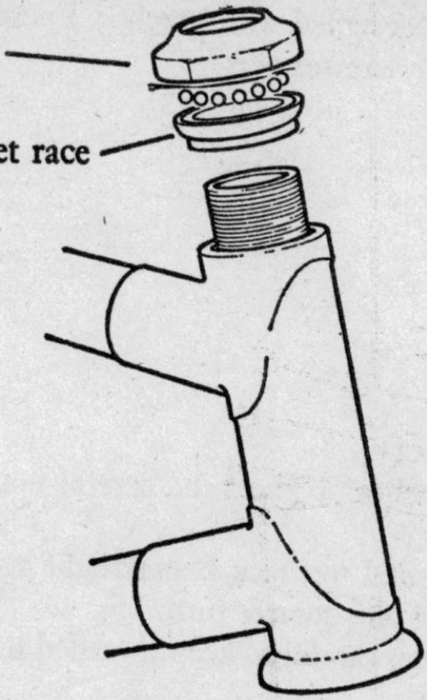

top race ————

top set race ————

A ————

B ————

This is capped by a washer, the cable hanger and/or other accessory mounts, if used, and a locknut to keep the top threaded race exactly in place:

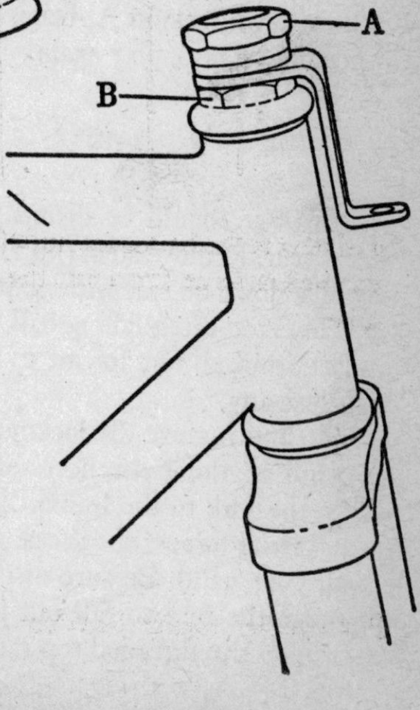

Forks should turn freely but without excessive up and down play. A simple test for looseness is to lock the front brake and rock the bike forward and backward. A clicking noise from the headset indicates loose bearings. To adjust, loosen locknut A (above).

Sometimes this locknut is designed with notches. Loosen with a hammer and centre punch or screwdriver:

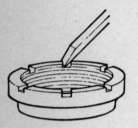

If you are using big wrenches or pliers, be careful not to bend nuts or races.

Now turn down the threaded top race B handtight against the bearings, and then back it off one quarter turn.

Snug down locknut A, being careful to keep threaded top race B in position. Check play again.

Lubrication and Disassembly

The headset should be dismantled, cleaned, and regreased about once a year. Remove stem (pp 211–12) and front wheel (pp 223–24). Lay bike down on side with newspaper or white rag under the headset. This is to catch falling ball bearings. There are many different headsets, and no way for me to tell you how many are in yours. So don't lose any.

Undo and remove the locknut, washer, cable clamp (if you have one), and anything else necessary to get to the threaded top race. Secure the fork to the frame. You can do this with rubber bands, elastic carrier straps, shoelaces, etc, but the simplest way is to hold it with your hand. Be sure to do something, or what you do next will cause the fork to fall out along with a rain of ball bearings. Next: undo the threaded top race A:

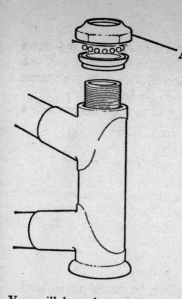

A

You will have loose ball bearings and are to follow instructions for (1), or bearings in a clip in which case follow (2).

(1) A few may stick to the threaded race, a few may fall on the newspaper, and most will probably stay in the top set race. Get them all together, count them, and put bearings and race into a box or jar. Next: make sure head tube is positioned over newspaper or rag. Slowly draw out fork tube. Ball bearings will fall out. Gather and count them, including any that are still stuck to the bottom set race, the fork tube, or whatever, and put them in a jar.

(2) Clipped bearings: Lucky you. Remove clip, noting carefully which side goes down against the top set race, and put in a jar or box. Now draw out fork tube and lift out clip for bottom race.

Further disassembly for routine lubrication is not necessary.

(1) & (2) Soak and clean thoroughly all parts in solvent. Use a rag to clean out the top and bottom set races, and the fork crown race. Ball bearings should be smoothed and unpitted. Clipped bearings should be securely in place. Races should be evenly coloured all the way around where the balls run. Place them on a glass surface to see if they are bent or warped. Replace any defective parts.

Reassembly: pack fresh grease in the top and bottom set races. Just fill the grooves; excessive grease will attract dirt.

(1) Push ball bearings into grease on bottom set race. Grease will hold them in place.

(2) Put some grease inside the clip. Slip it down over the fork tube to rest on the fork crown race.

(1) & (2) Carefully insert fork tube into head tube. Keeping it snug against the bearings, check that it turns freely. Hang on to fork so that it does not fall back out.

(1) Stick ball bearings into grease of top set race.

(2) Grease and slip on clipped bearings.

(1) & (2) Screw down top threaded race. These threads are fine, so do it carefully (see General Words, pp 168–69, for best technique). Set it hand tight, and then back it off one quarter turn. Pile on washer, cable anchor mount, etc, and locknut. Be careful to keep threaded top race in position when tightening locknut. Check for play.

Complete Disassembly

If the bike has been in a smash-up or if rust has got to the bearings, it may be necessary to do a complete disassembly.

Take fork and ball bearings out as for lubrication. Remove crown fork race from fork. If it is stuck, prise it up *gently* with a screwdriver, working around the edges a little at a time. Be careful – it is easy to bend:

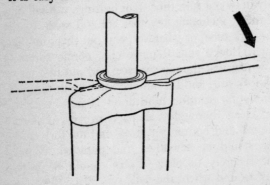

Remove top and bottom set races. You may possibly have threaded set races, in which case simply unscrew them. For force set races, insert a large screwdriver, piece of pipe, or stiff rod into the head tube and tap around the edges of the race:

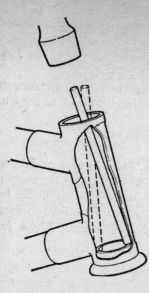

Clean all parts with solvent. Test races for uniformity by seeing if they lie flat on glass or other smooth surface.

Reassembly: screw in threaded set races. For force set races use a wooden block (to avoid denting or bending the race) and hammer:

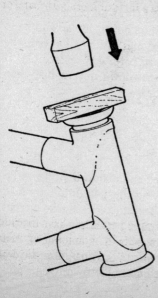

Make sure that it is seated fully into the frame. Use a wooden block also on the fork crown race if it is balky but be very delicate, and tap evenly all the way around the race.

Trouble-shooting

◎ Fork tube is extremely loose in the head tube. May just need adjustment (p 216), but if things have come to this pass I suggest dismantling and checking condition of parts.

Adjustment does not work: top threaded race or fork is stripped. Dismantle and see. It is unlikely that this is the result of excessive tightening, and likely that the top threaded race was screwed down off-centre. When you have your new parts review General Words, Threading, p 168, before starting.

◎ Fork binds or catches, or makes grating and rasping noises when you turn handlebars. Adjust as per p 216. No go? Something is broken or bent, completely worn out, or there are too many or too few ball bearings. Review the possibilities. Has fork or headset been whacked severely lately? A couple of months ago? Did you or someone else service the headset and lose a bearing or two, or place too many in one race and not enough in the other? Or perhaps the bike is simply ancient, and needs new races? In any case, disassemble (pp 218–20), clean, and check all parts. Are bearings evenly distributed (ask your bike shop how many should be in your headset), and free of dents, cracks, and pitting? Do races lie flat on a glass surface? Replace defective parts and reassemble. If you can find nothing wrong, take the parts down to your bike shop and see what they say.

Forks
How They Work

The fork holds the front wheel in place and allows the bike to be steered. The fork arms are curved, giving the axle drop-outs rake or trail from a line drawn through the fork tube. This rake or trail has two purposes: it makes the bike handle better and it helps the bike to absorb bumps and other road shocks. The amount of trail varies according to the purpose of the bike. Touring bikes have a slightly longer trail for a softer, more comfortable ride. Racing and

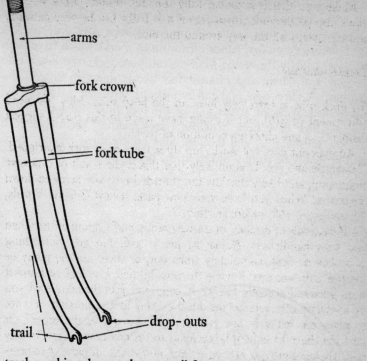

arms

fork crown

fork tube

trail

drop-outs

track machines have a shorter trail for greater efficiency in transmitting rider effort to the wheels. Additionally, the forks may be solid or tubular, the latter lighter and more flexible.

Lubrication and Dismantling

Covered under Headset, pp 216–20.

Trouble-shooting

◎ All problems with turning, grating noises, etc, are covered under Headset, p 220.

◎ Bent forks: replace them. Bending fatigues metal and makes it weak. The weakness does not show. What happens is that the fork suddenly gives up while you are tearing along at 30 mph. This does not happen very often, but once is enough. Bicycle shops do have special tools for straightening bent forks and if the bend in yours is slight, you may want to try it. Be aware that you are taking a calculated risk, however small.

Tests for bent forks: the bike will ride funny. If forks are bent to one side, the bike will always want to turn to the left or right. Test by taking your hands off the handlebars. Any decently set-up bike can be ridden hands off for miles. Forks which have been bent in, usually through a head-on collision, make the bike's ride choppy and harsh, and make it feel like it wants to dive in the corners. A sure sign of bent-in forks is wrinkled paint on the upper fork arms, or at the join of the fork tube and fork crown. Forks which have been bent out (rare) manifest themselves in a sloppy, mushy ride, and curious, long arcing turns. Again, there will probably be paint wrinkles at the bend point.

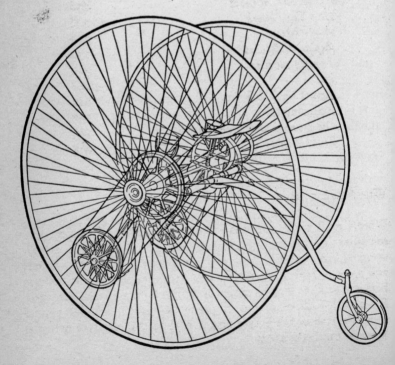

Contents

Wheel Removal

Wheels need to be removed often, for a variety of reasons, and sometimes on the road. So you can and will do this with a free-standing bike, but it is much easier if it is hung up. Most 3-speeds and some 10-speeds can simply be turned upside down on handle-bars and seat, as long as cables or shift selectors are not damaged. Bikes with calliper brakes in proper adjustment should require some slacking of the brakes (see p 182) so that the tyre will pass between the brake shoes.

Front Wheel, Any Bike

Wheel will be held to fork by hex nuts, wing nuts, or a quick-release lever:

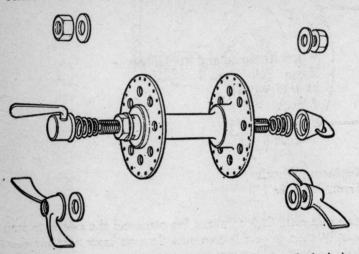

For nuts, undo both simultaneously (counter-clockwise) and unwind a turn or two. Levers, flip it. Remove wheel. Note washers go outside fork drop-outs.

Rear Wheel

10-speed Bikes: Run chain to smallest sprocket. Undo nuts or lever as for front wheel, and push wheel down and out. If you have a free hand, hold back the derailleur so that the freewheel clears it easily, otherwise just gently wiggle it by.

3-speed Bikes: Shift to third gear. Disconnect shift cable at rear hub by undoing locknut A and unscrewing adjustor sleeve B from pole (see opposite page).

Undo nuts simultaneously (counter-clockwise). Remove wheel, and note washers are outside drop-outs.

Single-speed Coaster-brake Bikes: Disconnect coaster-brake bracket from bike frame (metal arm at left end of rear axle), undo nuts (counter-clockwise), and remove wheel.

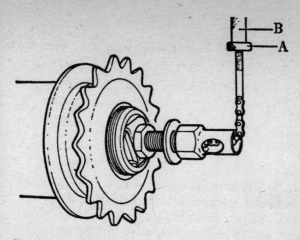

Replacing Wheels
Front, Any Bike

Axle with nuts: Back off nuts a few turns and slip axle on to drop-outs. Washers go outside drop-outs. Set nuts finger tight and check that rim is centred between fork arms before snugging them down. Re-set calliper brakes if you have them.

Levers: Slip axle on to drop-outs with lever on left side of bike. If this is difficult, hold knurled cone with one hand and unwind lever a couple of turns with the other. Slip axle on drop-outs and wind lever down just short of finger tight. Check that wheel rim is centred between fork arms, and close lever so that it points upward and backward. It should be firmly shut but not hysterically so. Re-set calliper brakes.

Rear Wheels

10-speed Bikes: Work axle into drop-outs, slipping chain over smallest sprocket on freewheel. Set nuts or lever for light tension. Pull wheel towards rear of bike until right end of axle hits the back of the drop-out. Use this as a pivot point to centre the rim between the chain stays, and tighten nuts or lever. Re-set calliper brakes.

3- and 1-speed Bikes: Work axle into drop-outs, slipping chain over sprocket. Lightly tighten nuts (washers are outside drop-outs), and pull back wheel so chain has $\frac{1}{2}$-in play up and down:

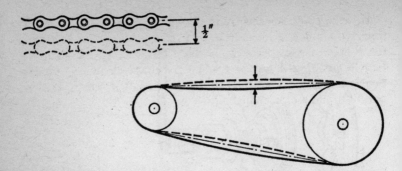

Centre rim between chain stays and tighten down nuts. Check chain tension. One-speed bikes: reconnect coaster brake bracket to frame. Three-speed bikes, with gear selector in 3rd: reconnect barrel sleeve to hub gear chain, and set locknut with cable slightly slack. Test gears and adjust if necessary (pp 270–71). Re-set calliper brakes.

Tyres
How They Work

Any pneumatic tyre works by supporting a casing, the part touching the road, with an inside tube which is filled with air like a balloon. With tubular tyres the tube is fully encased by the casing; with wire-on tyres the tube is held in place by a combination of two wire beads which run around the outside edges of the tyre, and the rim sides:

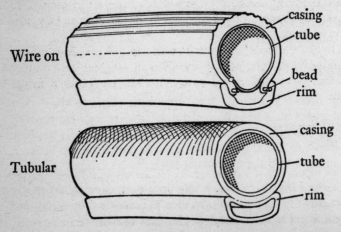

Air is pumped into the tube through a valve which comes in three types. Some wire-ons have Schraeder valves, the kind typically found on cars. Most have regular bicycle valves, requiring either a bicycle pump, or a special adaptor for petrol station air pumps. Some wire-ons and all tubulars have Presta type valves, also requiring a pump or adaptor:

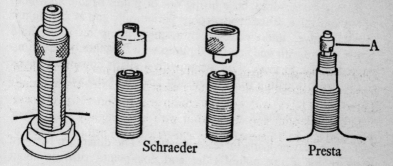

Schraeder

Presta

'Presta' valves need to have the locknut A undone in order to be pumped up.

Tyre Selection

There are tyres for nearly every purpose and condition: rain, mud, racing, touring, and carrying heavy loads. In tubulars heavy-duty 15-16 ounce tyres are about the only practical choice for touring and general use. Racers use lighter tyres which run 7 to 11 ounces. In wire-on tyres I suggest you explain your needs to a shop and try their recommendation.

Generally, 3-speeds are fitted with an all-purpose coarse-thread heavy-duty tyre, and 10-speeds with a lighter road pattern tyre. Better tyres cost only a little more and are worth it in the long run.

Routine Adjustments
Tyre Pressure

Use your own tyre pressure gauge (bike shops). Petrol station gauges are unreliable. When filling your tyres at a petrol station do it yourself. The proper pressure for your tyre may be as high as 100 pounds per square inch, but the total volume of air is small, and it takes only seconds to blow a tyre out. Some air pumps take a few moments to fill the tyre; others will do it instantaneously. Jab the air hose down on the valve for just a second, then release and test. Tyres should be hard enough so you can barely dent them with a finger, and bulge only very slightly when ridden. Consult chart below for proper pressure.

Bicycle pump: draw hose fitting out of pump handle and fit to pump and valve. Check connections periodically and as you pump. 'Presta' valve: undo valve locknut, push pump on valve, hold firmly to tyre with one hand, and pump with the other. Keep pump perpendicular to valve. Disengage with a sharp downward knock of the hand; wiggling will lose air and possibly bend valve.

Recommended Pressures

Note: for heavier loads increase pressure. The difference between pressure for a 125 pound rider and 200 pound rider is about 15 to 20 pounds per square inch.

Tubular 27 in — Rear, 85 to 100; front, 75–90.
Wire-on 27 in — 75 to 90.
Wire-on 26 in × $1\frac{1}{4}$ in — 45 to 60.
× $1\frac{1}{2}$ in — 40 to 55.
× $1\frac{3}{8}$ in — 40 to 55.
× $1\frac{3}{4}$ in — 35 to 45.
24 in   — 35 to 45.
20 in   — 45 to 50.
18 in   — 35 to 45.
16 in   — 30 to 40.
12 in   — 30 to 40.

Check tyre pressure often. Tubular tyres 'breathe' air through the sides and need filling frequently. Hot weather in the 80's and upwards may require that you bleed some air from the tyre to avoid over-inflation and a possible blow-out.

Riding

Most tyre problems are the result of picked-up debris working into the casing as you ride. Going over rocks, through pot-holes, and on and off kerbs will cause ruptures. Cultivate an eye for these hazards, and if you are forced to go through a patch of broken glass, for example, check and see that the tyre has not picked any up. A useful gadget for tubular tyres is a nail-catcher (bike shops) which rides lightly over the tyre and brushes off particles before they can cause damage:

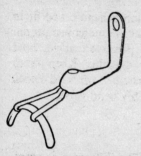

Keep oil away from tyres. It rots rubber. Grease, do not oil, bicycle pumps. Oiled bicycle pumps can vaporize and blow oil inside the tube. Check cement on tubulars about once a week.

Care and Storage

Keep wire-on spares in a dry place. Tubular spares should be carried folded so the tread is on the outside and not folded back on itself. Under the seat is a dandy place. Secure with straps or rubber bands:

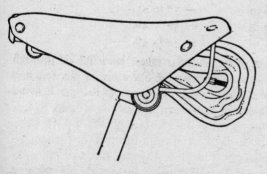

Every two weeks or so inflate a folded spare and let it stand for a while. Refold in the opposite direction.

Flats

Flats take the form of violent blow outs (rare), or punctures (common) which leak air with varying degrees of speed. Blow outs are usually terminal, doing so much damage that the tube and sometimes the tyre must be replaced. Punctures which are not gaping wounds can be repaired. There is debate as to proper policy for this and some bike shops maintain that any patching is 'temporary' and prefer to install a new tube. I suggest that you patch newish tubes and throw out older ones.

Wire-on Tyres

You will need a tube patch kit containing patches, glue, an abrasive surface, tyre irons (the kind which hook on to spokes are handiest), and chalk.

First check valve by inflating tyre slightly and placing a drop of spit on the end of the valve stem. A leaky valve will bubble or spit back. Tighten valve if necessary with valve cap or suitable part of pressure gauge:

Hooray if the problem was a loose or defective valve. If not, spin the wheel and look for an obvious cause like a nail or piece of glass. Yes? Dig it out and mark the spot.

What you do next depends on circumstances. It is easier to work on a puncture with the wheel off the bike (see pp 223-25). However, you may not have the tools to accomplish this feat, or perhaps you know exactly where the puncture is. At any rate, the basic procedure is the same.

Deflate tyre and remove valve stem locknut if you have one. Work the tyre back and forth with your hands to get the bead free of the rim. If the tyre is a loose fit on the rim you may be able to get it off with your hands. This is best, because tyre irons may pinch the tube and cause additional punctures. To do this make sure that the bead is free of the rim all the way around. Take a healthy grip on the tyre with both hands and pull it up and off-centre so that one bead comes over the rim:

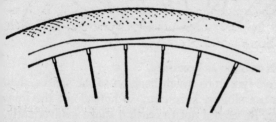

Then go around the rim working the bead completely off.

You will probably need to use tyre irons. Use tyre irons, not screwdrivers, as these are likely to cut the tube. Free bead from rim. Insert tyre iron under bead, being careful not to pinch the tube, and lever it over the side:

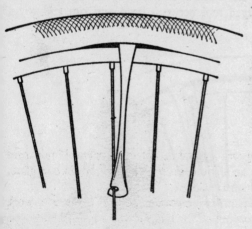

Insert second iron 2 in or 3 in away from first iron, and past where bead is over side of rim. Lever iron. For most tyres this will do the job. No? A third iron. If this doesn't work, use the now free 2nd iron for a fourth attempt:

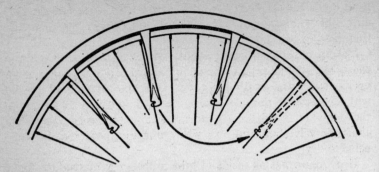

and repeat process as often as necessary.

If you don't have tyre irons which hook on to the spokes, then you will need to use elbows, knees, etc, to hold down the irons as you work away. Be careful not to crush a spoke inadvertently, and keep your face away in case something slips and tyre irons start jumping about.

If you have only two tyre irons and need a third, scrounge something up. In the country a flat rock or a stick. In the city a pencil, a beer can-opener, or something from the garbage. Look around. At any hour there will be *something*. Prise up bead with a tyre iron. Insert foraged tool between bead and rim and wiggle iron out:

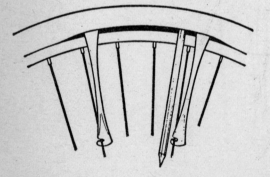

Use tyre irons to make two prises on either side of foraged tool.

One bead is off rim. Push valve stem up into tyre, and remove tube. Use chalk or eidetic memory to make note of which way tube was in the tyre. Inflate tube and rotate it past your ear. If you can locate the puncture through the hiss of escaping air, mark it with chalk. No? Immerse tube in water and look for escaping air bubbles. Dry tube with a rag while holding finger over puncture then mark with chalk.

Take sandpaper or metal abrader supplied with patch kit and rough up the area around the puncture. Spread a layer of cement over this area and let dry tacky. Peel the paper backing off a patch without touching the surface thus exposed, and press it firmly on the puncture. Hold for a moment next to tyre with valve stem alongside valve hole and note where puncture occurred. Set tube aside to dry.

If puncture was on inside of tube probably a protruding spoke caused it:

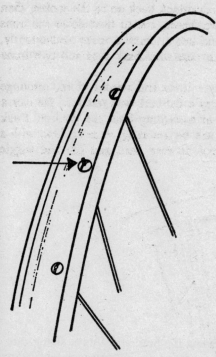

File the spoke flush with the rim. Check other spokes.

If the puncture was on the outside of the tube find what caused it by rubbing your fingers around inside the casing. Check the rest of the casing for embedded particles, and for ruptures or breaks:

Replace the tyre at the first opportunity if it has these.

To install the tube, first inflate it slightly to prevent it from folding and pinching itself. Push the part of the tube with the valve stem into the tyre, and the valve stem through its hole on the rim. Fit valve stem locknut loosely. Stuff rest of tube into tyre being careful not to pinch or tear it. Check that valve stem is still straight.

Push valve stem part way out, and slip bead of tyre at that point back over the rim. It is important that you hold the base of the valve stem clear of the rim as you do this, or the bead may catch on it, creating a bulge in the tyre:

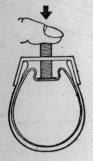

Work around the rim replacing the bead and always taking care not to pinch the tube. Ideally you can do the entire job with your hands. Check that the valve stem is still straight. The last bit will be hard. Just keep working at it with your thumbs, first from one side, then from the other. When about 2 in of bead remains give it the grand mal effort. Don't wonder if it will go over; decide that it will. If you have to use a tyre iron, be very careful not to pinch the tube.

Tubular tyres

You will need:

Patches
Needle
Thread
Rubber cement
Sandpaper
Talcum powder
Chalk
Screwdriver
Sharp knife or razor blade

Remove wheel (pp 223–25). Deflate tyre completely by opening locknut A on valve and holding down:

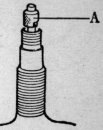

Remove tyre from rim with your hands. Inflate and immerse in water a little at a time. Do not be misled by air bubbles coming out by the valve. Since the tyre is sewn, the valve hole and puncture hole are the only places air can escape. Hold finger over puncture when located, dry tyre, and mark puncture with chalk.

With a screwdriver or similar implement pry away about 5 in to 6 in of the tape of the inner side of the tyre at the puncture area:

Next cut stitching about 2 in to either side of puncture. Make only two cuts to avoid numerous bits and pieces of thread, and cut upward to miss tyre:

Gently remove tube and locate leak. A mixture of soap and water will pin-point elusive ones. Dry tube if wet. Abrade area around puncture with sandpaper. Apply cement and let dry. Peel protective paper from patch without touching surface thus exposed and apply to puncture. Dust with talc to prevent tube from sticking to casing. Get whatever caused puncture out of casing. Insert tube, inflate, and check for leaks. Do this carefully. You are going to be mad if you get it all back together only to discover it still leaks.

Thread the needle and knot the two loose ends of thread. In a tight situation, 12-pound linen thread or silk fishing line will do. Using the old holes, start with an overlap of about $\frac{1}{2}$ in, i.e. $\frac{1}{2}$ in past where thread was cut. Pinch the sides of the casing between thumb and forefinger to keep the tube out of the way:

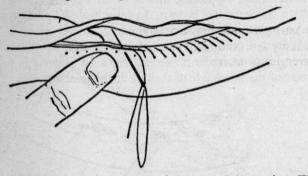

Pull stitches firm, but not so tight as to cut casing. Finish with a $\frac{1}{2}$-in overlap into original stitching. Layer cement on casing and inside of peeled-away tape and keep apart until dry. Position carefully and press together firmly.

Mounting a tubular

New rims and tyres: inflate tyre, deflate, place on rim (see opposite page), inflate, deflate, remove.

Repaired tyres and/or old rims: clean off old cement from rim with shellac thinner or solvent (bike shops).

There are two methods of mounting a tubular.

(1) Slow but sure. Deflate tyre. Insert valve. Stand rim on soft surface with valve stem up, and working from above, work tyre down over rim:

Be careful to distribute tyre evenly around rim.
Finish by grabbing with both hands and getting
the last bit over by main force:

Check again that tyre is evenly distributed and centred on rim.
Roll back a portion of the tyre and brush glue on rim and lining.
Repeat all the way around and from both sides. Check again for
evenness. Inflate hard. Allow half a day to dry before using or tyre
may creep (bunch up in spots) or simply come off the rim in a
corner.

(2) Fast method. Apply glue to rim and tyre and allow to dry
tacky. Wear old clothes and assemble as above.

Road repairs: use the old cement on the rim and don't lean hard
into corners going home. Double-sided rim tape (bike shops) is
very handy.

Rims and Spokes

How They Work

The rim which supports the tyre is laced (held) in position by the spokes, which are held fast at the hub and screw into the rim, so that they are adjustable:

Adjustments

The tension on the spokes relative to each other determines both the strength and position of the rim. Positioning the rim correctly, both up and down, and side to side, is a long job requiring lots of patience and skill. Most times it is much more efficient to leave this to a bike shop. If you have no alternative however, or are determined to go it alone, here's how:

Hang up the bike or place the wheel in a jig. Spin the wheel while holding a pencil or something similar at a fixed point like the fork arm or a seat stay with the point near the rim to see how bad the wobble is. If it is over ½ in, pack up the entire project and take the wheel to a bike shop. If they think they can save the wheel, fine, otherwise get a new wheel.

With a less than ½-in wobble: deflate tyre. If job looks to be major, it will be easier if you just remove the tyre altogether. Pluck the spokes with your fingers – they should all 'ping' – and tighten any that are slack so that they all have an even tension. Spokes are tightened by turning *counter-clockwise*. If in the course of doing this you find spokes with frozen nipples (the part which holds the spoke to the rim) they must be replaced (see below). If it is more than three or four spokes I once again suggest resorting to your friendly bike shop.

Hold a chalk or pencil at the *outer edge* of the rim while you spin the wheel so that the high spots are marked. Working one-half to one turn at a time, tighten the spokes at the chalk mark (*counter-clockwise*) and loosen them opposite the chalk mark. Continue until wheel is round.

Hold pencil or chalk at *side* of rim so that side to side wobbles are marked. Working one half to one turn at a time, and in groups of four to six spokes, tighten up the spokes opposite the chalk mark and loosen the ones next to it:

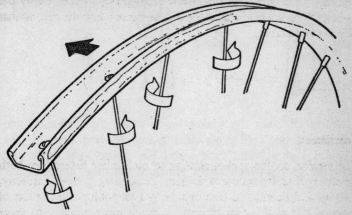

Tighten or loosen the spokes which are in the centre of the chalk marks a little more than the ones at the edges of the marks. When you have finally succeeded, or compromised, run your finger around the rim and check for protruding spoke ends. File protruders down.

Replacing Spokes

Remove tyre (pp 230–35). If you are dealing with spokes on a free-wheel-equipped rear wheel that go to the freewheel side of the hub, the freewheel will have to be removed (pp 266–67). Take broken spokes out of the hub and rim. Get replacements which are exactly the same; many different kinds are available.

New spokes should go into the hub so that head is on opposite side of hub from adjoining spokes and spoke is pointed in opposite direction:

Be sure that it is correctly positioned in the hub with respect to the bevels:

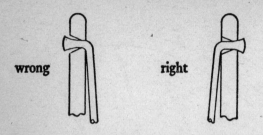

On almost all bikes the spokes touch where they cross. Weave new spokes through old as per other spokes on wheel. Place nipples on spokes and tighten. True wheel (see above), file down any protruding spokes which might puncture the tube, and remount tyre.

Trouble-shooting

◎ For side-to-side wobbles and elliptical wheels see pp 238–39.
◎ For bulges in the rim caused by piling into kerbs, stones, etc: you will need vice-grips, channel-lock pliers, or a C-clamp. If bulge is equal on both sides of rim, place implement over bulge and squeeze *gently* until the rim is even again:

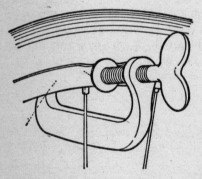

If the bulge is on one side of the rim, distribute the pinching force of your implement on the non-bulge side with a block of wood or some such:

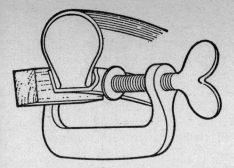

Fixing bulges almost invariably leaves a slight dimple because the metal itself was stretched, but the wheel will probably be usable.

Hubs

We are talking here about any front wheel hub or freewheel equipped rear wheels. Multi-speed hubs are too complicated to service.

How They Work

A hub consists of an axle, two sets of bearings, and a casing. The axle is held fixed, and the casing, to which the spokes are attached, spins around it riding on the ball bearings:

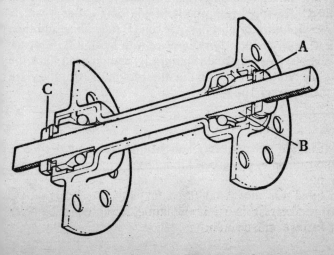

Adjustments

Wheel bearings are out of adjustment if, with the axle held firmly in place, the wheel can be wiggled from side to side (usually with a clicking noise), or if the wheel will not turn easily. Wheels held with nuts or lever nuts can be adjusted while on the bike. Generally speaking however, the best procedure is to remove the wheel (pp 223–25). Wheels with quick-release hubs must be removed. You will need special thin hub wrenches (bike shops).

Undo locknut A from cone B:

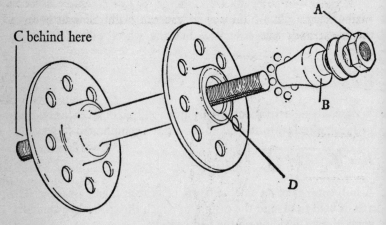

Holding axle or axle housing (quick-releases) still with wrench at locknut C (ten-speed rear wheels: if you can't get at it with a wrench use vice-grips or pliers), screw cone B fully home and then back off one quarter turn. Lock in place with locknut A. Test for side to side play. Wheel should spin freely, and on good hubs the weight of the tyre valve will pull the wheel around so that the valve rests in the six o'clock position.

Lubrication

Any front hub or 10-speed rear hub with oil clips or caps: $\frac{1}{2}$ teaspoonful oil a month. If a grease fitting, one or two shots of grease per month.

Multi-speed rear hubs: 1 tablespoonful oil.

Coaster brake rear hubs: if oil fitting, 2 tablespoonfuls per month; if grease fitting, two or three shots of grease.

Hubs need to be cleaned and re-greased every six months for bikes in constant year-round use, and once a year for bikes retired for the winter or used only moderately. This requires disassembly.

Disassembly and Replacement

Remove wheel from bike (pp 223–25). Ten-speed rear wheels, remove freewheel (pp 266–67). Lay wheel down on rags or newspaper to catch ball bearings. Undo locknut A from cone B and remove both while holding on to axle at C (see opposite page).

Remove dust cover D. To do this, it may be necessary to let the axle drop in just a little way so you can prise the dust cover off with a screwdriver:

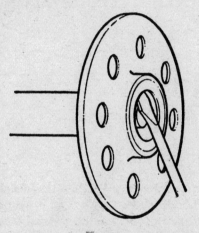

Prise out the loose or clipped ball bearings (or turn the wheel over and dump them out), count, and place in jar. Now slide axle all the way out and dump out remaining bearings. Garner and count. Undo remaining locknut and cone and remove from axle. Clean all parts in solvent. Examine bearings to see that they are not cracked or pitted. Clipped bearings should be secure in clip. Cups and cones should be even in colour all around where bearings run and free of pitting. Test axle for straightness by rolling on glass surface. Replace any defective parts.

Reassembly: pack cups with grease. Not too much, excess will attract grit. Replace and lock one cone and locknut on axle. Slip dust cover on axle. Pack bearings into cup on one side of wheel.

Gracefully insert axle and turn wheel over. Pack bearings into cup, replace dust cover, screw on cone and locknut, and adjust as per above.

Trouble-shooting

If something goes wrong it is usually because
  (1) the hub hasn't been serviced, or
  (2) a cone and locknut have come adrift.
  In either case, if routine adjustment will not solve the problem, completely disassemble hub and replace broken or defective parts as per above.

Contents

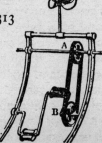

Pedals
How They Work

A pedal consists of a platform of metal or metal and rubber for the foot, an axle (called a spindle) which screws into the crank, and two sets of ball bearings on which the platform rides as it spins around the spindle.

Adjustment

If pedal can be wiggled back and forth on the spindle, it needs tightening. Remove dustcap A (prise with a screwdriver if it is the wedge type):

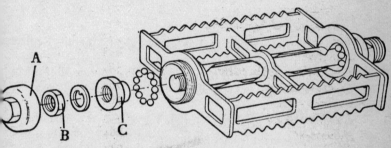

Undo locknut B from cone C. Screw cone C fully home and back off one-quarter turn. Secure with locknut B. Check for play and that pedal spins easily. Replace dustcap A.

Lubrication and Disassembly

Pedals lead a hard, dissolute life and need cleaning and regreasing every six months, more often if you ride a lot or favour wet weather. This requires disassembly. Remove pedals from crank. *Note :* right-hand pedal has a conventional right-hand thread and unscrews by turning counter-clockwise, but left-hand pedal has a left-hand thread and unscrews by turning *clockwise*. Work with pedal over newspaper or rag to catch ball bearings. Remove dustcover A (see illustration above). Undo and remove locknut B and cone C while holding platform and spindle together with hand. Get all bearings out of dust cover end and place in jar. Remove spindle and place all bearings from crank end in jar. Clean all parts in solvent. Check ball bearings for pitting, cracks, disorderly conduct; cups and cones for uneven wear, pitting; spindle for straightness.

Reassembly: pack grease into cups on platform. Pack ball bearings into cup on crank side of platform (grease will hold them in place), and slide on spindle. Pack bearings into dust cover side cup. Screw down cone C fully home and back off one-quarter turn. Secure with locknut B. Check for play and that pedal spins easily. Replace dustcover.

Note: When replacing pedals on bike be sure that left-side pedal, stamped 'L' on end of spindle shaft, goes to the left side. It screws on *counter-clockwise*. The right-hand pedal is stamped 'R' (surprise!) and screws on *clockwise*.

Trouble-shooting

◎ Pedal is tight to crank but askew. Bent spindle. Replace immediately.

◎ Grinding noises, hard to turn pedal. Try routine adjustment as above. No? Something is probably broken. Disassemble as above and replace defective parts.

◎ Loose pedal. Check that it is tight to crank. Left pedal tightens *counter-clockwise*, right pedal tightens *clockwise*. No? Loose bearings. Adjust as per above.

Cranks

Cranks support the pedals and transmit pedalling power to the front sprocket(s). They are attached to a bottom bracket axle which rides on two sets of ball bearings inside the bottom bracket shell. There are three types of cranks: one-piece; cottered three-piece; and cotterless three-piece (see opposite page).

Since one-piece cranks include the bottom bracket axle, they are covered under Bottom Brackets. To test a cottered or cotterless crank for tightness, position the pedals equidistant from the ground. Press firmly on both pedals with hands and release. Rotate crankset one half turn and press pedals again. If something gives, one of the cranks is loose.

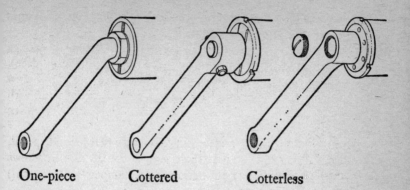

One-piece   **Cottered**   **Cotterless**

Adjustment and Removal

Cottered Cranks Support the crank with a block of wood which has a hole or V-notch into which the cotter pin A fits:

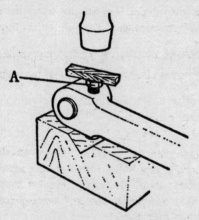

A—

Be sure that the support block touches only the crank and is firmly in place. Otherwise what you do next will damage your bearings by driving the balls into the sides of the cup and scoring it (called Brinelling). Next: if you are tightening, give the head of the cotter pin A two or three moderate blows with a wooden mallet or hammer and wooden block combination. Then snug down nut firmly, but not with all your might or you will strip it. If you are removing, undo cotter pin two or three turns and then tap threaded end of cotter pin. Repeat if necessary. Be careful not to damage the threads as you will want to use the pin again. If you use a new pin and it does not fit, file down the flat side until it does.

Cotterless Cranks You will need a crank installer and extractor which fits your particular brand of crank. Cotterless cranks are made of an aluminium alloy called dural and must not be tightened with the same force as steel parts. To tighten or loosen, first remove the dust cover A:

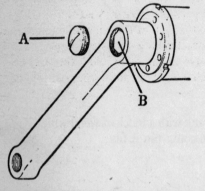

To tighten, apply socket wrench of installer to nut B and turn down, wiggling crank arm to make sure it is seated all the way. For new cranks retighten every 25 miles for the first 200 miles of use. To remove, first get chain out of way. Remove nut B. Back inner bolt A of extractor all the way out:

Screw extractor into crank, and then tighten down inner bolt A. *Do not do this with all of your might or you may strip the threads.* If the crank does not come loose with a firm tightening on the extractor bolt, give it two or three taps with a hammer, and tighten it one-eighth of a turn. Repeat until crank comes free. When replacing crank, be sure to wiggle it around a lot so that it is fully home before you give it the final tightening.

◎ There is a 'click' as you bring the pedal around on the upstroke and then a momentary dead spot and another 'click' as you push it down. It may be a loose pedal (p 247), bottom bracket (p 252), or crank. If it looks to be the crank, test and tighten if necessary as per above.

◎ Stripped holding bolt on a cotterless crank. Get a new bottom bracket axle. If this is impossible, a machine shop may be able to re-thread the axle to accept a larger bolt. Be sure that the head of the larger bolt is small enough so that you can still use an extractor.

◎ Stripped thread for the extractor on a cotterless crank. First ask your bike shop if they can solve the problem. No? You may be able to find a substitute tool which will do the job. I have one which looks like:

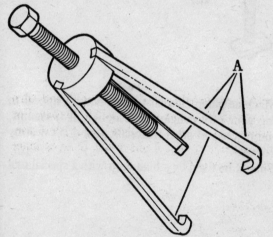

I have no idea what it is used for, although I think it has something to do with plumbing. It may be a flywheel remover. Anyway, the arms A will hook on to the crank or sprocket while the bolt passes against the bottom bracket axle.

If you can't find a substitute tool you and a machine shop may be able to manufacture a new extractor. It will be some trouble, but at upwards of £40 for fancy new cranks it is probably worth taking a stab at saving the old ones. Take your bike to a machine shop and explain that you want a steel plate or bar threaded in the centre for an extractor bolt, and with holes drilled so that other bolts can be slid through and in turn be attached to metal plates which will hook behind the front sprocket:

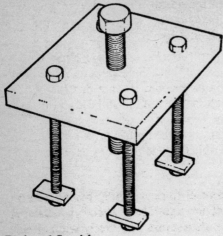

Backyard Special

If this Backyard Machine Shop Special Gizmo doesn't appeal to you, try jury-rigging your own conglomerate design of C-clamps, bolts, levers, bits and pieces and other materials. Just don't destroy your bike in the process.

◎ Bent crank. Should be fixed by a bike shop with a special tool for the job.

Bottom Bracket
How It Works

The bottom bracket axle (called a spindle) spins on two sets of ball bearings contained within the bottom bracket shell, and holds the cranks. On the Ashtabula type one-piece crankset, the two cranks and spindle are one unit. Three-piece cranksets (cottered and cotterless) consist of two cranks and a separate spindle. Although service techniques are fundamentally similar, we will discuss one-piece cranksets and spindles for three-piece cranksets separately.

Ashtabula One-piece Crankset
Adjustment

If axle is hard to turn, or slips from side to
side in bottom bracket shell, first remove
chain (p 259). Then loosen locknut A by
turning it *clockwise*:

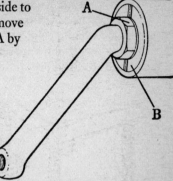

Use screwdriver in slot of cone B to turn it fully home (*counter-clockwise*), and then back it off one-eighth turn. Resecure locknut A
(*counter-clockwise*), and check that cranks spin freely without side
to side play.

Lubrication and Disassembly

Bottom bracket axles should be cleaned and re-greased once a
year. This requires disassembly. Bearings for one-piece cranksets
are held in clips so don't worry about losing them. Remove left
pedal (*clockwise*) and chain from front sprocket (p 259). Undo
locknut A (*clockwise*), and unscrew cone B (*clockwise*):

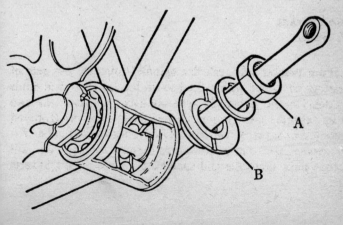

Remove ball bearing clip. Slide all parts off crank and place in a jar. Now move axle to right and tilt to slide whole unit through bottom bracket and out of frame. Take right side bearing clip off axle. Clean everything thoroughly with solvent. See that ball bearings are secure in clips and free from pitting or cracks; cups and cones are even in colour where ball bearings run and free from pitting or scoring. If cups are deeply grooved, replace. Remove with hammer and steel rod or screwdriver

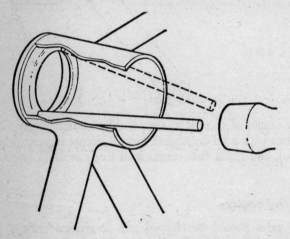

and make sure the new cups are well seated by tapping them in with a hammer and wooden block:

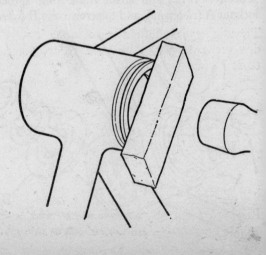

To reassemble: pack grease into bearing clips and cups. Slide one clip on axle with solid side against right cone. Gracefully insert crankset through bottom bracket shell from right side. Slide on ball bearing clips with balls in, solid side out. Screw on cone (*counter-clockwise*), and turn it fully home, wiggling and spinning the crankset as you do this. Reverse one-eighth turn and secure with locknut (tighten *counter-clockwise*). Check that crankset spins freely without side to side play. Replace pedal (*counter-clockwise*) and chain.

Three-piece Cranksets
Adjustment

Bottom bracket axle (spindle) should be free from side to side play and spin freely. To adjust, first disconnect chain from front sprocket (p 259). Loosen notched lockring C on left side of bracket with a 'C' wrench (bike stores) or hammer and screwdriver combination (*counter-clockwise*):

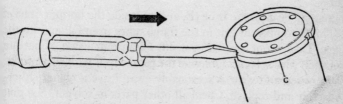

Then tighten (*clockwise*) adjustable cup D fully home with a screwdriver or centre-punch inserted in hole or slot and *very light* hammer taps:

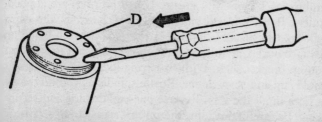

Reverse one eighth turn and secure with lockring C. Check that spindle spins freely and has no side to side play.

Bottom bracket assembly should be cleaned and re-greased once a year. This requires disassembly. Remove chain from front sprocket (p 259) and cranks (p 249). Lay bike right-side down on newspaper or rags to catch loose ball bearings. Undo lockring C with 'C' wrench or hammer and screwdriver combination and remove. Carefully holding axle in place against right side bearings, remove adjustable cup D:

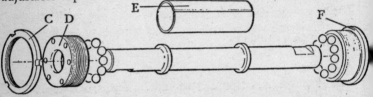

Look out for the ball bearings! Some will fall out, others will stick to various parts. Gather, count, and place in jar. Make sure you have them all. If your bearings are clipped, lucky you. Now pull spindle straight out. Garner all the right side ball bearings and jar 'em.

There may be a plastic tube (E, above) inside the bottom bracket shell. This is to prevent grit in the frame tubes from falling into the bearings. Take it out and clean it off. Clean out inside of bottom bracket shell with solvent. Examine the fixed cup F with a flashlight. If it is unpitted and wear is reasonably even, leave it alone. Otherwise unscrew and replace. Clean all other parts in solvent. See that ball bearings have no pits or cracks, and, if clipped, are secure in retainers; inside of adjustable cup and cones on spindle also have no pits and wear is even; spindle is straight. Replace defective parts.

Reassembly: pack cups with grease. If ball bearings are clipped, pack retainers. Replace plastic sleeve. Pack ball bearings into cups. Grease will hold in place. Clipped bearings go with solid side on cone (balls face out). Carefully insert spindle, long end to sprocket side of bottom bracket shell. Without jarring loose ball bearings fit on adjustable cup and screw home. Rotate spindle as you do this to be sure it goes in all the way. Reverse one-eighth turn and secure with lockring. Be careful threading this on as it is easy to strip. Check that spindle spins easily with no side-to-side play. Replace cranks (p 249) and chain (p 259).

◎ Tight or loose crankset, grinding noises. Try adjustment as above. No? Disassemble and replace defective parts as per above.

◎ 'Click' on pedal upstroke followed by dead spot and second 'click' on downstroke. Could be a loose spindle, but more probably a loose crank or pedal (p 247).

Front Sprocket(s) (Chainwheel)

The front sprocket is the business with all the teeth attached to the right crank which pulls the chain around to deliver power to the rear wheel.

Adjustment

The only maintenance needed is to check periodically for bent or chipped teeth. Remove chain (p 259). With a strong light behind the front sprocket, rotate it, looking from the side for chipped teeth, and from above or in front for bent teeth:

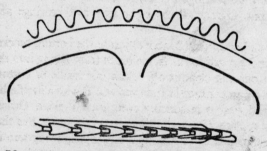

If teeth are chipped, replace sprocket (see overleaf). If bent, take an adjustable wrench, snug it down over the bent tooth, and bend it back:

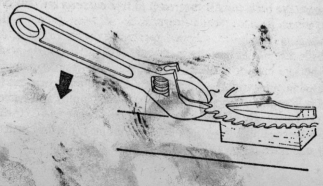

It helps a lot if you can brace the sprocket as you do this to avoid bending it.

Replacement
If it is necessary to replace your sprocket, take a look at the chapter on gearing (pp 78–85). You might be interested in changing the number of gear teeth.

Ashtabula one-piece cranksets require replacing the whole unit (pp 253–55).

1-speed and most 3-speed bikes have a one-piece right crank and sprocket. To remove see pp 249–50.

10-speed bikes generally have a sprocket which is bolted to the right crank:

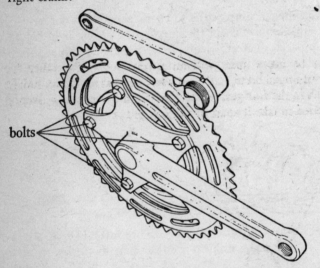

bolts

Simply undo the bolts (or Allen screws) to remove sprocket.

Trouble-shooting

◉ There is a 'clunk' every time you bring the front sprocket around. One possible cause is a bent tooth. Check by hanging bike up and slowly running sprocket. If chain suddenly jumps up where it meets the sprocket – bent tooth. Fix as above.

◉ Sprocket wobbles from side to side, hitting front derailleur cage or rubbing chainstays. If this is not due to incredibly loose bottom bracket bearings (p 255), the sprocket is warped. Fixing is a job requiring both great delicacy and considerable force. Techniques vary so much according to the exact problem that I strongly suggest you leave it to a bike shop.

Chain

The chain is that innocent and simple-looking business which transmits power to the rear gear(s). There are two kinds: one is used on non-derailleur bikes, is $\frac{1}{8}$-in wide, and held together with a master link:

which can be taken apart without special tools; the other for derailleur-equipped bikes, is 3/32-in wide, and has no master link (it would catch in the rear gear cluster), so that a special chain riveting tool is needed to take it apart or put it together:

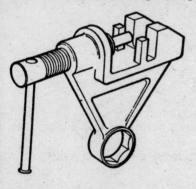

Removal and Replacement

Chains should be replaced every two years on bikes that see constant use, and every three years on bikes that see average service. Although the chain may look perfectly sound, the tiny bit of wear on each rivet and plate adds up to a considerable alteration in size. A worn chain will chip teeth on (expensive) gear sprockets. To test for wear, remove chain (see below) and lay on table with rollers parallel to surface. Hold chain with both hands about 4-5 in apart. Push hands together, and then pull apart. If you can feel slack, replace chain.

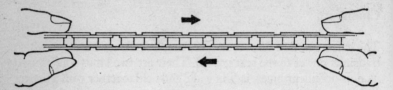

Test also for side to side deflection. It should not be more than 1 in:

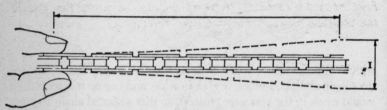

To remove and replace a master link chain find the master link and prise it off with a screwdriver.

To remove a derailleur chain drive out a rivet with a chain tool:

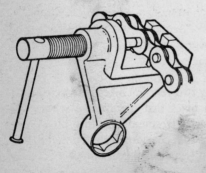

Be sure that the point of the chain tool centres exactly on the rivet. *Do not drive the rivet all the way out.* Go only as far as the outside plate. Stop frequently to check progress. Once rivet is near chain plate I like to free link by inserting a thin screwdriver and twisting gently:

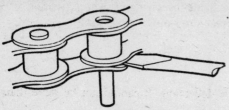

Another method is simply to twist the chain. Be careful that you do not bend the plates. To replace rivet, reverse tool:

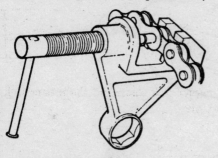

Again, be careful how far you go, or the link will jam (see Trouble-shooting to fix).

Fitting

Most new chains need to be shortened in order to fit properly. On a non-derailleur bike it should be set so that there is ½-in up and down play in the chain with the rear wheel in proper position:

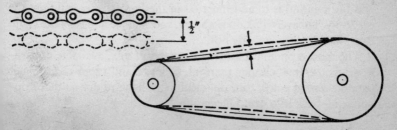

On a derailleur bike, the chain needs to be long enough to fit over the large front and back sprockets, and short enough to fit on the small front and rear sprockets. The less tension the better, but be careful the derailleur does not double up on itself. Remove links from end of chain that has two plates with no roller between them. Some adjustment can be made by changing wheel position with adjustable blocks on the rear drop-outs:

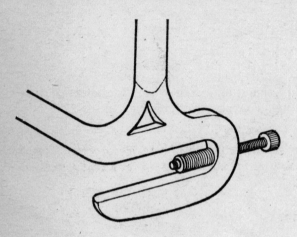

Lubrication

The scheme for lubrication depends on what kind of lubricant you use.

In my opinion the best is a petroleum distillate spray like WD-40 or LPSW-1. The greatest advantage of this stuff is that it is clean, does not attract dirt, and goes on in a flash. Apply every 1 or 2 weeks, and remove and soak chain clean in solvent every 2 or 3 months.

Oil is the common lubricant. The problem is that it attracts grit and the solution is to add more oil in the hope that it will float the grit away. Oil every link once a week, and remove and soak the chain clean in solvent once a month.

The most economical lubricant is paraffin wax, available in hardware shops. It is cleaner than oil. Remove and clean chain. Melt paraffin wax in coffee can, dip chain, and hang to dry so that drippings fall back into can. Once a month.

◎ Jammed link. Use chain tool to free tight links by working the rivet back and forth a quarter-turn on the chain tool at a time. If your chain tool has a spreader slot (handy), use that:

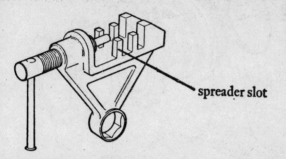

spreader slot

◎ 'Klunk' sounds and/or chain jumping sprockets. Test chain for excessive wear as per above. May also be a bent sprocket tooth (see p 257).

Rear Sprocket

All chain drive bikes have a rear sprocket. On 1- and 3-speed bikes this is a single sprocket and is extremely simple. Derailleur-equipped bikes use several sprockets (also called cogs) mounted on a freewheel.

How It Works

The freewheel is in two parts, and there are two basic designs:

C B

The inside part B threads on the hub. Sprockets slide or are threaded on the outside part C. The freewheel is ratcheted so that when the outside part C is driven clockwise by the chain, the inside part B (and hence the hub) is driven too. But when the bike is coasting, with the chain stationary, part C holds still while part B spins merrily along. This ratcheting is accomplished through the use of a clever maze of ball bearings, pins, springs, and other minute and complex parts inside the freewheel.

Adjustment

Periodically check for chipped or bent teeth by looking at them in profile:

Replace cogs that have chipped or broken teeth, or an uneven U between teeth. Straighten bent teeth by removing cog (see below), gripping the bent tooth with an adjustable end wrench, and straightening:

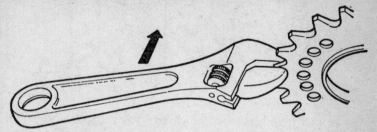

Alignment between front and back sprockets is important. Standing at the front of the bike and sighting between the two front sprockets, you should see the centre cog of the back gear cluster:

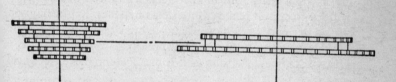

If back sprocket is too far out, so you can see the 2nd or 1st largest rear cog, the front sprocket must be moved out. This can only be done by installing a longer bottom bracket axle (p 256). If you have Ashtabula one-piece cranks (p 253) there is nothing you can do at all.

If back sprocket is too far in, so you can see the 4th or 5th largest rear cog, it must be moved out. This is done by removing the freewheel (see overleaf), installing a shim (bike shops), the freewheel again, and then possibly another shim so that the freewheel will clear the drop-outs. All this stuff usually makes it hard to put the wheel back in and may necessitate a little judicious bending. It is better to let a bike shop deal with problems of this sort.

Lubrication

A bi-weekly shot of petroleum distillate spray like WD-40 or LPSW-1 is best. Remove freewheel (see overleaf) and soak clean in solvent once a year.

Oil: a few drops once a month. Remove and soak clean in solvent every six months.

Removal and Disassembly

This requires a freewheel remover. There are two types, pronged and splined:

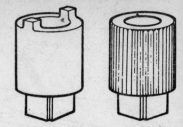

Look at your freewheel to see which kind you need. Remove wheel (p 223). Remove nut and washers from freewheel side of axle. Quick release hubs: remove conical nut and spring from shaft of skewer and place spring in a jar. Fit freewheel remover. If it won't go on, you may have a spacer nut. Remove with a wrench while holding axle stationary with another wrench on the left-side cone or locknut. Fit freewheel remover into slots or splines. Replace nut on axle or skewer and screw down hand-tight. Use a wrench on the freewheel remover to break the freewheel loose (*counter-clockwise*). This may be difficult. As soon as it comes loose, remove freewheel and spin it off by hand.

Replacing freewheel. *Note :* a new freewheel or sprockets requires a matching new chain, especially if the existing chain is more than a year old. A stretched chain will probably kick up on new sprockets. Also, if you are getting a new freewheel, read the chapter on gears. You may be interested in changing gear ratios. If you do this, be sure to check chain tension after installing freewheel (p 261). To replace a freewheel, simply screw it on, being extremely careful not to strip the threads on the hub. Snug down with the freewheel remover secured by the axle bolt but do not bear down hard; it will tighten as you ride.

Changing cogs. For this you need a sprocket remover (bike shops) and, if you are removing all the sprockets, a freewheel vice (ditto). Incidentally, if you want a number of different gear ratios it is much simpler to have two fully set-up freewheels with different gear ratios than to keep diddling with individual sprockets. However, if you are experimenting to work out the combination of cogs which is best for you and are impatient with bike shops (they can do this job very quickly), then by all means proceed. Removing a cog is simple –

it unscrews or slides off the freewheel – but tools for the job vary considerably in design. Follow the instructions given with your particular tool. If you change the small or large cog, be sure to check chain tension (p 261) after reassembly.

Dismantle freewheel. Uh-uh. This is another of those profitless jobs. If the freewheel goes, replace it.

Trouble-shooting

◎ A 'klunk' two or three times per complete revolution of the front sprocket. May be a bent tooth on a freewheel sprocket. Check as per above.

◎ Freewheel won't freewheel. Try soaking in solvent to free up innards. No? Replace it.

◎ Freewheel turns but hub doesn't. Spin cranks while holding bike stationary and look carefully at freewheel. If both parts spin around the hub, threads on hub are stripped. New hub. If outside part of freewheel spins around inside part, freewheel is clogged up (frozen) or broken. Try soaking in solvent. No? Replace.

Gear Changer Systems

Except for the two-speed pedal-operated rear hubs, gear changer systems typically include a shift trigger, lever, or twist-grip, a cable, and the gear changing mechanism, of which there are two kinds, internal rear hub, and derailleur.

Multi-speed Internally Geared Rear Hubs

These come in 2-, 3-, and 5-speed versions, with planetary or sun gears inside the hub. I consider these units too complicated to be worth disassembling, and so does any bike shop I have asked about doing such work. Here, for example, is an exploded view of a Sturmey-Archer 3-speed hub and coaster brake combination (see overleaf). Believe me, if you run into trouble with your hub and can't solve it with routine adjustment or trouble-shooting (below), the best thing to do is remove the wheel (p 223) and take it to a bike shop. The chance of problems arising is quite small. A regularly lubricated hub should last the life of your bike.

Sturmey-Archer 3-speed hub

No adjustments are possible with 2-speed pedal-controlled hubs. There are two major brands of 3-speed hubs, Sturmey-Archer, and Shimano. Service techniques for both are virtually identical, and so we will concentrate on one, the Sturmey-Archer.

How They Work

Shift trigger A connects to cable B, which in turn connects to toggle chain C on hub. Position of trigger determines gear.

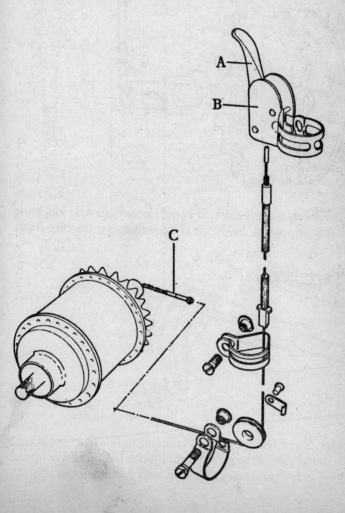

Three-speed Hubs To adjust a hub, first run the shift lever to 3rd or H. Then take up slack in cable by loosening locknut A and screwing down barrel sleeve adjustor B:

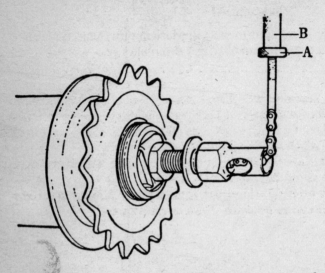

Leave cable very slightly slack. If barrel sleeve cannot do job, move the fulcrum clip which holds the cable housing on the bike frame forward:

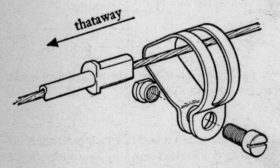

Test gears. No? Check position of indicator rod by looking through the hole in the side of the right hub nut. With the shift lever in 2nd or N position it should be exactly even with the end of the axle:

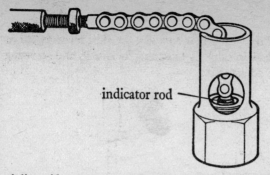

indicator rod

Adjust if necessary with barrel sleeve. Test gears. No? Remove barrel sleeve altogether. Check that indicator rod is screwed finger-tight fully into hub. Reassemble and adjust as above. No? Turn to Trouble-shooting, this section (p 275).

Five-speed Hubs For the right-hand shift lever, follow the same procedure as for the 3-speed hub, above.

For left-hand shift lever, set it all the way forward and screw cable connector to bellcrank B two or three turns:

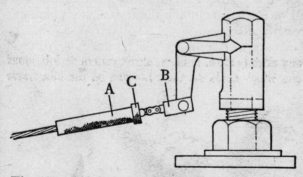

Then run shift lever all the way back, and take slack out of cable with cable connector. Secure with locknut C.

Lubrication

A tablespoon of oil inside hub once a month. I strongly recommend a quality oil such as is sold in bike shops and by gunsmiths. Some household and other cheap oils leave behind a sticky residue when the oil evaporates. This is the last thing in the world you want. Once a month use a little petroleum distillate spray or a few drops of oil on the trigger control, cable, and inside the cable housing.

Hub : Remove wheel (p 223) and take it to a bike shop.
Cable : Needs replacement when it becomes frayed, the housing kinked or broken, or exhibits suspicious political tendencies.

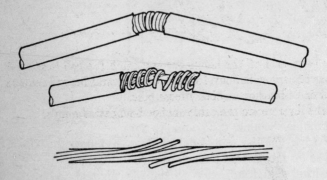

Run shift selector to 3rd or H. Disconnect barrel sleeve from indicator and loosen fulcrum clip (for illustration, see Adjustment above). To free cable from a:

Trigger: shift to 1st or L, prise up holding plate A with a small screwdriver, and push cable *in* until nipple clears ratchet plate:

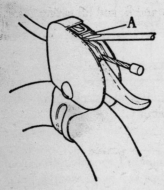

and then pull cable out. Remove entire cable and housing assembly from bike and set aside fulcrum sleeve.

Twist-grip: first take off the spring S with a screwdriver:

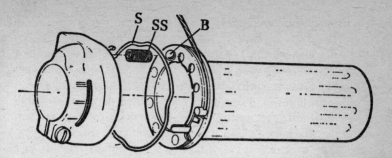

Slide the twist-grip off the handlebar and catch the ball bearing B and spring SS if they fall out. Release nipple from slot, and remove cable and cable housing assembly from bike.

Top tube lever: undo the cable anchor bolt near the hub:

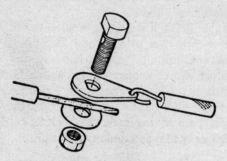

Unscrew the two shift lever halves A and B, and lift casing C away from bike:

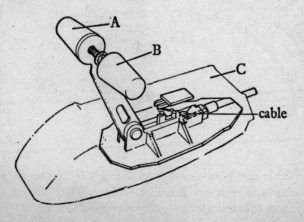

Push cable in to free nipple from slot and thread out cable.

Note: Take the old cable with you to the shop when buying replacement. This kind of cable comes in a variety of lengths. To replace a cable to a:

Trigger: place the fulcrum sleeve on cable housing and thread through fulcrum clip. Prise up trigger control plate, insert cable through hole in trigger casing, and slip nipple into slot on ratchet. Run cable over pulley wheel if you have one, and attach to toggle chain. Shift to 3rd or H. Position fulcrum clip so cable is just slightly slack and tighten. Adjust if necessary as per above.

Twist-grip: insert nipple into slot. Grease and replace spring and ball bearing. Slide twist-grip on handlebar and secure with spring clip. Use a small screwdriver to work the spring clip in. Run cable over pulley wheel if you have one, and attach to toggle chain. Shift selector to 3rd or H and adjust as per above.

Top tube lever: thread cable through slot until nipple catches. Replace cable housing or run cable over pulley wheel, depending on the kind of system you have. Connect cable to anchor bolt, shift to 3rd or H, and adjust as per above. Replace casing, and screw together handle halves.

Shift Control: If you have a bashed or recalcitrant shift control the best thing is to replace it. They are not expensive. To replace

Trigger: disconnect cable (see p 272) and undo bolt B:

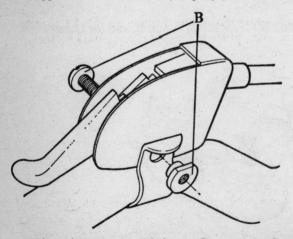

Twist-grip or top tube lever: I recommend replacing with a standard handlebar trigger, which is a much better mechanical

design and more reliable. To remove old unit disconnect cable (see p 272) and undo bolt B:

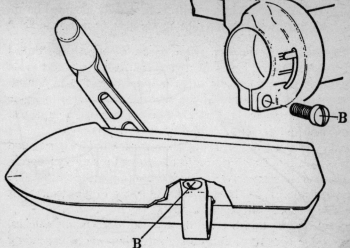

B

Trouble-shooting

No gear at all (pedals spin freely) or slips in and out of gear.

◎ Is gear in proper adjustment (pp 270–71)?

◎ Is cable binding? Check by disconnecting barrel sleeve at hub (p 270) and working cable back and forth through housing. Replace (pp 272–74) if it binds.

◎ Is shift mechanism together and functioning? Stick and twist-grip models are especially prone to slippage after the track for the ball bearing becomes worn:

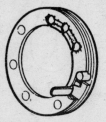

◎ Insides of hubs may have got clogged through the use of too heavy or household oils so that pawls are stuck. Try putting in paraffin or penetrating oil and jiggling everything around. No?

◎ Give up. Remove wheel (p 223) and take to a bike shop.

Derailleur Systems

A derailleur system includes a shift lever, usually mounted on the down tube, but also on the top tube, or the stem, or at the handlebar ends,

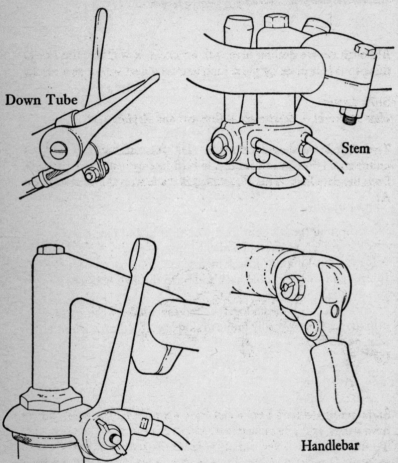

Down Tube

Stem

Top Tube

Handlebar

a thin cable and (sometimes) cable housing, and a front or rear gear changer (derailleur) through which the chain passes. When the shift lever is actuated, the derailleur moves sideways and forces the chain on to a different sprocket:

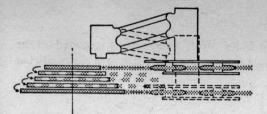

Although we are dealing here with a system, it will simplify everything to take it piece by piece first, and then deal with it as a whole.

Shift Lever
How It Works – Adjustment – Removal and Replacement

The shift lever should be set so that you can move it without undue strain, but be stiff enough to hold fast against spring pressure from the derailleur. This adjustment is made with the tension screw A:

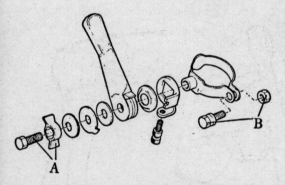

Some tension screws have a slot for a screwdriver (or coin), others have wings, and others have wire loops. All function the same way. To dismantle the lever, simply remove the tension screw. Be sure to keep all parts in order. To remove a down-tube-mounted lever unit, undo bolt B above.

To make a top tube lever unit come off, remove the stem (p 211). A stem-mounted unit comes off by undoing bolts A and B (overleaf):

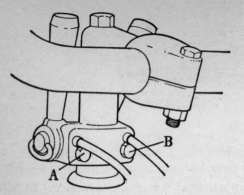

A handlebar end unit requires first removing trim nut A (below):

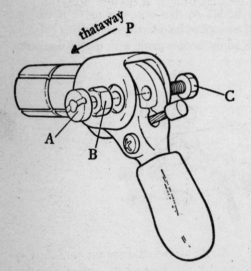

then nut B and screw C. Then loosen Allen screw (6 mm) located at point P inside selector body, and remove unit.

Cables
Adjustment

Cables of derailleur systems are frequently exposed, thin, and take a hell of a beating. Check them often for fraying:

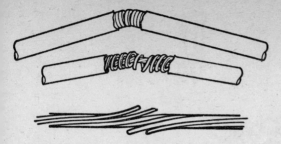

Adjustment is needed when the shift lever has to be pulled all the way back to engage the large sprocket. Place the shift lever forward so that the chain is on the smallest sprocket. Some systems have a barrel adjustor, either at the derailleur or at the shift lever:

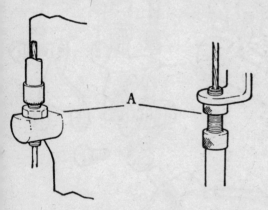

Undo the locknut A and move the barrel adjustor up until slack is removed from cable. If this will not do the job, turn barrel adjustor back down fully home, and reset cable anchor bolt.

All derailleurs, front and back, use a cable anchor bolt or screw to hold the cable. Here is the location (CB) on four representative types (overleaf):

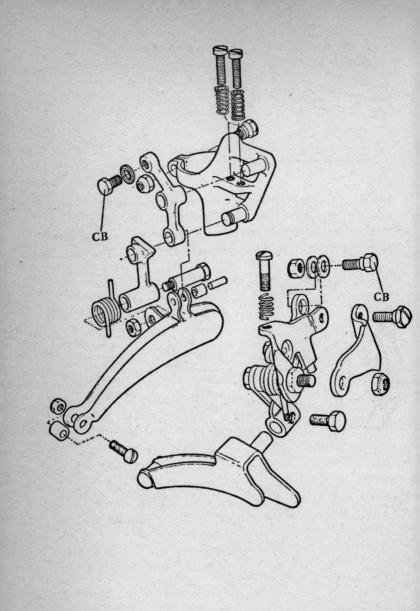

CB

CB

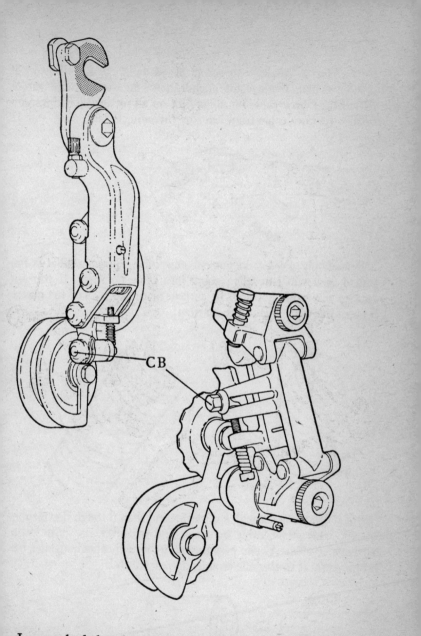

CB

Loosen the bolt, take the slack out of the cable, pulling it through with pliers if necessary, and retighten bolt.

Run chain to smallest sprocket. Screw home barrel adjustor, if you have one. Undo cable anchor bolt and thread cable out of derailleur. Check cable housings (not on all models) for kinks and breaks. Remove cable from lever by threading it out:

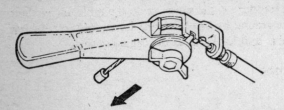

Reassembly: *Note:* do not cut new cable to size until it is installed or it will jam when going into cable housings. If you are cutting new cable housing, be sure to place the jaws of the cutter *between* the wire coils of the housing:

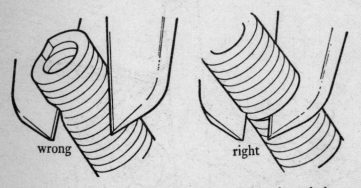

wrong   right

Start by threading through shift lever, and then through down tube tunnel, cable stops, cable housings, and whatever else is in your particular system. As you pass the cable through cable housings, be sure to twist it so that the strands do not unravel:

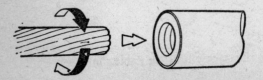

Finish at derailleur. Move shift lever to forward position, make sure that cable housing ferrules (if you have them) are seated properly, and attach cable to cable anchor bolt.

Trouble-shooting

Cable problems are evinced by delayed shifts, or no shifts at all. In any case, the procedure is the same: undo the cable anchor bolt and slide the cable around by hand, looking for sticky spots. Check carefully for fraying, and for kinks in the cable housing.

Derailleurs – Front
How They Work

There is a metal cage through which the chain passes as it feeds on to the front sprocket. The cage can be moved from side to side, and by pressing on the side of the chain, shifts it from sprocket to sprocket:

Virtually all derailleurs are built as a parallelogram. Heh. This design is used to keep the sides of the cage A straight up and down as the cage is moved from side to side on the pivot bolt P:

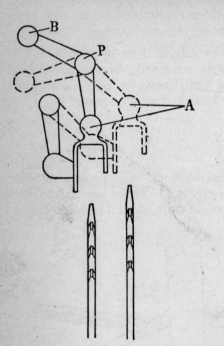

The cage is moved by pulling with a cable at point B, and when the cable is released, spring tension pushes it back. Details may vary, but this is the basic design.

Adjustment

The changer as a whole must be properly positioned, with the outer side of the cage about $\frac{1}{4}$ in to $\frac{1}{2}$ in above the sprocket:

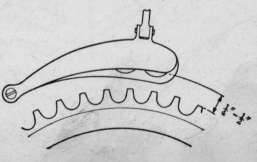

Raise or lower the unit by undoing the mounting bolt (B). The sides of the cage should follow the curvature of the sprocket. Some cages are adjustable in this respect, others (perfectly good ones) are not. Those that are usually swivel on a post between the cage and changer. Sometimes the post comes off the changer, and sometimes off the cage. Either way, there will be a locking bolt like C:

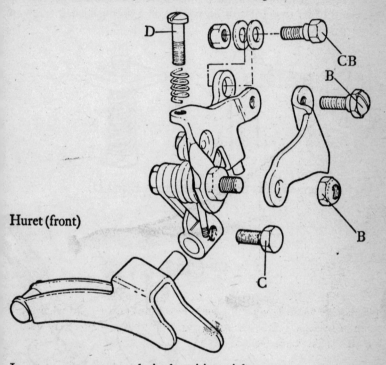

Huret (front)

Loosen, rotate cage to desired position, tighten.

Side to side travel of the cage must be set. First check that cable is properly adjusted (p 278). Front derailleurs fall into two design categories, those with two adjusting screws, and those with one. Look at yours to determine the type.

One-screw derailleurs Run chain to largest back and smallest front sprockets. The first adjustment is made with the cage positioning bolt C (above). Loosen it, and move the cage so that the left side just clears the chain. Tighten. Now loosen the adjusting screw D three or four turns. Run the chain to the smallest back and largest front sprockets.

Using the shift lever, position the cage so that the right side just clears the chain. Turn down adjusting screw D until resistance is felt, and stop.

Two-screw derailleurs If you can't find your adjusting screws easily, get down close to the unit and watch it carefully as you wiggle the shift lever back and forth. Each time the body of the changer reaches the end of its travel it will be resting on a spring-loaded screw or knurled ring:

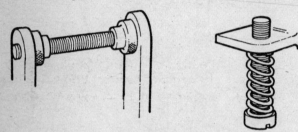

On Campagnolo units they are the screws E and D:

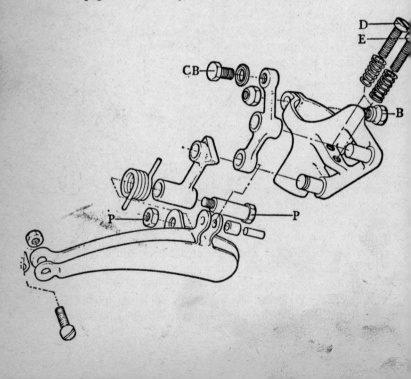

Run chain to largest and smallest front sprockets. It should just clear the left side of the cage. Adjust left side (low gear) adjusting screw (D, opposite) as necessary until it does. Now run chain to smallest back and largest front sprockets. It should just clear the right side of the cage. Adjust right side (high gear) adjusting screw (E, opposite) as necessary until it does. Test operation of gears. Sometimes it is necessary to set the high gear adjustment a little wide to make the chain climb up on the big sprocket – but be cautious, or the chain will throw off the sprocket.

Lubrication

A little petroleum distillate spray or a few drops of oil on the pivot bolts once a month. If the unit becomes particularly dirty, take it off (see below) and soak it clean in paraffin or other solvent.

Replacement

Remove chain (p 259). Undo cable anchor bolt CB and slip off cable (p 282). Now undo mounting bolt(s) B and remove unit:

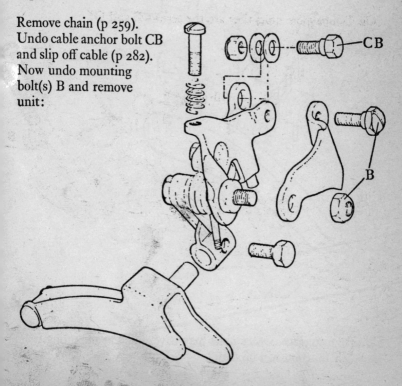

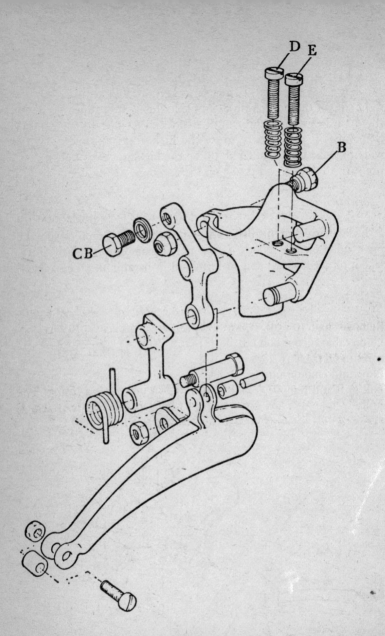

Reverse to replace. Other units may have different mounting bolts but their function will be clear.

Most of the difficulties experienced with the front changer are actually caused by problems elsewhere in the power train. I am assuming that you have already set your changer as per Adjustment, p 284.

Chain rubs side of cage
◎ Is shift lever tight (p 277)?
◎ Can you stop rubbing by diddling with shift lever? For example, the amount of right travel necessary to shift the chain from the left (small) sprocket to the right sprocket may leave the cage too far to the right when the chain is on the large back sprocket, and cause the chain to rub the left side of the cage. In fact, it is frequently necessary with front changers to move the cage back just a trifle after a shift has been completed (p 277).
◎ Is the sprocket warped (p 257)? Or loose (pp 263, 265)?

Chain throws off sprocket
◎ Is shift lever tight (p 277)?
◎ Cage travel may be set too far out. Adjust it slightly (pp 284–87).
◎ Is chain old? Test (p 259).
◎ Are sprocket teeth bent (p 257)?
◎ Are front and rear sprockets in alignment (p 264)?
◎ If chain continually over-rides big front sprocket, take an adjustable end wrench and bend the leading tip of the outside cage in very slightly – about $\frac{1}{16}$ in:

Delayed shifts or no shifts at all

◎ Are pivot bolts clean? Try a little spray or oil.

◎ Is spring intact and in place?

◎ Is cable sticking or broken (p 278)?

◎ If pivot bolts are adjustable, as P is on this Campagnolo unit, undo locknut, back P off one eighth turn, reset locknut.

Derailleurs – Rear
How They Work

As the chain comes back off the bottom of the front sprocket it passes through the rear derailleur on two chain rollers. The cage holding the rollers is fastened to the main body of the changer by a pivot bolt P, and is under constant spring tension so as to keep the chain taut:

The lower roller is the tension roller (TR), the upper the jockey roller (JR). The position of the cage, and hence of the chain on the rear gear cluster, is determined by the changer body:

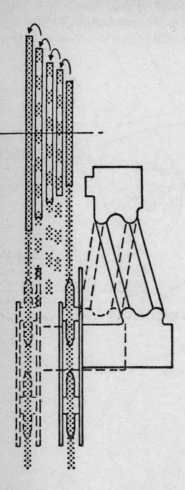

The changer body is under constant spring tension to carry it to the smallest sprocket. It is restrained from doing so by a cable and shift lever.

Derailleurs come in two basic designs, box, like the Huret Allvit or Simplex, and bare parallelogram, like the Campagnolo:

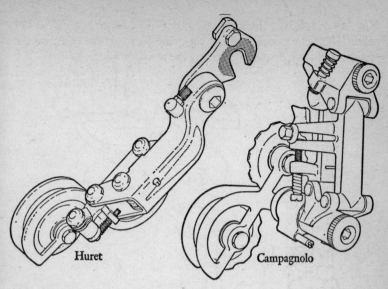

Huret   Campagnolo

Adjustment

Position of changer with respect to bike: The body of the changer should form an angle with the vertical of about 20° to 30°. Many derailleurs are not adjustable in this respect and are held by spring tension against a stop (Campagnolo, Simplex). Others like the Huret Allvit can be adjusted by loosening locknut A and then pivot bolt P (see next page).

Chain rollers should align with the chain:

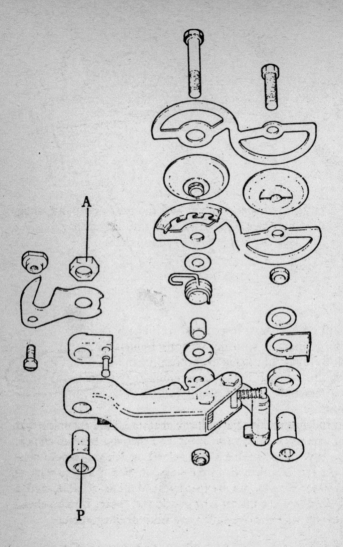

If your derailleur is fastened to a mounting plate, remove it (see opposite), clamp in a vice, and bend it with an adjustable end wrench:

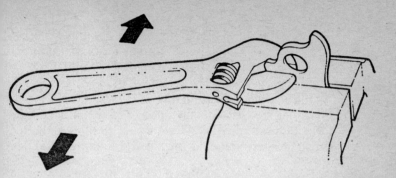

If your derailleur is bolted straight into the frame drop-out, snug wrench around the chain rollers and bend into alignment:

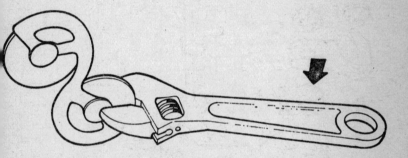

Bear in mind that this is a fairly drastic measure. I am assuming that the derailleur was bent in an accident, and that you have no choice. The alternative is replacement (see below), which you should consider if the old derailleur is on the way out. Box changers such as the Huret or Simplex are inexpensive and quite reliable, and a working derailleur, no matter how plastic and cheap, is miles ahead of a fancy job which is one shift away from disintegration.

Note: if it is a brand-new derailleur which is out of alignment, then the fault is with the frame drop-out. You can bend this into line yourself with an adjustable end wrench the same as you would bend the derailleur mount (above), but this is a very serious matter which should be left to a bike shop. Bending does cause metal fatigue, and if the rear drop-out were to shear unexpectedly you might have an accident.

Side to side travel of derailleur:

First check with chain on smallest rear and biggest front sprockets, and with rear derailleur shift lever all the way forward, that there is only a little slack in the cable. Take up or give slack through barrel adjustor and/or cable anchor bolt (p 278).

The derailleur needs to be set so that side to side travel is stopped short of throwing the chain into the wheel or off the small sprocket. This is done with two adjusting screws or knurled rings, and here is their location on six typical units (high gear – E, low gear – D):

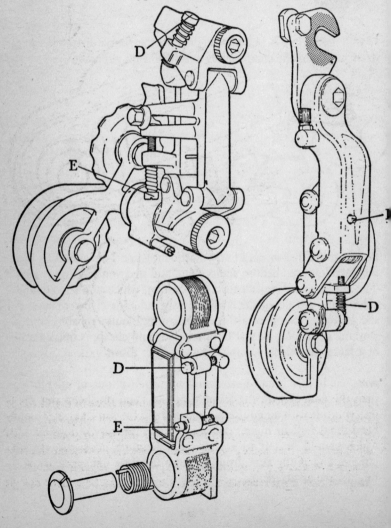

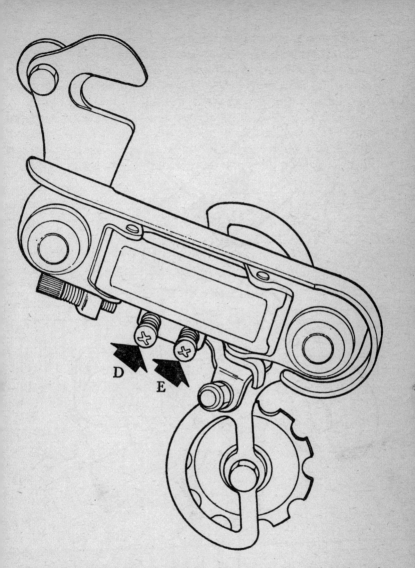

D   E

If your derailleur isn't included here, get down close to it and run it
back and forth, seeing which adjusting screw does what. OK, now:
if derailleur goes too far, throwing chain off, set in position with
shift lever so that jockey wheel lines up with sprocket on the side
you are working on, and turn in appropriate adjusting screw or
knurled ring until resistance is felt. Stop. If derailleur does not go

far enough, back the appropriate
adjusting screw off until it does. If this
does not work, check to make absolutely
sure adjusting screw is backed off. Yes?
Turn back to Trouble-shooting, p 289,
for what to do next.

Spring tension for roller cage:

Spring tension on the roller cage should be sufficient to keep the chain taut when in high gear. No tighter. Excess tension will cause unnecessary drag and rapid wear. On the other hand, too loose a chain will skip. If you have this problem and the chain tension seems OK, check the chain itself for wear (p 259). Worn chains skip.

Adjustment procedure varies according to type of derailleur. Many have the spring set on a hook on the roller cage:

Move it carefully with pliers or screwdriver.

On a Campagnolo unit, first remove wheel. Then remove tension roller by undoing bolt G:

Use one hand to hang on to the chain roller cage and prevent it from spinning, and unscrew the cage stop bolt SB. Now let the cage unwind (about one-half to three-quarters of a turn). Remove cage pivot bolt with Allen wrench and lift off cage. Note that protruding spring end engages one of a series of small holes in the cage. Rotate cage forward until spring fits into next hole (see opposite page). Replace pivot bolt. Wind cage back one-half to three-quarters turn and replace cage stop bolt. Replace tension roller and go back to the races.

On the Simplex, remove screw and dust cap (not on all models) from bottom pivot bolt A. Loosen locknut B, use a metric Allen wrench to turn A clockwise for more tension, counter-clockwise for less, reset locknut.

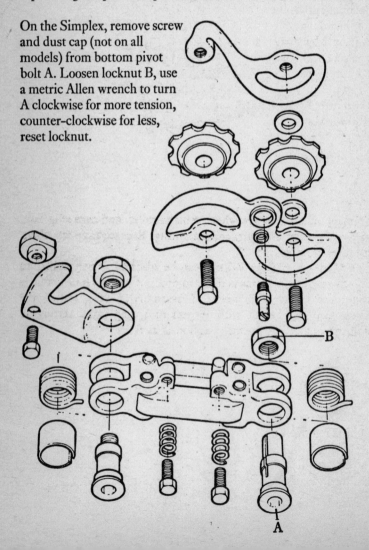

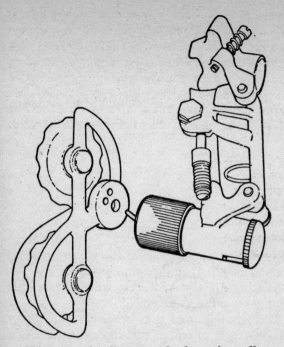

Shimano units: Remove wheel, tension roller, and cage stop bolt. Rotate entire cage one turn against spring. Replace cage stop bolt, tension roller, wheel.

The Madea Sun Tour V-Luxe can be adjusted as per procedure for Shimano units, but this is likely to produce too much or too little tension. For a finer adjustment, disassemble (p 311), noting the relative position of cage with respect to spring catch setting in castellated nut. If the normal position is as A:

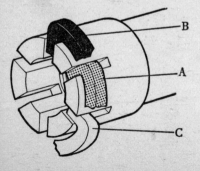

spring tension may be increased by moving spring catch to position B, and decreased by moving to position C.

Lubrication

Petroleum spray: once a month on the jockey and tension rollers, pivot bolts, and cables. Once a year remove and soak clean in solvent.

Oil: a few drops monthly on chain rollers, pivot bolts, cables. Soak clean in solvent every six months. Regrease wheel bearings, if you have them (p 303).

Removal and Disassembly

Disconnect cable from anchor bolt (p 278).

Remove tension roller by undoing bolt G (below, and pp 303, 305). Undo mounting bolt B (Campagnolo) or slacken axle nut and remove adapter screw AS (Huret Allvit) according to how your unit is mounted (opposite and next pages).

Disassembly: the parts that need this regularly are the chain rollers. Otherwise do it only to replace parts. Chain rollers: take off jockey roller (tension roller is already off).

On the Campagnolo this is done by undoing the jockey roller bolt just like the bolt for the tension roller. On the Huret it is necessary to first unsnap the cage spring:

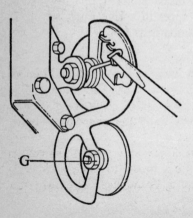

and then unscrew the cage mounting bolt CB:

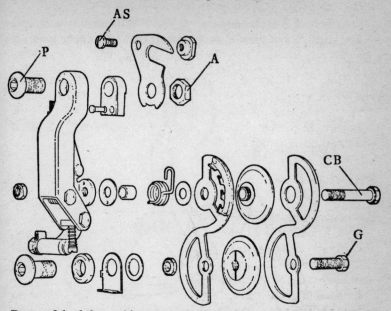

Be careful of those shims and whatnots! Keep track of their order.

There are two kinds of chain rollers, those with washers and a metal sleeve, and those with a hub and ball bearings:

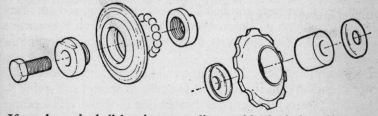

If you have the ball-bearing type, disassemble the hub and remove the bearings. Both types: clean in solvent. Ball-bearing type reassembly: lay one cone flat on table, place chain roller over it. Apply petroleum spray or grease. Put in ball bearings. More lubricant. Screw on second cone.

For the rest of it, the degree of disassembly possible, as well as the technique, varies somewhat from model to model. We'll do six: the Huret, Campagnolo, Simplex, Crane, Eagle and Sun Tour V-Luxe.

Undo locknut A and remove pivot bolt P with Allen wrench (previous page). Keep parts in order. Next: undo the upper lever arm bolt D:

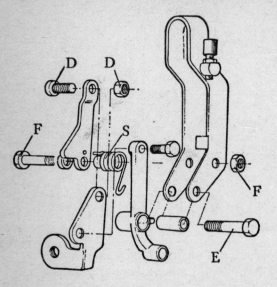

and then lower lever arm bolt E. Remove lever arm, and use pliers to prise spring S off changer body. Then remove bolt F to remove spring S. Replace any parts to be replaced. Clean everything in solvent.

Reassembly: *Note:* Be sure to set all locknuts with sufficient play for smooth derailleur operation. Assemble movement arm spring S, bushing, spacer, at housing and insert bolt F, secure with locknut. Replace spring hook on changer body. Put lever arm in place and secure with bolts D and E.

Reassemble cage (see p 303 for illustrations): mounting bolt CB, outside cage, jockey roller, inside cage (has hooks for cage spring – these face changer body), washer, cage spring and bushing, washer; screw this assembly into the cage mounting plate. Set cage spring with screwdriver. Replace pivot bolt, stop plate, mounting plate. Mount derailleur on frame. Replace tension roller. Re-engage cable. Adjust side to side play as necessary (p 293).

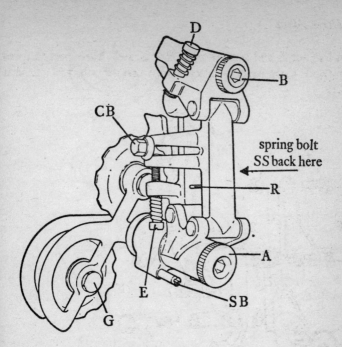

D

B

CB

spring bolt
SS back here

R

A

E

SB

G

The Campagnolo

Hang on to chain roller cage to prevent it from spinning and remove cage stop bolt SB. Let cage unwind (about one-half to three-quarters of a turn). Remove cage pivot bolt A with Allen wrench and lift off cage. Slide out pivot bolt A and spring. Back off high gear adjusting screw E to minimize changer body spring tension, and undo spring bolt SS. Replace parts, clean everything in solvent.

Reassembly: screw in spring bolt SS while holding changer body spring R in position. Replace cage spring and slide in pivot bolt. Put cage on changer with two half-moon sides next to changer. Put nut on pivot bolt. Rotate cage back one-half to three-quarters of a turn and screw in cage stop bolt SB. Replace jockey roller. Mount derailleur on frame. Replace tension roller, cable. Adjust side to side travel as above (p 293).

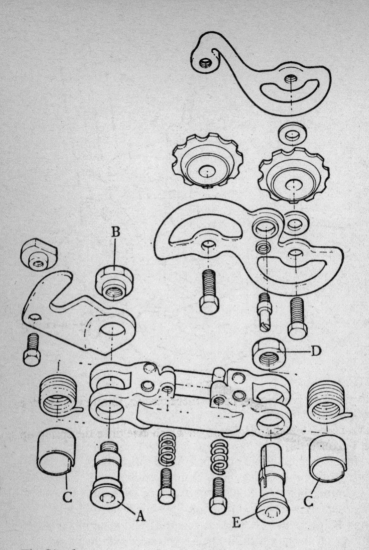

The Simplex

Remove dust caps from pivot bolts A and E. Spring off clips C (not all models). Undo locknut B for main arm pivot bolt A and remove bolt and spring. Ditto for locknut D and cage pivot bolt E. Some Simplex models have a circlip which can be removed so the anchor bolt F will slide out (overleaf):

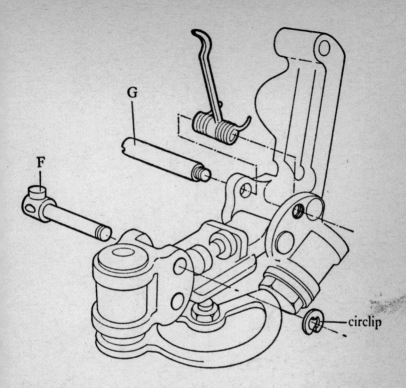

With the outer arm hinged up to relieve tension, unscrew the spring pivot pin G.

Other models lack this feature, in which case prise the spring up with a screwdriver

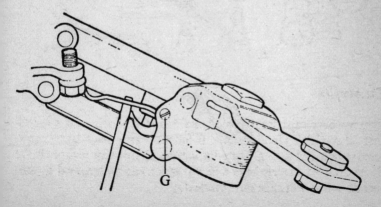

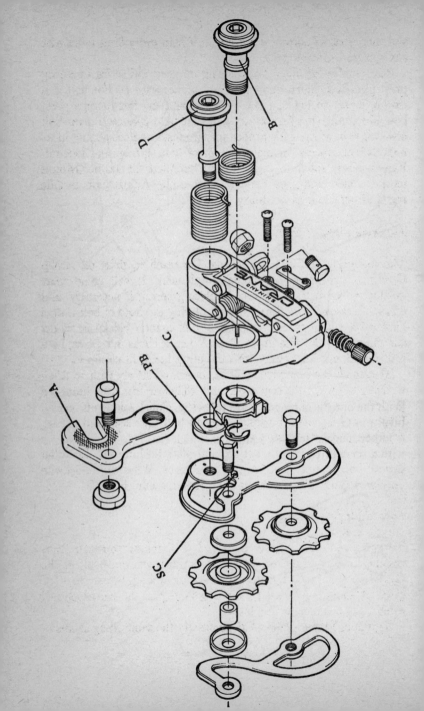

and then unscrew spring pivot pin G. Clean everything in solvent and replace defective parts.

Reassembly: Put main body spring in place and screw in spring pivot pin. Push down outer arm and secure with anchor bolt and circlip, or set spring in place with screwdriver. Put in cage pivot bolt and spring. Put on locknut and cage, and give cage pivot bolt one-half turn to right for proper spring tension before setting locknut. Repeat process for main arm pivot bolt, spring, and locknut. Fasten jockey roller to cage. Mount derailleur on frame. Mount tension roller, and then connect shift cable. Adjust side to side travel of derailleur as necessary (p 293).

The Crane (*opposite page*)

The mounting bolt B has a spring. To reach it, prise off circlip C with a screwdriver or similar implement. It will come apart quickly. Clean parts in solvent, replacing spring if necessary, and grease. Reassemble by fitting spring, placing the head of bolt B on a hard surface, and twisting the bracket A counter-clockwise whilst simultaneously pressing downwards. When it clicks into place, hold it firm with one finger and, with the other hand, fit circlip C.

To remove the cage pivot bolt D, back it off slowly with an Allen wrench, and when the cage stop catch SC clears the little bump on the frame, let the chain roller cage unwind. Finish taking off bolt D. Remove spring, plate bushing PB, and bolt D. Clean and grease, replacing parts if necessary.

Reassembly: fit bolt D, spring, and plate bushing PB. Fit roller cage to bolt D and turn down $1\frac{1}{2}$ to 2 turns. Wind cage clockwise until stop catch SC passes bump on frame, secure bolt PB.

Eagle SS (*next page*)

To undo mounting bracket pivot bolt PB, remove dustcap D by twisting off or prising up with thin screwdriver, prise off circlip C, and unwind bracket gently. When reassembling, be sure that CC catch on mounting bracket plate is wound past the corresponding catch CD on the derailleur body.

To remove the cage bolt CB do exactly the same thing as above.

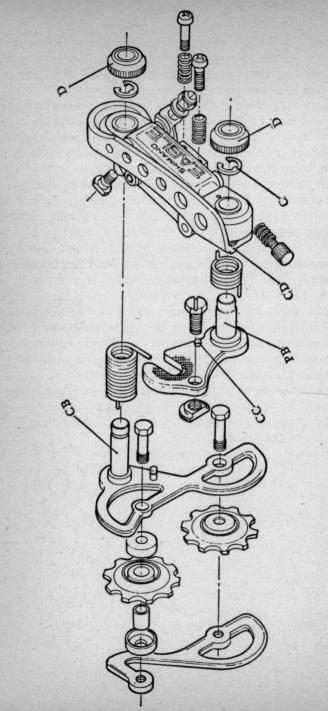

To undo mounting bracket pivot bolt PB, slack off locknut N and then back out bolt PB.

To remove cage bolt CB, first undo cage stop screw SS and allow cage to unwind. Next, while holding cage and main body together, undo cage bolt CB and withdraw. Note position of spring S in slots of cage axle A, and of cage relative to main body. Separate cage and main body. Withdraw spring S, noting which of two holes the end catch fits into. Clean and grease, replacing parts as necessary.

Reassembly: place in spring S, fitting to appropriate hole. Refit cage. If the spring tension of the cage has been weak, start from a position anti-clockwise of the original, and if it has been too strong, from a position clockwise of the original. A little diddling will achieve what you want. Fit cage bolt CB. Wind cage clockwise until cage stop screw SS can be fitted.

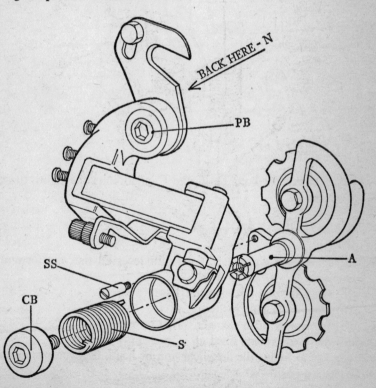

Trouble-shooting
Derailleur is sticky, won't always shift, sometimes shifts unexpectedly

◉ Is shift lever working smoothly but with enough friction to hold derailleur in place (p 277)?

◉ Are cables sticking (p 278)?

◉ Are pivot bolts lubricated and clean? On some models (Campagnolo, Huret, among others) these bolts can be adjusted:

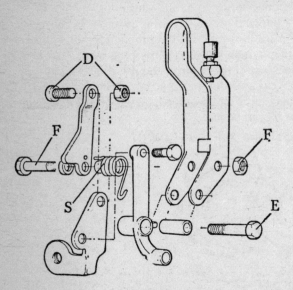

Undo locknuts for bolts D, E, and F, undo bolts one eighth turn; reset locknuts.

Derailleur will not go far enough

◉ Is cable slightly slack with shift lever all the way forward (p 296)?

◉ Are adjusting screws properly set (p 293)?

◉ Does cable slide easily (p 278)?

◉ Is pivot or main changer spring broken?

◉ Are chain rollers lined up with chain (p 293)?

◉ Try to wiggle the derailleur unit by hand. Can you push it to the desired position?

Yes:

works are gummed up. Clean in solvent and lubricate with spray or oil. Adjust (not possible with all models) by undoing pivot bolts one eighth turn and resetting (opposite page).

No:

if it won't reach the big rear cog, remove mounting plate and bend it in a vice.

if it won't reach the little rear cog, bend mounting plate, or put in shims at the mounting bolt.

Chain throws off cogs

◎ Are adjusting screws set properly (p 293)?
◎ Are any teeth worn or bent (pp 257, 264)?
◎ Is chain good (p 259)?
◎ If chain is skipping, is spring tension for roller cage sufficient (p 299)?
◎ Is roller cage aligned with chain (p 293)?

P is the chain pulley, one being placed at either end of the crank-shaft, and capable of freely revolving thereon, except when jambed by the shallow rollers, R. These rollers lie in a cavity formed by a circular recess in the pulley and a steel disc, D, which is shaped off on four sides so as to form alternately hollows and wedges. The disc, D, is a fixture on the crank-shaft. When the latter moves forward in the direction shown by the arrows, the rollers, R, are jambed between the disc and the inner surface of the pulley, P, and the whole of the parts, pulley included, run solid. The machine is then driven. On the contrary, when D is turned in the opposite direction, the rollers pass into the hollow spaces, and there simply rotate without jambing. This also happens when the crank-shaft, with the disc D, is held stationary as in running down hill, in which case the pulley P runs on, rotating the rollers in the hollows as already explained.

Power Train – Trouble-shooting Index
Noises

First make sure that noise is coming from power train by coasting bike. If noise continues it is probably a brake (p 170) or hub (p 241) problem. If noise persists, try to determine if it comes from the front (crankset), the chain, or the rear sprocket(s). Do this by disconnecting the chain (p 259) and spinning the various parts.

Grinding noises

Front:
- ◎ Bottom bracket bearings OK (pp 253, 255)?
- ◎ Pedal bearings OK (p 247)?
- ◎ Chain rubbing derailleur?
- ◎ Front sprocket rubbing cage or chainstays (p 257)?

Back:
- ◎ Wheel bearings OK (p 242)?
- ◎ Freewheel OK (p 264)?

Clicks or Clunks

One for every revolution of crankset:
- ◎ Pedal tight (p 247)?
- ◎ Crank(s) tight (p 249)?
- ◎ Bottom bracket bearings OK (pp 253, 255)?
- ◎ Are teeth on sprocket(s) bent (pp 257, 264)?

Two or three for every revolution of the crankset:
- ◎ Are teeth on rear sprocket(s) bent (p 264)?
- ◎ Is chain worn or frozen (p 259)?

No go. Pedals and chain spin uselessly:
3-speeds, see p 275.
10-speeds, see p 267.

Delayed shifts, no shifts, or not all gears:
3-speeds, see p 275.
10-speeds, see p 312.

For all other problems consult the trouble-shooting section for the part which is malfunctioning.

Tricycle carriers like this late 1800s model
are what we need now.

6. Dream * Ramode * Sunfighter * Dream * Birthright *

This is a chapter about bikeways and dreams and transportation wonderlands in which we go and are carried about quickly and with ease. By way of living on the wild side I want first to reproduce the American version of this chapter:

Everybody has dreams and here is one of mine: cars are banned from central areas of all major metropolitan regions. Each city provides free bicycles (with adjustable seats and handlebars) scattered about to be used as needed. Because cities can buy enough bikes at a time to make special orders feasible, each city has a bike with a unique and readily identifiable frame design. All bolts and screws have left-hand threads, like the light bulbs in subway stations, to discourage the stealing of parts for private use. There are repair centres throughout town, as well as special racks in which bikes in need of servicing can be left.

Schemes something like this are already working with a fair degree of success in Europe. Amsterdam is a blizzard of public and private bicycles. The chances for such a sequence here are remote. There is just too much money to be made from cars and petroleum products. That you and I pay a stiff price in life and health for this profit-making is immaterial.

In the struggle of bike versus car the bike emerges an obvious winner in economic and ecological terms. Logic would suggest that the bicycle be favoured as a mode of transport, but as anybody knows this is not so. This is the age of the motor car. It is also a period in which ecological causes have become as sound as mother's milk. Hardly a Sunday goes by without some politician hopping on the ecological bandwagon and puffing his way on a bike through the opening of a special 'Bikeway'. But rare indeed is the politician who rides to work.

A classic example was provided by John V. Lindsay, Mayor of New York, who led a parade of bicyclists for fourteen blocks before returning to his limousine. The occasion was the creation of 'Bikeways' on some major avenues. What this means is that there are little signs posted along the avenues which say 'Bikeway'. Practically speaking, these make absolutely no difference whatsoever, as any bike rider who has to mix it up with NYC traffic can testify.

All is not gloom however, and the 'Bikeways' boom has a lot to recommend it. Bikeways come in different classes:

Class I — A separate lane for bikes only.
Class II — A restricted lane in a street with no autos allowed.
Class III — Streets with slotted speed bumps to slow down but not eliminate autos.
Class IV — Painted lane on a pedestrian path.
Class V — Signs on regular thoroughfares which say 'Bikeway'.

Class I and II bikeways are the only meaningful types, and where implemented have been a great success. The city of Davis, California, for example, has had Class I bikeways on the University of California campus, and Class II bikeways throughout town, since 1966. Davis has a population of 24,000 and approximately 18,000 bicycles. One survey found that during rush hour 40 per cent of the traffic was bicycles, and 90 per cent of the riders were adults.

There are approximately 15,000 miles of bike paths in the US of A, with 200,000 'planned' for 1975. These come in all shapes and sizes. Many national parks such as the Cape Cod National Seashore in Massachusetts feature Class I bikeways. Wisconsin has a 300-mile mixed class bikeway through cities, towns, back roads, abandoned railroad beds, and the like. A number of towns make instant bikeways by closing parks to autos on weekends and selected weekday nights. A really enterprising town is Littleton, Colorado, which created 23 miles of bikeways. One side of the street is reserved and specially marked for two-way bicycle traffic. Cars are not even allowed to park on that side of the street, and violators get tickets. So do bike riders who disobey traffic regulations. The Littleton venture has been a great success (they should have about 50 miles of bikeways now), and inspired by this example other cities in Colorado — Boulder, Lakewood, Aurora, Denver, Englewood, Northglenn, Aspen, and Fort Collins — have either created or are creating bikeways.

Bikeways are a good idea. The Bicycle Institute of America, 122 East 42nd Street, New York, NY 10017, will send you free a blizzard of information and workable plans for how to get bikeways in your community. Despite the fact that some bikeways are sheer tokenism distinguishable in no way whatsoever from a regular highway or street, there are some good ones, and the idea is sound, especially if you push for Class I and II bikeways. I hope that you will engage in such activity.

At the same time the shape of things to come may be a little hairier than Sunday rides with Mr Lindsay. No major concessions will be made to cyclists as long as the automotive and petro-chemical industries hold the economic clout. A glimpse into the future has been provided recently in France.

Paris is famous for traffic. Cars are everywhere, moving in a constant rushing stream, and creating an incredible din. Cars have the right of way and pedestrians have to fend for themselves. In Paris the auto is King. Mr Pompidou even announced, 'We must adapt Paris to the automobile and renounce a certain aesthetic idealism.'

Not all Parisians agree. They want alternate means of transportation and an end to noisy traffic jams. On 23 April 1972, the organizations Les Amis de la Terre, Comité Anticuléaire de Paris, Comité de Libération Ecologique, Etre, Objectif Socialiste, and the Federation of Users of Public Transport staged a massive bike-in to dramatize their demands. It was beautiful.

Some 10,000 bicycles of every conceivable type and condition rendezvoused at Porte Dauphine. A few forward-looking Frenchmen showed up on roller skates! Harried police tried to route the demonstrators to exterior streets, but the procession went straight down the Champs-Elysées to the Place de la Concorde, up the Blvd St Germain, and on to Bois de Vincennes (a park). Bus loads of riot police tried to stem the tide on the Champs-Elysées but failed, possibly because they did not want to be violent in full public view. As the procession wound along replete with signs and streamers, some sympathetic motorists blocked side streets with their cars to add to the confusion, and pedestrians shouted 'Bon Courage!'. One spoilsport who refused to be stymied ran into several bicycles with his car. Surrounded by several thousand angry bicyclists he paid damages on the spot.

When the cyclists reached Bois de Vincennes, they were greeted with victory hymns by the Grand Magic Circus troupe. An hour of dancing, singing, and good times followed. Then the CRS riot police arrived. Helmeted troops on motorcycles charged the crowd and tear gas flew. Efforts at reason failed. About fifty people were arrested. The CRS used the shelter of the woods to smash up bicycles with their nightsticks.

Now Les Amis de la Terre and other groups are pressing on with their demands: the creation of pedestrian streets*; one million free bicycles at the disposition of Parisians; non-polluting public transportation à la Rome; the closing of Paris to more automobile traffic, and a halt to the creation of inner-city expressways. *Yeah!*

The French experience points the way to real victories. Theirs was an *ecological* demonstration stressing the needs of both pedestrians and bicyclists. Bikeways are not enough. What is needed is the elimination of polluting transportation. In urban areas the car accounts for up to 85 per cent of the air pollution, and for 85 per cent of the noise pollution. The absolute elimination of internal combustion engines from urban areas is the practical solution which benefits everybody. The bicycle and roller skate are wonderful pollution-free adjuncts to such a campaign.

As the existence of good bikeways attests, it is not necessary to get tear-gassed or clubbed in order to get something done. But the industries with vested interests in maintaining a motor age are large and powerful to the extreme. Petro-chemical companies are a law unto themselves. They routinely buy and sell governments. Steel, mining, rubber, textiles, cement, and plastics are automotive-related industries, each with a profit and make-work situation to protect. Each, curiously enough, is a major pollutor in its own right. Ultimately, the only solution to this vicious conglomerate of vested interest and power will be to take the profit out of their activities by nationalizing all transportation – bicycles, cars, trucks, buses, trains, aeroplanes – and all related service industries. In the technology-oriented US of A this is economic and psychological revolution.

What we are more likely to see is a long series of minor reforms, tokenism, and other concessions to public unrest. If we are lucky, there will be a major smog disaster in which thousands of people will suddenly die all at once, instead of piecemeal as they do now. This might spur improvements which would ultimately save more lives than were lost. But the power of vested interests in maintaining a motor age is such that there will probably be a long, drawn-out struggle, and concessions will not be won without a fight.

So don't be too surprised if you are beaned at a bike-in by a club-swinging cop who calls you a dirty communist, and don't back off because of it. *You have a right to live.* Arguments which present the roller skate or bicycle as more economical, efficient,

*They have some now.

320

etc, are all well and good, but the situation is extremely simple: present transportation systems are filling the air with deadly fumes and noise and recklessly wasting a dwindling supply of natural resources. *They are killing and injuring people.* You have a right to live – it is your birthright – but you will have to fight for it.

Do it!

Lucky you! You don't have to ride around in demonstrations and be clubbed by police. In fact, if the bitter resistance to coercion that the British have demonstrated in the past is any guide, trying for improvements by making trouble is a sure way to get nothing done at all. But this is not relevant, because, seemingly, the British government and assorted municipal and county authorities are responsive to the needs of the public, and can be depended upon to act in a more or less rational if not always competent fashion. As an American I find this degree of civilization so novel that I am a bit mistrustful, a feeling jaundiced by having a London bobby try to kick spokes out of my bicycle wheel in the course of a peaceful (I have been to enough to know the difference) demonstration. But he was clearly the rotten apple in an otherwise good barrel. The case for designing integrated transportation systems with special provision for cyclists, motorists, and pedestrians as being of great benefit to the overall community and society is so solid, with absolute evidence immediately to hand, that it seems only reasonable to presuppose that any planning organization, once appraised of the facts, would be appropriately influenced.

Stevenage, Hertfordshire, a town of some 72,000 souls situated 32 miles north of London, is a transport dream-world, a kind of magical Walt Disney fantasy in which everything flows with perfect smoothness and problems evaporate. Stevenage was the first designated New Town under the provisions of the New Towns Act, 1946, and development is through a Development Corporation whose expenditure is directly financed by the state with loans on a sixty-years' repayment basis at the current rate of interest. Most or all of the credit for the design and engineering of the town, and in particular the transport systems, goes to Eric Claxton, now retired as Chief Engineer for the Stevenage Development Corporation, and a man who must be reckoned a one-of-a-kind genius.

With a population of 72,000 on 6,000 acres, Stevenage has a population density greater than that of Central London. Yet there is not one single traffic, cycle, or pedestrian stoplight or sign in the entire town. The flow of these different kinds of traffic, even at rush-hour periods, is so smooth and even that there does not appear to be anybody around. What rush hour? one asks, looking around for queues or packs of traffic. There are none. There is no congestion because nothing ever holds still.

The basic reason for the success of the Stevenage system is that there has been the design of a *total* transport system in which pedestrian, cycle and moped, and motor vehicle carriageways are separate and never conflict. It is possible to drive a motorcar throughout the town without once encountering a cycle or pedestrian. As a result the average speed of rush hour traffic is 20 mph, double the average of other cities, and better still than the average in major metropolitan regions, such as London. You are guaranteed a parking space right near your destination except on the two Saturdays before Christmas. Bus services operate to and from the absolute centre of town, literally only steps away from shopping and munici-pal centres. There are no dwellings more than five minutes' walk from a bus stop. Most are much closer.

If you are cycling it is also possible to go anywhere you wish in town via the cycleways or footpaths (on which pedestrians, cycles, and mopeds have mingled freely and without incident for twenty years), and never encounter a motor vehicle. For pedestrians, in addition to a comprehensive network of footpaths, the town centre and many sub-centres are completely pedestrianized, with no vehicle traffic and complete protection from the weather.*

The official cycleway system is 25 miles long, and is shared by all types of cycles, mopeds up to 50cc capacity, and pedestrians. The cycleways frequently run alongside main roads but are separated by grass verges and trees from both the roads and footpaths. There are in addition a number of cross-town cycleway links which run independently of roads. Some were originally country lanes from which vehicular traffic has been withdrawn. Additionally, cycles make free use of over 100 miles of footpaths so that most cycle journeys are door-to-door. There are no rules or regulations (and hence no need for the police to concern themselves with traffic

*Traffic bans increase business in shopping areas. The Organization for Econ-omic Cooperation and Development reports that vehicle bans increased business by 25–50 per cent in Vienna, 15–35 per cent in Norwich, and 10–15 per cent in Rouen (1972).

regulation) governing the use of the cycleways and pedestrian footpaths, no 'cycles must or must not'. Cyclists are free to use the vehicle carriageways if they prefer. The existing cycleway system is so attractive, however, that only the odd racer in training buzzing along at 25 mph plus chooses to mix it up with the cars.

The different types of carriageways are kept separate through the generous use of underpasses. These are a study in sensitive design and architecture. An overpass for cycles must rise at least 16 ft over the road, necessitating either a long or steep gradient. An underpass for cycles only requires a 7 ft 6-in headroom. By excavating to a depth of only two metres, and using the excavation material to raise the road gently by one metre, the differences in gradient are still further minimized. The cycleways are normally 12 ft wide and carry two-way traffic. Construction is similar to a footpath, with minimal lighting and drainage. The main costs derive from the earthworks resulting from segregation at intersections with car-

The Stevenage roundabout

riageways and the concrete underpasses which carry the carriageways over the cycleways.

Equal in importance with underpasses to the success of the Stevenage system is the frequent use of ingeniously improved roundabouts, described here as part of the Good Ideas To Keep In Mind Campaign.

In the classic roundabout vehicles must fairly well stop before entering, and the tendency is for journey paths through the round-about to conflict, creating four cross-roads where formerly there was only one (as shown below).

The 'classic' roundabout

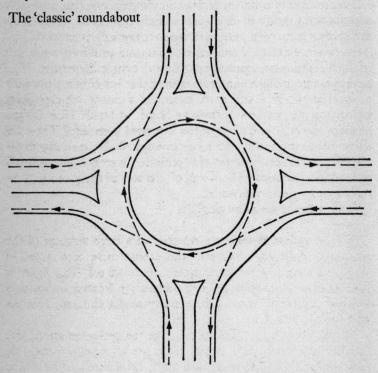

When the right of way of vehicles already on the roundabout is observed, traffic flow is improved, but heavy traffic from one road will impede lighter traffic from another for long periods of time.

Under the Stevenage system the cross-road conflict points are re-placed by weaving areas (p 323). Before arriving at the roundabout the motorist positions him/herself in the correct lane for the intended route. It has been found that at busy periods most of the motorists know where they are going. Those few who need to read signs before selecting a lane can manage a shuffle without difficulty.

Vehicles then enter the roundabout at between 15 and 25 mph, the same speed (by design) as traffic already on the roundabout. Merging is simple, and under the Stevenage system vehicles may go before or after vehicles already on the roundabout as long as there is no abrupt dislocation. Vehicles turning left have no problem at all and can just motor through. For the sceptics, I can only say that I have tried this system myself and it works like a charm.

The benefits of a system such as Stevenage's are often intangible and not easily reckoned on a balance sheet. What is the worth of the fact that there is never, ever, obstruction or aggravation in travelling? That whole series of abrasions, conflicts, and problems for which most of us armour up each day just doesn't exist in Stevenage. What price a mother's peace of mind, knowing that her children can walk or cycle anywhere – and never encounter a motor vehicle? Sixty per cent of the workers in town go home for lunch. How do you measure the value and effect of this increased home life? These are alterations in the quality of life, perhaps describable as similar to the relaxed pastural peacefulness of a 'primitive' society – but with full technological benefits! The worth of this sort of thing can only be determined by each individual.

Other benefits are more tangible:

◎ The cycleways serve the interests of a large segment of the population aged six to sixteen who cannot drive cars. 1,420 of 16,760 children (8·4 per cent) cycle daily to school. This figure is low because Stevenage's primary schools are located within easy walking distance of home. Of secondary school children, 17·4 per cent cycle to school.

◎ Such few accidents as do occur on the cycleways are minor. Pedestrians, cyclists, and moped riders are all equally vulnerable and take equal pains to avoid each other. Stevenage's safety record is four casualties per 1,000 population per year as against a national average which is more than 50 per cent greater. The direct saving in medical service costs is considerable, to say nothing of life and limb.

◎ By encouraging cycling and walking, the Stevenage system promotes mild exercise. There are 4,000 regular cyclists, about 11 per cent of the people working in Stevenage, and 10,000 recreational and shopping cyclists. This health benefit may seem minor, but for many people it is their only exercise, and as such may extend their longevity by up to five years.

⊚ An immense amount of time is saved. There is a car ownership rate per household of ·80, which is no lack of cars. People walk and cycle because it works better. Stevenage fairly well buries the utterances of cynics who point out that due to population increase there has actually been a decline in the use of cycles, despite increased sales. The national rate of decline 1966–71 was 39 per cent, but Stevenage's was 29 per cent. And as the cycle is utilized increasingly for recreation and sport this decline will reverse.

As a New Town, Stevenage has had a considerable freedom in designing and implementing a transportation system. But the difficulties encountered with already existing towns are surmountable. For example, Peterborough is currently creating a 72-mile-long system of cycleways at a cost of £1·7 million. The cycleways are four types: cycle path, completely separate from motor traffic; cycle lane, by the side of a road and separated by a painted line or kerb; cycle route, low traffic streets marked with signs giving priority to cyclists; and cycle trail, through park, countryside and forest, and utilizing bridle paths, disused railway tracks and footpaths. The proper cycle path is the ideal of course, and at £1·50 per square yard, one-sixth the per square yard cost of a carriageway, with a 12-ft wide cycle path yielding five times the carrying capacity of a 24-ft carriageway, it is a bargain. In existing built-up areas however, cycle lanes, routes, and trails are often a better compromise. Construction of a proper cycle path can await general redevelopment although sometimes, if there is no suitable alternative, it cannot. This costs, but in the end a lot less than sticking with what we have, and can be spread out over a period of time. For the most part, a great deal of special provision for cyclists can be made right away, with minimal construction and expense.

Action. Write to your local authority and ask them what they are doing to encourage cycling. What about cycleways? What about parking for cycles? Sixteen cycles will fit into the same space as one car.

Design a cycleways system for your area. Mark on a map all the schools, factories, offices, shops, and places of interest that need to be served by a cycleway. Work out routes from residential areas to these areas which are as direct as possible, going along back streets, footpaths, bridlepaths, etc, and necessitate the minimum of construction. Some conflicts are unavoidable, and once the plan is accepted, will be resolved with traffic lights, bridges, or underpasses. Provide for recreational cycling and access to leisure facilities and the surrounding countryside. Cycle the routes yourself. Note where parking should be provided and what major problems, if any, exist. You can get help and advice with this project from

> All Change to Bikes,
> Greater London House,
> Hampstead Road,
> London NW1 7QP.
> Tel: 01-387 0116

and do not hesitate to call on them, because promoting cycling is their job.

Once you have completed your plan/proposal, send it to your local authority asking for their comments, and send copies to the All Change to Bikes and your local newspapers. If you have done your homework – and the All Change to Bikes will inundate you with a blizzard of information on the advantages of cycleways – you'll get action. Such an enterprise might somehow seem childish – and indeed, it is a perfect school project – but at the moment it is the most useful thing you can do. So please,

DO IT!

What a safe note to end on. And dull. Another go:

An integrated traffic system such as Stevenage's is a masterful study in efficiency where each modality of transport complements the other. The question arises: should efficiency be the prime value? What about the need to preserve health, or to expend energy wisely? Stevenage clearly shows that the car is not the enemy of the bicycle unless they share the same road. Create an integrated system, and this problem evaporates. But the car remains an enemy of man, a tool with a backlash of millions of dead and grievously injured. More Britons have died in accidents since the inception of the auto than in World War II. The simple fact is that humans cannot master the safe operation of motor vehicles. And even if they could, the motor vehicle is interdictable on account of air and noise pollution and energy waste.

We may mourn the loss of an early morning run into a rising sun, the thrill and satisfaction of fast motoring, the love and fury we feel for our machines – but the price is too stiff. There is a curious rationale: the actions of a Jack-the-Ripper style sniper or mass murderer, while a predictable outcome of the society, are seen as aberrant and 'unacceptable', whereas the thousands killed and mangled by motor vehicles are seen as unhappy but necessary by-product casualties of transport needs.

Bilge. It is not a necessity on two counts. One, that we do not need such mobility, and two, even if we insist on having it, there are other, safer ways to get it.

Let us start with the idea of banning the motor vehicle as an unwarranted assault on human rights and life. Many must feel that such an action would have a severe price in depreciated quality of life, and is completely unrealistic. Not so. The precise point is that an excess of transport efficiency is not good for us, but bad. We do not own our transport; it owns us.

Mobility and the nuclear family are factors of alienation, con-comitants of an industrial society. The extended kinship family is not necessarily the model for relationships, and relationships are not needed by everyone, but relationships must exist for most people most of the time. An industrial society, particularly a hyper-industrial society such as ours, inhibits relationships. Men and women are sorted into worker and non-worker groups. Employ-ability is privileged, and non-workers, who include females, the old, the foolish, the poor, the incompetent, and the uncooperative of whatever form and for whatever reason, are discriminated against. They simply have fewer human rights.

It is the nature of industrial processes that it is difficult to employ groups or families or even couples. For the sake of worker mobility, males are given the dominant central economic role in a nuclear family, and females, less desirable in the labour pool, are made accessories.

So there is a situation where a large segment of the society has been relegated inferior status and rights, and where even the structure of relationships is subordinate to industrial needs. And the reward is not job satisfaction, or a furtherance of the interests of the society, but consumerism. The use of the products and services created by this particular method of organizing society. And, quite simply, we have no choice. We do not reap benefits; rather, we are compelled to adopt certain behaviours if we wish to live. We do not own the machines and the technology and the products therefrom; they own us.

It is my feeling that some loss of mobility would be a good thing. Negatively, in that employment for the sake of consumerism is worthless and destructive; and, positively, in that it may encourage relationships and foster wholesome goals together with greater self-awareness. The consumer society is built on promises and a hoax of future progress. Expectancy blinds us to the realities of the moment. The 'primitive' societies that functioned without technological innovation or expectancy that the future would be different enjoyed a far richer here and now.

But it goes deeper than not perpetuating the evils of consumerism. If the members of the society are to engage management and share privileges and responsibilities, there must be a relative equality of experience. The creation of privilege – in this example, mobility – for the purpose of administering, coordinating, or whatever worthwhile activity, is a terrible mistake which confers discriminatory power. And power corrupts and perpetuates. It is more important to maintain power equality.

Ivan D. Illich in his wonderful book *Tools for Conviviality* (Calder & Boyars Ltd, 18 Brewer Street, London W1; £2·25) says that the upper limit of transportation technology should be the bicycle. A genuinely socialist society cannot support anything more advanced. Properly limited technologies 'serve politically inter-related individuals rather than managers'.

The point of this discussion is to show that 'alternate transportation' does not necessarily mean just another way of doing the same thing. This is more than a matter of perspective, because the form, i.e., the transport engineering, and the content, the culture, are interrelated. If we are conscious of the desirability of other goals besides employment mobility, then transport design may be influenced in evolution.

But I. D. Illich directs his ideas towards influencing the potential lifestyle for countries which have not yet industrialized. No one standing by the endless streams of motorcars blaring through our cities and countryside can realistically hope that it will end quickly. The energy crisis is a boondoggle, a hoax, not the harbinger of a new and different time, but a manipulation by the petro-chemical companies and governments to maintain consumerism – and power.

So I think the fight against the motor vehicle has to be simple. Not an abandonment of mobility, which is too large a pill to swallow, but that mobility is attainable by safer means.

The hunting of game in countries like America and Italy is a process in which a considerable number of people are hurt. However, most of the injured are participants rather than innocent bystanders. The victim of the motor vehicle is all too often blameless in the case of an accident, and defenceless in the case of pollution. These are real issues: the Vienna inter-city ban has reduced air pollution levels by 70 per cent; a 1971 closing of New York City's Madison Avenue resulted in a threefold drop in carbon monoxide levels. In Stevenage there is a casualty rate of four per 1000 population as against a national average which is more than 50 per cent greater. There is no such thing as a 'right' to endanger life, and especially when no offsetting advantage is gained by so doing. In urban areas the motorcar hinders mobility. Leaving aside health and safety considerations, it plain just doesn't work.

Alternatives to the motor vehicle must be utilized, and most exist already. Trains, buses, cycles, roller skates, electric- and steam-powered low-speed delivery vehicles are more than adequate – they are better. At present motor vehicles are very heavily subsidized by the general public, and if the users of this form of transport were to bear the full cost they could not afford it. Support must now go to alternative (and cheaper) methods. Trains and buses must have racks for the free carrying of cycles. Stations and terminals must have overnight storage facilities for cycles. Parks must have cycle paths. Instead of squandering funds on motorways and heavy streets and traffic regulation, cities must provide free, simple, easily adjustable bicycles for inter-city use. And as for the motorcar, in urban areas

Ban it.

Index

Richard Ballantine has no academic education he considers worth mentioning. He has engaged in, for greater and lesser durations, a stimulating variety of occupations and professions, among them busboy, chef, shooting gallery attendant, electronics technician, door-to-door salesman, book editor, community organizer and anarchist. He is the co-author, with John Cohen, of *Africa Addio* (1966), a noble attempt to rationalize a bloodcurdling film of the same title; and, with Joel Griffiths, of *Silent Slaughter* (1972), a survey of radiation hazards, with emphasis on emissions from electronic products such as radar, television sets and microwave ovens. Forthcoming epics include *The Moroccan Journey*, an article on skiing in the Atlas Mountains; *Alone*, a book of short stories; and, with Dr Shyam Singha, *The Book of Health*, a detailed study of the definition of health and its relationship to various health disciplines, including alleopathy, osteopathy, acupuncture and homeopathy, together with a manual of herbal, dietary and manipulative self-treatments.

Mr Ballantine is fond of skiing, travel and skiing. He was last seen, together with wife and three bicycles, aboard a fast sloop bound for South America.

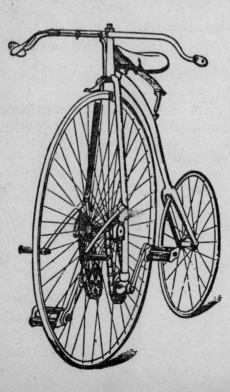

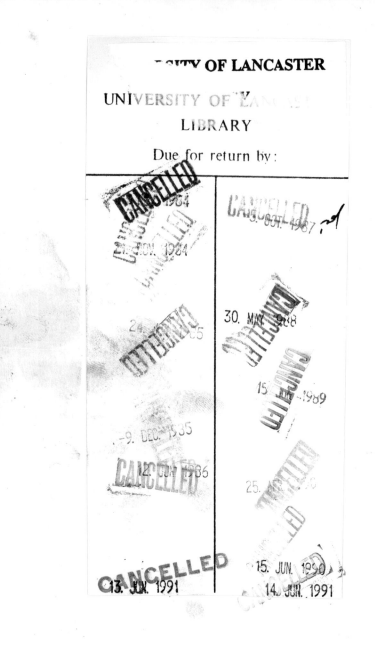